TABLE OF CONTENTS

i	Foreword
1	Chapter 1: The Journey Begins
5	Chapter 2: Understanding "The System"
17	Chapter 3: Therapeutic Foster Care
29	Chapter 4: Certification & Beyond
39	Chapter 5: Home & Self Care
53	Chapter 6: Child Development & Behavior
81	Chapter 7: Ready, Set, Go!
87	Chapter 8: Cultural Awareness
93	Chapter 9: Unique Challenges of Children & Youth in Foster Care
113	Chapter 10: Guiding Principles
145	Chapter 11: In Case of Emergency
149	Chapter 12: Prepare, Prevent & Protect
163	Chapter 13: Healthy Kids
179	Chapter 14: Off To School
191	Chapter 15: Adolescence to Independence
217	Chapter 16: A Forever Family
227	Chapter 17: Success…
235	Terms & Definitions

FOREWORD

Thank you for choosing to read and explore *The Therapeutic Parent*. This Handbook was originally developed by the Family Care Network in 1992 as a tool for our therapeutic foster parents. The agency's goal was to create a practical, easy to follow "cookbook" style workbook for therapeutic foster parenting. Over the years this book has gone through many changes, coinciding with changes in the law, regulations and, most importantly, techniques, methods and best practices. This book now incorporates all of the evidence-based, evidence-informed and promising-practices available to the therapeutic foster care industry at this time. Why? Because these practices produce the best outcomes for foster children and youth!

Therapeutic Foster Care (TFC) is a family-based, evidence-based treatment service which serves as a very effective alternative to group home or institutional care. TFC is the integration of foster care with mental health therapeutic services delivered through a single provider, supported by a collaborative, team-driven process. What's more – it works; dramatically improving the wellbeing, health and success of traumatized foster children and youth.

The Therapeutic Parent was created for you—the foster parent who works day in and day out to help foster children and youth heal and become successful. We are confident this book will be a very valuable, time tested, resource for you; helping you to become a successful therapeutic foster parent!

The following is a brief background about Family Care Network, Inc., to help you understand the experience, philosophy, motivation and practices influencing this Handbook.

FOREWORD

FAMILY CARE NETWORK, INC.

HISTORY

Family Care Network, Inc. (FCNI) was founded as a California public benefit corporation in August of 1987 by the current CEO, Jim Roberts, for the purpose of creating family-based and community-based treatment programs as an alternative to group home or institutional care of foster children and youth. The agency currently serves California's Central Coast through multiple programs designed to strengthen and preserve families and individuals, and are delivered in partnership with public and private agencies and the community. FCNI has been a state certified Mental Health Services provider since 1998.

Presently, the Family Care Network provides 17 distinct programs in five service divisions, including: Therapeutic Foster Care Services; Family Support Services; Transitional Age Youth Services; Early Intervention and Prevention Services; and Community-Linked Services.

Over the years, FCNI's CEO, Jim Roberts, has contributed to the development of legislation, program models and state policy and procedure for Therapeutic Foster Care, Transitional Age Youth Services and Family-Based Services.

MISSION

The mission of the Family Care Network is to "Enhance the wellbeing of children and families in partnership with our community."

OUTCOMES

Since 1988, the Family Care Network has served over 10,000 children and youth in its therapeutic foster care programs, with an 89% success rate. Success is defined as:
- Discharged to parent
- Discharged to family/kin
- Discharged to adoptive/guardian family
- Discharged to Transitional Age Youth Services program
- Discharged to self, aged out of foster care
- Successfully stabilized and stepped down to a lower level of care

ACCREDITATION

In 2006, FCNI was formally accredited through the California Alliance of Child and Family Services, having met the highest industry standards of excellence as a state licensed Foster Family Agency, mental health services, family-based services and transitional age youth services provider and was reaccredited in 2009. In 2014, all FCNI programs will become nationally accredited through The Joint Commission.

BEST PRACTICES

All Family Care Network programs are delivered utilizing industry established "Best Practices," as well as evidence-based, evidence-informed and promising-practices. "Best Practices" services are:
- Family-Centered
- Solution-Focused
- Strength-Based
- Community-Based
- Needs-Driven

FCNI's evidence-based, evidence-informed and promising-practices include:
- Therapeutic Foster Care
- Wraparound Services
- Managing and Adapting Practices (MAP)
- Trauma Informed Interventions including TF-CBT
- Therapeutic Behavioral Services (TBS)
- Cognitive Behavioral Therapy (CBT)
- Transition to Independence (TIP)
- Family-Centered Intensive Case Management

Permanency

The goal of the Family Care Network's programs is to establish permanent, lifelong, supportive relationships for the children and youth we serve. All foster children and youth served are assisted in securing a permanent family, either with biological parents or extended family, or through adoption. Transitional age youth are assisted in establishing permanent, lifelong supportive relationships with positive adult role models. Families served are provided the skills to maintain strong, supportive familial connections.

Therapeutic Foster Care Goals

- Therapeutic Foster Care is a short-term, treatment intervention, designed to stabilize behaviors, promote healing and facilitate a rapid reunification or move to permanency.

- Place children/youth singly or at most in pairs, with a foster parent who is carefully selected, specialty-trained, supervised and specifically matched with the child's needs and strengths in mind;

- Create, through a team approach, an individualized treatment plan that builds on the child's strengths and addresses his/her needs;

- Train and empower the therapeutic foster parent to act as a central agent in implementing the child's treatment plan;

- Make available an array of therapeutic interventions for the child, the child's family and the foster parent (family);

- Provide intensive oversight of the child's treatment, often through daily contact with the foster parent; and

- Enable the child to successfully transition from therapeutic foster care to placement with the child's family or alternative family placement by continuing to provide therapeutic interventions that support the youth's permanence.

A Few Points Before You Begin Reading

Sunbeam Icon

Throughout this Handbook, you will see this sunbeam icon used to highlight critical information and supportive notes pertaining to foster parenting and your role as a Therapeutic Foster Parent. These key points are emphasized to clarify difficult or complex information, as well as to provide you with a deeper insight into main concepts.

Exclamation Point Icon

Similar to the use of the Sunbeam icon, you will also see an "Exclamation Point" icon throughout this Handbook which is used to highlight critical information that is also sensitive in nature.

The California Connection!

As we have described in the Foreword, this Handbook was written and is distributed by Family Care Network, Inc. (FCNI), a California-based child, youth and family services agency. While every effort has been made to make this material understandable to Therapeutic Foster Care (TFC) parents across the United States and internationally, there may be some limited references to policies, procedures and programs specific to California or to FCNI. This is especially true with Chapter 10 – "Guiding Principles." Chapter 10 of this Handbook provides a detailed discussion of licensing regulations, standards and best practices. A purposeful decision was made to include citations to the applicable California licensing regulations for the benefit of California-based TFC parents. It should be noted that California licensing standards are some of, if not the most detailed in the nation and that licensing regulations/standards are very similar state to state. Additionally, we have added cross-references to the Foster Family-based Treatment Association (FFTA) 2013 Program Standards for Treatment Foster Care, a nationally recognized, venerated Standards Manual. These will be identified by the FFTA logo and applicable Standard number.

It is essential that every TFC Parent know and understand your Foster Care Provider's licensing regulations and the standards which apply to them.

CHAPTER 1

THE JOURNEY BEGINS
Your Decision to Open Your Heart and Your Home to a Child in Need

CHAPTER 1

THE JOURNEY BEGINS
Your Decision to Open Your Heart and Your Home to a Child in Need

The decision to share your home and your family with a foster child is one of the most life changing decisions you will ever make. It is life changing for the child certainly, but also life changing for you and your family. Everyone involved will have new experiences, some wonderful and some challenging, and each experience will allow for personal growth and will add a new depth and richness to your lives. All along the way, you will have the assistance and support of the staff from your Foster Care Provider, the professionals who are dedicated to the success of every foster child and foster family under its supervision.

Foster parents are amazing and incredibly special people. There is probably no greater demonstration of compassion and love than in opening your home to a complete stranger who is experiencing some degree of trauma. And the impact you will have on the children and youth in your care will be for a lifetime.

Throughout this Handbook, we emphasize how competent, qualified foster parents are the most significant individuals in the life transforming process of foster children and youth—they key ingredients being "competence" and "qualified". Foster parenting needs to be taken as seriously as any other profession. It's so much more than just providing a safe and comfortable place to sleep, good food and love. As you consider your choice to be a foster parent, here are seven points to keep in mind:

- **It Takes Time** to become a "competent" and "qualified" foster parent. We don't expect you to memorize this handbook—just to use it. The material contained within this text comes from research and years of training, education and experience. This Handbook is designed as a resource to help you grow into your role as a foster parent, so we encourage you to invest the time and be willing to learn, continually striving to do your best.

- **You are a Professional Parent.** We use the term "Therapeutic Foster Parent," to emphasize the significance of your role. Don't minimize the influence you have. By "professional" we mean: Possessing specialized knowledge, skill and ability, and being substantially committed to the endeavor as a primary vocation or pursuit.

- **You are a Therapeutic Change Agent.** As a therapeutic foster parent you can and do contribute substantially to the healing process of the foster child(ren) placed in your home. You help equip them to meet life's challenges, to overcome adversity and to make a successful transition to adulthood. Your home is a place for healing, learning and growing.

- **Relationship Is the Key to Success;** no effective change can take place without it. Make it your primary goal to establish a genuine relationship with your foster child. Remember, you may be able to control and manipulate behavior externally, but lasting change, the kind that occurs within, comes only by way of relationship. Through relationships, people change because they want to, not because they have to. Your Foster Care Provider will provide you with all of the training needed to establish effective relationships.

- **Commitment** is another building block to success. Any growth and positive change takes time. Patience and endurance are essential when you are a foster parent. Too often children in foster care experience being passed from placement to placement when people give up too soon. This repeated rejection and loss causes them to trust no one, and they aren't given the opportunity to properly heal. We encourage foster parents to have the attitude: "No matter what, I'm going to stick it out with this child, because if I don't, who will?" You will have lots of support and guidance from your team, which will help you and your foster child on your journey together.

- **Network.** "Lone Rangers" don't do well as foster parents, but team players do! Learn to become a dynamic team member and use every resource available to you. Call. Ask questions. Seek assistance and advice. Get involved with every aspect of your foster child's treatment plan. You're the professional parent. Who knows better about some issues and behaviors than you?

- **Relax!** We know it can be overwhelming to give your heart and soul to being a foster parent. You will find yourself under a multi-agency "looking glass" and your home life may drastically change as you integrate a new child into your family. You will make mistakes, every parent does. But rest assured, your Foster Care Provider is there to help you, consult with you, and train and support you. Make it a goal to have a peaceful, fun-filled home. Most foster children have never experienced a truly happy family environment. Make a deliberate plan to minimize stress and promote peace and tranquility in your home.

Please use this Handbook as your "Owner's Manual" for foster parenting. Read it carefully and make it your reference and guide. Most of the questions you might have are answered in here! As laws/regulations change, or new and better techniques are developed, your Foster Care Provider will keep you informed and appropriately trained. Our goal is for you to be the best trained, best equipped, most competent, and (most importantly) the most effective foster parent you can be!

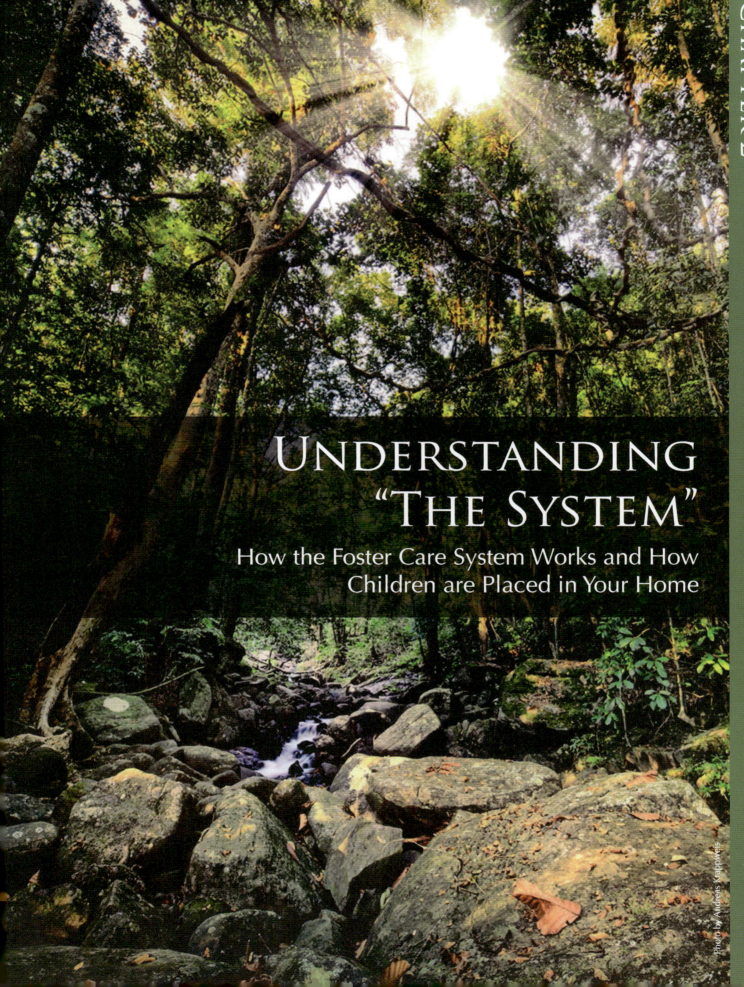

CHAPTER 2

Understanding "The System"

How the Foster Care System Works and How Children are Placed in Your Home

CHAPTER 2

UNDERSTANDING "THE SYSTEM"
How the Foster Care System Works and How Children are Placed in Your Home

Every year, over a half million children in California come to the attention of child welfare officials through reports of suspected child abuse or neglect. On any given day, more than 175,000 children and youth are involved in the child welfare system: 39,000 receive emergency services and other forms of assistance to keep the family together safely, and over 50,000 live in foster homes, relative homes and residential care facilities. Today's welfare system faces many challenges, including rapidly diminishing resources in the face of increased social responsibility to investigate reports of abuse and neglect; to protect victimized and vulnerable children; to assist children who are removed from their parents' care; and to support families in their efforts to stay together.

Over the last 15 years, child welfare services have done an excellent job of diverting children from the "system" by placing children in need of out of home care with relatives and friends. Unfortunately, the number of older youth within the system continues to increase, primarily due to their elevated emotional and/or behavioral needs. Institutional group care has produced poor outcomes in "helping" these foster youth. For this reason, Therapeutic Foster Care, along with other family-based services, has emerged as the preferred treatment intervention.

BASIC "SYSTEM" OVERVIEW

The foster care system is made up of multiple federal, state and county agencies, all of which share the goals of providing for the safety, permanence, and wellbeing of children and their families. Both federal and state laws establish the legal framework that governs the roles and responsibilities of agencies and organizations for children that enter and leave the foster care system.

FOSTER CARE AGE ELIGIBILITY

Until January 1, 2012, all children 0-18, or foster children/youth able to graduate high school before turning 19, were under the jurisdiction of the Juvenile Court System. After January 1, 2009, states have the opportunity to permit foster youth, ages 18-21, to voluntarily choose to remain under the jurisdiction of the Juvenile Court in order to receive services specifically designed to promote self-sufficiency and a successful transition to independent living.

STATE RESPONSIBILITIES

All states offer a collection of programs and services aimed at safeguarding the wellbeing of children and families in order to strengthen and preserve families, encourage personal responsibility and foster independence. The state's primary role is to establish laws, regulations and a framework for monitoring Child Welfare Services. Some states give their counties responsibility for delivering direct Child Welfare Services, including adoptions services.

COUNTY RESPONSIBILITIES

In many states, counties are the primary governmental bodies that directly interact with children and families to address child abuse and neglect. Children and families involved in the Juvenile Court system receive services from several county-level departments:

Juvenile Court

Every state has a Juvenile Court System, regionalized in counties or geographic regions. A child cannot be removed from his/her home and placed in foster care without a Juvenile Court order.

Department of Social Services or Human Services

The Department of Social/Human Services (DSS/DHS) is the primary state or county agency responsible for the county foster care program. All payments to Foster Care Providers come from DSS/DHS, and they are responsible for all children and youth taken into "protective custody." Other related responsibilities include:

- Providing Child Protective Services (CPS), a 24/7 emergency response service to investigate any reports of child abuse and/or neglect.

- Social Work services which include providing case management and supervision of all children under the jurisdiction of the court.

- Independent Living Program (ILP) which delivers transitional services to foster youth aging out of the foster care system, and supportive services to former foster youth up to age 24.

- Early Intervention and Prevention and Family Maintenance services.

- Most Social/Human Services Departments also provide foster home licensing under state authority, and oversee placement of children and youth in these homes.

- Some Social/Human Services Departments also serve as licensed adoption agencies and run local foster-adoption services.

Juvenile Probation

It is the responsibility of the state or county Probation Department to oversee all children and youth who are involved in criminal conduct, delinquency, truancy or incorrigible behavior. Some youth placed into foster care are actually Wards of the Court, placed and supervised by Probation. Even though it is the youth's behavior which brings them to the attention of the Juvenile Court, very often there are dysfunctional family circumstances as well. Unlike Court Dependents, Wards can be sent to Juvenile Hall, or a similarly secure facility, should negative behavior persists. Probation Officers are "Peace Officers" in contrast to CWS Social Workers who are not.

Behavioral Health Services

Every state or county provides Mental Health and Drug & Alcohol Services. This is generally referred to as Behavioral Health Services, conforming to standard healthcare terminology. The basic behavioral health services include:

- Children's Mental Health services (up to age 21), either provided by the County or by a state approved contract provider.

- Therapeutic Behavioral Services (TBS), is an individualized, one-on-one, behavioral management service every foster child is entitled to receive when it is determined to be medically necessary.

- Therapeutic Foster Care (TFC) is another entitlement service available to every foster child. TFC includes specially trained foster parents, mental health services, behavioral supports and augmented care and supervision.

- Psychiatric assessment, medication administration and monitoring.

- Psychiatric hospitalization in either a temporary local facility or in a hospital setting located in a neighboring jurisdiction.

- Outpatient drug and alcohol treatment services.

Health Care Services

All foster children are automatically eligible for health care coverage under the Federal Medicaid program (Medi-Cal in California). Health care services can be received through regional hospitals, private physicians willing to accept Medicaid, and publicly funded health care clinics. State or County Health Departments may provide some or all of these hospital and/or outpatient services, and may also provide:

- Prenatal and well-baby services
- Healthcare screening
- Case consultation for medically fragile or high-risk children
- Nutrition, weight loss and tobacco cessation programs

How Children Come Into Foster Care

All children in foster care, including children receiving services through a private, not-for-profit Foster Care Provider, are processed through the Juvenile Court. Children are most often placed in foster care after they have been removed from their home by a child welfare agency and the Juvenile Court has found their parents cannot care for them. Additionally, a child who has been declared a "ward" of the court for committing a violation of law may also be placed in foster care if the court finds that returning the child home would be contrary to the child's best interest.

The Juvenile Court process involves a series of hearings within specified periods, and is basically the same for both Dependents (abused/neglected) and Wards (criminal conduct). Judges rely on investigation reports, assessments and information from social workers, probation officers, service providers, and others to reach decisions regarding a child/youth appearing before the Court. **Legal Council** must be appointed by the Juvenile Court Judge to represent the interests of every child/youth throughout the court proceedings.

The court may also appoint a **Court Appointed Special Advocate** (CASA) to represent the best interests of a child and provide the court with independent information regarding the case. A CASA worker is a trained volunteer who advocates on behalf of the child, giving him/her a "voice" in the court process. The CASA worker can be helpful if your foster child has concerns/questions or does not feel like they are being "heard" while going through the court process.

One of the responsibilities of the foster parent is to be aware of where the child is in the court process and to ensure that the child receives answers to their questions regarding the process. There are many individuals involved in your foster child's life who can assist in supporting him/her and answer any technical questions they may have. Foster parents must know who these individuals are and be able to assist foster children in contacting them should they have a need.

Foster Care Placement Options Available to the Juvenile Court

Relative or Kinship Home: Federal law, but more importantly "Best Practices," requires child welfare agencies to place children removed from their home with a relative or non-relative family friend before making a foster care placement. A substantial number of California's foster children and youth are placed with kin or with a non-relative family friend.

Wraparound Services: Provide a unique placement option, allowing a high-needs foster child/youth to remain in a family setting, usually their own, while receiving very intense services. This strength-based, needs-driven program is an extremely effective intervention which serves and supports not only the foster child/youth, but the entire family, even siblings. Wraparound is a volunteer program designed to empower families and help them create community connections and supports.

Foster Family Home: A licensed family residence that provides 24-hour care for no more than six children total (eight if sibling groups). The California Department of Social Services (CDSS) is responsible for licensing and monitoring a foster home's compliance with the licensing standards. CDSS has delegated the licensing function for foster homes in most counties to the county child welfare agency.

Private Foster Care Provider: Refers to foster family homes that are recruited and certified by a state-licensed private, not for profit agency. These agencies, referred to as "Foster Care Providers" in this Handbook, provide social work and other supports to their certified homes, including payments to foster parents. The state monitors all Foster Care Providers and has authority to investigate complaints against certified foster families and initiate corrective action, including decertification.

Therapeutic Foster Care (TFC): A specialty service provided by licensed Providers. TFC is an optional program which serves as a family-based treatment option to group home or institutional care. The primary components of TFC are:

- Smaller social worker caseloads
- Specially trained professional foster parents
- Intensive foster parent support, guidance and assistance 24/7
- Intensive In-Home Support Services, potentially seven days per week and at times which best serves the foster child/youth and the foster family
- Mental Health services and other augmented treatment services (i.e., mentors, tutors, life-skill development, etc.)

Transitional Housing Programs: In some states, like California, foster youth have several options for supportive transitional housing designed to help them successfully transition from foster care to independent self-sufficiency, including:

- **Transitional Housing Placement Program (THPP):** A program offered to youth in foster care between the ages of 16 and 19, allowing them to live independently with supervision, intensive one-on-one life skill development instruction and guidance, case management and social work assistance, mentoring and a variety of other services to help them successfully transition to independent living.
- **Supported Independent Living Program (SILP):** Available to foster youth ages 18 to 21. SILP is a voluntary program which basically provides participating youth with a monthly stipend to be applied to rent and basic necessities. SILP participants must be enrolled in college or engaged in full-time employment.
- **Transitional Housing Placement–Plus Foster Care (THP+FC):** A voluntary program for foster youth ages 18 to 21 which operates like THPP. Youth are provided housing, one-on-one life-skill development instruction, case management, mentoring and other supportive services to assist them in obtaining self-sufficiency and independence.
- **Transitional Housing Placement–Plus (THP+):** Another voluntary program for former foster youth, ages 18 to 24. THP+ is identical to the THP+FC program, with the exception that participants are not current Dependents or Wards of the court, and access to the program is very limited. Participation is limited to two years, but can provide continued support to a foster youth exiting the THP+FC program.

Group Homes & Institutional Care: An option for children and youth who present serious behavioral challenges, suffer from severe mental illness, and/or are a danger to themselves or others.

Whenever the Juvenile Court determines that a child cannot be safely returned to parents, the court issues an order terminating parental rights. Once parental rights have been terminated, the child is free to become adopted.

Chapter 2

The Foster Care Referral and Placement Process

Children are referred to foster care a number of ways:

- Most are referred by a Social/Human Services or Child Welfare Services (CWS) agency.
- The Probation Department may refer a child to foster care for placement if they are not a risk to the community or the foster family.
- In some states, a child may be referred by the Behavioral Health Department.
- Additionally, parents or other individuals can refer a child without any involvement in the juvenile justice system on a "private pay" basis. (This may be funded by health insurance.)

Once the Provider receives a referral, the following screening process is initiated:

- Any history and vital information available (including health information, risk factors, past trauma, psychological evaluations, therapist comments, court reports, school reports, etc.) is obtained and evaluated by the placement coordinator and/or supervising social worker.

- The referral is "staffed" and evaluated considering several important criteria:
  - Can the agency meet the child's needs?
  - Is the child a risk to themselves or others?
  - Can s/he be treated in an open, foster family setting?
  - Is there an available family where an appropriate match can be made?
  - Does the agency have a Social Worker with caseload space to work with the child?

- Sometimes a pre-placement visit is scheduled to allow both the foster parent and child to get to know each other before placement; however, this is not the norm. It should be a placement agency's policy, as well as the county's, to cause as little disruption to a child as possible as some children are coming straight from their biological home to a foster home.

Why Children Are Referred To Foster Care

Children who are referred to foster care can be 0 to 18 years of age (in some states up to 21), and come from diverse backgrounds with varying needs. All children referred to foster care have experienced some form of trauma in their lives; as just the experience of being separated from their families, no matter the circumstances, is extremely traumatic for a child. These emotionally fragile children may experience stress from even the simplest activities and environments. Their behaviors, especially those that appear negative, indicate the level of stress they are experiencing.

Common Characteristics of Traumatized, Emotionally Fragile Children

- These children may produce strong negative statements and may send off continuously strong rejection signals.
- They may lack self-control and may be impulsive.

- The trauma they have experienced has physically changed the parts of their brains that help them regulate stress, so changes in their behaviors may take a longer time and progress may seem slow.
- They often do not perform at a level that a foster parent might expect or at a level indicative to their individual potential.
- They can challenge foster parents' skills, energy and commitment.

SOME REASONS FOR REFERRAL

- **Circumstances Beyond Their Control:** Parents or relatives have made choices that affect the safety and wellbeing of the child and the child must be placed in a safe environment until the family stabilizes.
- **Problem Behaviors:** Physically acting out (hitting, biting); lying; stealing; bedwetting; soiling; sexual play; masturbation; anger and rage; chronic truancy; drugs and alcohol abuse; running away; self-mutilation; suicidal gestures or attempts; hyperactivity; defiance; etcetera.
- **Educational Needs:** Refusal to attend school; severe learning disabilities; non-compliance and defiance; and fighting and attention deficit. Schools may provide services through an Individual Education Plan (IEP).
- **Medical Needs:** Physical handicaps; epilepsy; diabetes; allergies; asthma; fetal alcohol syndrome; eating disorders; children born drug dependent.
- **Psychological Needs:** Psychotic episodes; delusional thinking; dissociation; tic disorder; depression; identity disorder; anxiety; reactive attachment.
- **Independent Living Skills Training:** For older children, the need to learn skills to be self-sufficient, including: employment skills, managing money, paying bills, obtaining insurance, renting housing, cooking, grocery shopping, transportation, etcetera.
- **Permanency:** Children are placed in foster care to prepare them for a permanent living situation.
- **Family Reunification:** Interventions are provided to children and parents to support the goal to reunite the family.

Note: Federal law requires a time period of up to 18 months of attempted family reunification for all children removed from their family of origin. This period may be shortened for younger children, and varies from state to state.

"My foster parents are my super heroes because they take care of me and love me and keep me safe!"

—Youth age 9

CHAPTER 2

THE PLACEMENT PROCESS

Once a decision has been made to place a foster child in a particular foster home, the child and his/her belongings are transported to the home. Some important priorities within the first 30 days:

- **School Enrollment:** This is usually done by the foster parent as soon as possible after placement, however, the Foster Care Provider's Social Worker or other designated staff may assist with the process. School enrollment is covered in detail in Chapter 14: Off to School.

- **Visitation:** The Juvenile Court sets forth a case plan which normally includes court ordered visitation with the child's biological family. It is usually very specific as to frequency, length of time, type of supervision and parents (or other relatives) involved.

- **Services:** Within the first 30 days, the Foster Care Provider's Social Worker assigned to the child will meet with the child, foster parents and county placement worker to set up a Child & Family Needs & Services or Treatment Plan. This plan will identify what services the child needs including counseling, tutoring, behavioral services, or services for mental or physical disabilities.

PEOPLE AND AGENCIES THAT WORK WITH FOSTER CHILDREN

Depending on the child's status and needs, as well as the Foster Care Provider's services model, most children in foster care will interact with:

- Foster Care Provider's Social Worker
- State/County Placement Agency Workers (CWS & Probation)
- Adjunct Services Providers (i.e., Mental Health, Health Department personnel, Drug & Alcohol Services, etcetera)
- Provider's In-Home Support Counselors or Behavioral Specialists/Coaches (only in agencies providing Therapeutic Foster Care or mental health authorized rehabilitation services)
- Their Attorney

Additionally, they may also work with:

- Private therapist, psychologist or psychiatrist
- Independent Living Program (ILP) Coordinator/Worker
- Special Education resource teachers
- Volunteer mentor, tutor and/or student intern
- Court appointed special advocate (CASA)
- Child Development Specialist

STATE OR COUNTY PLACEMENT WORKER

Every child in foster care will have a State or County placement worker. Children placed by Child Welfare Services will have a CWS Social Worker assigned to them. Children who are placed by the Probation Department will be assigned a Deputy Probation Officer. The government placement workers act as the "eyes" and "ears" of the Juvenile Court. They must participate in all of the team meetings concerning the child, see the child face-to-face at least once a month, monitor their progress, report the child's status to the court and make recommendations for further court action. Additionally, they must authorize out-of-area travel and home visitation, as well as unsupervised time for teens. Out-of-state travel, medical/surgical treatment authorization, and authorization to administer psychotropic medication requires a court order obtained by the placement worker.

The Foster Care Provider's Social Worker

Every child placed with a private Foster Care Provider will be assigned an agency social worker. Foster children may be seen weekly or more frequently, but should be visited at least every two weeks, depending on the needs of the individual child. The Social Worker's major responsibilities are:

- Screen all referrals for foster placement; match referred foster youth with appropriate foster families; fully inform potential foster families about the child's needs, behaviors and case plans; and make placements within agency foster homes.

- Organize and facilitate Child & Family Team (CFT) meetings

- Utilize the CFT process to create the foster child's required case plans (Safety, Child & Family [Needs & Services Delivery] Plan, and/or mental health Treatment Plan) based on the foster child's needs and strengths.

- Coordinate services and monitor progress made towards meeting the child's goals set forth in the Child & Family/Treatment Plan.

- Provides each foster parent a Safety Plan which outlines any specific risk factors the child may have, and describes specific actions to be taken to minimize risk and/or respond to crises.

- Provide and/or coordinate authorized, medically necessary mental health services.

- Coordinate with government placement workers the scheduling and approval of all family visits and outside contacts with the foster children.

- Provide support, guidance, training and problem solving to the foster parents and their family.

- Liaison with the government placement agency, the child's biological family, school, outside therapist, attorneys and others as required.

- Prepare written progress reports; routinely update treatment objectives and Child & Family/Treatment Plans.

- Provide crisis and emergency assistance to the foster family and foster child.

- Maintain on-going case notes in the agency files for each child.

Therapeutic Foster Parents must work closely with their Provider's Social Worker for the success of a foster placement, and there may be times when a foster parent disagrees with their decisions. Remember, Social Workers have a broader perspective and understanding of clinical issues, court expectations and other information which you may not be aware of. On the other hand, the Social Worker may not have all of the information that you have, making your ongoing feedback and input into the CFT process critical.

Should you, as a foster parent, disagree about a particular decision, please do not hesitate to talk with the Provider's Social Worker. As a best practice, always:

- Be solution-focused and address issues professionally and directly.

- Never place your foster child in the middle of a disagreement you might have with another.

- Remember, you are your child's role model and they will learn appropriate communication from you.

- Approach the situation with the idea of improving everyone's base of information to arrive at a mutual understanding.

- Remember, it's OK to disagree on an issue as long as this doesn't negatively impact the child or case plan.

- Always know that you can request a meeting with the supervising Social Worker to work out any differences.

Other Possible Agency Staff Involved with the Child and Foster Family

As foster parents you should know that you will be in regular contact with your Foster Care Provider. Besides regular weekly (or every other week) contact with the Provider's Social Worker, there will be some contact with the following:

- **Placement Supervisor:** Screens and coordinates new referrals.

- **Supervising Social Worker:** Supervises all of the agency Social Workers.

- **Foster Care Administrator:** Is responsible for the day-to-day operation of the Provider, certifying/decertifying foster families, monitoring incident reports and interfacing with state licensing.

- **In-Home Support Counselors:** Are available in the Therapeutic Foster Care (TFC) programs. They are trained behavioral specialists who provide a vital resource by working one on one with children to provide skill development or enhancement in the home setting, at school and in the community.

- **Educational Coordinators:** Some Providers employ staff who are responsible for communicating with the schools, enrolling students, attending special education meetings, monitoring academic progress, providing or coordinating tutoring, and other related educational or vocational activities.

- **Family Development Specialist:** Are responsible for screening all foster parent applicants and guiding them through the certification/licensing process. Once a home is certified, they monitor on-going compliance and provide assistance, mentoring and support. This person also coordinates foster parent training and training resources.

- **Volunteers:** College graduate and undergraduate interns, as well as members of the community, may be used to augment services. They serve as mentors and tutors or reading specialist; they can transport, schedule appointments, supervise foster children, help with special projects and assist agency personnel in case management activities.

- **Clerical Support Staff:** Involved in record keeping, making sure foster parents are reimbursed for expenses, sending out important information concerning clients, training, etcetera.

Foster Child/Youth Case Plans

Every child referred to your Foster Care Provider for placement will have a Juvenile Court ordered Case Plan which governs the child and their family. Juvenile Court case plans frame a timetable for family reunification or another plan for permanency, i.e., adoption. Case plans also detail visitation requirements, counseling or any other service required to bring the case to a successful termination. It is a court order that all parties comply with Case Plans.

There will also be a specific "Needs & Service Delivery or Treatment Plan," sometimes referred to as a Child/Youth & Family Plan, developed by the agency Social Worker in collaboration with the child's Youth and Family Team. It identifies specific treatment objectives and activities for meeting each of these objectives. Foster parents provide input and are responsible for assisting the child in following the plan.

Whenever a foster child/youth is receiving Mental Health services, whether from the Foster Care Provider, State, County, or another provider, there will be a Medicaid/MediCal required Client Coordinated Care Plan. This plan is also developed by the treatment team, and designates all of the medically necessary mental health services the child/youth is entitled to receive, when and how they will receive them, and who will be delivering them.

The Foster Parent's Role in the Treatment Process

Foster parents have a very important role as a member of the child's treatment team. The foster home is the place where the most therapeutic work is done. The child's trusting, loving relationship with their foster parents is where they heal the wounds that occurred from past relationships. It is where they begin to learn new ways to respond to stress and where they can develop hope for the future. Foster parents:

- Provide a safe, caring, healthy and calming home environment.

- Understand that behavior is an indication of stress and work to relieve and calm the stress, rather than focus on changing the behavior.

- Are willing to develop healthy, bonded relationships with their foster children.

- Reflect on their own past trauma and stress triggers and develop personal strategies for regulating their own stress. A dis-regulated foster parent cannot give what a dis-regulated child needs to come back into balance.

- Work closely with the Child & Family Team, such as the agency Social Worker, In-Home Support Counselors, government Placement Worker, etcetera on specific treatment issues, following case plans and staff suggestions.

- Participate in team meetings.

- Keep the child's records current and up-to-date.

- Maintain open communication with their Foster Care Provider, sharing impressions, observations and opinions of how the child is doing. The Provider needs to know immediately if a problem develops or there are any abrupt changes in the child's behavior.

- Provide transportation for medical/dental needs, school functions, clothes shopping, recreational activities, etcetera.

- Participate regularly in training/educational programs, attend foster parent educational workshops, use the Provider's library resources, and attend support group meetings in order to fulfill initial and ongoing annual training requirements.

Other Information about Therapeutic Foster Care

- Funding for foster care is part Federal and part State/County. Federal participation is determined by the financial status of the child's family. Foster care rates are established by the state and are standardized statewide. Biological parents may be billed and are liable for the reasonable care and supervision costs of a child in foster care if the parents have the ability to pay.

- Clothing is primarily covered by the care and supervision reimbursement received by the foster parent. Foster children may receive an initial clothing allowance and an annual supplemental clothing allowance, but this is a state option.

- Most states have a "Foster Youth Bill of Rights" (See Figure 4) that provides children in care with a variety of protections for their health, safety and general wellbeing. Additionally, foster youth have more protections under other state statutes and regulations.

- **Complaints:** If a child/youth in foster care, or any interested party, believes that there is something wrong with the child's foster care placement, care or services, or believes the child is being discriminated against based on their sex, race, color, religion, or for any other reason, they may contact:

- **The Office of the State Foster Care Ombudsman**, established in most states to advocate for the needs of all foster children/youth. Check your state website for contact information.
- **State/County Child Protective Services** is required by federal and state law to receive and investigate allegations of child abuse against a foster child/youth.
- **State Licensing Agency** governs all licensed foster care facilities and the health and safety of foster children/youth; and investigate any alleged violations of foster children's Personal Rights, and/or allegations against foster parents. State licensing contact information is available on your state's website.

- **Grievance Procedures:** Foster parents, parents, legal guardians and children in foster care can file a grievance with their county child welfare agency concerning the placement or removal of a child from a foster home with certain limitations. A complaint must be filed within ten (10) calendar days of the action complained of in the complaint. Unless the child is in immediate danger, they will remain with the foster parent(s) pending the county's decision when removal is the basis for the complaint.

Therapeutic Foster Care

Chapter 3

Chapter 3

Therapeutic Foster Care

The role of the Therapeutic Foster Parent is substantially different from the traditional foster parent who only provides basic care and supervision. This chapter is designed to clearly delineate those differences and help Therapeutic Foster Parents understand the value and responsibilities of being a "Professional Therapeutic Foster Parent," including what to expect when serving in this capacity.

What is Therapeutic Foster Care?

Therapeutic Foster Care (TFC) is a medically necessary treatment service for foster children and youth with special medical, psychological, emotional and/or social needs who can accept and respond to the close relationships within a family setting and require intensive therapeutic services. TFC is distinguished from "traditional" foster care, "kinship" foster care and "specialized" foster care, where the fundamental need is for placement. **TFC is the integration of foster care with mental health therapeutic services delivered through a Foster Care Provider, supported by a collaborative, team-driven process.**

TFC is provided by a state licensed Foster Care Provider, that is responsible for providing leadership and highly-trained staff to support the therapeutic foster parent in the implementation of the child/youth's treatment plan goals. Therapeutic Foster Care teams and trained therapeutic foster parents work in full partnership with the child, the child's family and all other persons on the Child & Family Team (CFT).

TFC is extremely effective, and years of research have shown that children who receive treatment and support in a family setting, rather than in an institution, have much better outcomes. TFC serves a specialized population of children and youth, including:

- High-risk, high-needs
- Victims of abuse or neglect
- Diagnosed with a mental illness
- Juvenile justice involvement
- Substantial emotional needs
- Traumatized
- Behaviorally challenged
- Emotionally fragile

Any child entering into foster care has been traumatized to some degree—just the fact that the child was removed from his/her home is extremely traumatizing! Foster parents are in the unique position to provide these children with the safety and security to begin the healing process.

TFC foster parents are trained to understand the effects of trauma on the child's brain and recognize that the behaviors a child exhibits are symptoms of deeper feelings of fear, anxiety, grief, etcetera. TFC foster parents focus on building a trusting, loving, bonded relationship with the child, and provide a home environment that is stress reducing. This combination of relationship and a calm environment provides the essential elements for a child's healing.

TFC Program Goals

- Place foster children singly or, at most, in pairs, with a foster parent who is carefully selected, trained, and supervised and matched with the child's needs and strengths in mind;

- Create, through a team approach, an individualized treatment plan that builds on the child's strengths and addresses his/her needs;

- Empower the foster parent to act as a central agent in implementing the child's treatment plan;

- Provide intensive oversight of the child's treatment, often through daily contact with the foster parent;

- Make available an array of therapeutic interventions to the child, the child's family and the foster family (interventions include behavioral support services for the child, crisis planning and intervention, coaching and education for the foster parent and the child's family, and medication monitoring); and

- Enable the child to successfully transition from therapeutic foster care to placement with the child's family or alternative family placement by continuing to provide therapeutic interventions that support youth permanence.

Essential TFC Program Services

All TFC programs will offer a variety of services and supports to meet the specific needs of the foster children/youth placed in the program, as well as to the TFC foster parent who serves as a substantial "therapeutic change agent." Following are the Essential Services necessary for an effective TFC program.

- **Therapeutic Services:** Foster Care Providers must be authorized as Early and Periodic Screening Diagnosing and Treatment (EPSDT)–Mental Health Services providers and have the ability to bill all allowable mental health services offered in the TFC constellation of services in order to be a viable therapeutic program. TFC therapeutic service plans must address all underlying mental health needs, prioritizing those needs related to safety, permanence and stability. Mental health services can include:
    - Assessment
    - Plan Development
    - Intensive Case Coordination
    - Individual/Group Therapy
    - Individual/Group Rehabilitation
    - Collateral
    - Crisis intervention/stabilization
    - Medication Support Services
    - Therapeutic Behavioral Services (TBS)

- **Case Management:** The Foster Care Provider's Social Worker facilitates Child & Family Team meetings which function as a family/group multi-system planning session. Other areas for Case Management include home visits for the purpose of assessing progress, urgent needs and/or crisis consultation, etcetera, in addition to ongoing case management issues. Case management also includes coordinating services and progress with significant persons related to the child (example: parent, caregiver, sibling, teacher, therapist, etcetera).

- **Intense TFC Social Worker Visits:** Families need intensive on-going supports, services and weekly home visits to ensure success and that standards are being met. In-home Support Counselors/Behavioral Specialist must be available on a daily basis, including weekends and evenings, in order to stabilize foster child/youth behavior and preserve the foster placement.

- **Specially Trained Foster Parents:** Due to the high-needs and behaviors of children/youth entering TFC, and the key role they play in implementing the child's treatment plan, foster parents must be well-trained and highly skilled. Every effort should be made to support, nurture, train and validate these foster parents.

- **Foster Child/Youth Placement:** There should be no more than one TFC foster child/youth placed per foster family. Exceptions may be made for a second child/youth or for siblings, with the approval of the placing agency and after a determination is made that such an arrangement would not be detrimental to the foster children or foster family. Approvals for exceptions require a Compatibility Study and a Safety Plan that illustrates the protective and risk factors associated with the placement.

- **Rehabilitation:** At the direction of the Foster Care Provider's Social Worker, In-Home Support Counselors (also referred to as a Behavioral Specialist, Rehabilitation Specialist, Coach, etcetera) will provide support services as identified in the Child & Family Plan. The time and location of these services are based on the child's and family's needs. They can spend time with the child at your home, on activities or in school. Their primary role is to help their clients learn how to manage their behaviors and to provide training in activities needed to achieve the child's goals/desired results/personal milestones, etcetera.

- **Augmented Care & Supervision:** TFC program staff must have the capacity to work with TFC youth in all venues where problematic behaviors arise, including but not limited to: school, foster home, community, biological parents' home, etcetera.

- **Foster Parent Partner Support:** Foster Parent Partners are available to provide support to the foster parents from the parent's perspective. They co-facilitate regular foster parent support meetings and also assist foster parents on an individual basis per the unique needs of each family. As the child and his/her family move towards reunification, Foster Parent Partners can assist the family in navigating the system of services, linking them to resources as well as assisting the parent/caregiver with the development of life skills and parent skill enhancement.

- **Community Resources Development:** The child's community can provide the team with resources which can assist the child and his/her family or relative caregiver as needed during the reunification process. These resources will assist them in meeting their unmet needs with the overall goal of linking the child and family to sustainable resources within their community. Utilization of community supports is specific to their culture, faith and community. Examples may include affordable housing, budgeting, food, automobile repair, transportation, vocational training, etcetera.

- **24 Hour On-Call Social Work and In-Home Support Services:** The child and foster family will have access to a Social Worker and In-Home Support Services 24 hours a day, 7 days a week to assist with crisis stabilization.

- **Mentoring:** Provides mentoring relationships in order to strengthen children/youth and families by assisting with stabilization of children in their homes and increasing the child and family's positive connections within their community.

- **Tutoring:** Provides tutorial services to children/youth and family member(s) to assist in achieving their educational and/or vocational goals.

- **In-Depth Training for Foster Parents:** TFC foster parents are required to attend specific training opportunities which are designed to enhance parenting and communication skills.

- **Temporary/Respite Care:** The Foster Care Provider must work with the foster parents to develop their natural resources to provide a sustainable plan for temporary/respite care. During this plan development or when an urgent need arises, In-Home Support staff, mentors and/or approved community volunteers may assist with this need.

Unique TFC Models

TFC can and is used in a variety of ways to serve the treatment needs of foster children and youth; especially as an alternative to group or institutional care. Here are some TFC-based programs currently being used:

- **TFC-based Emergency Shelter Care:** Provides 24/7 foster care for children/youth who might otherwise be institutionalized or hospitalized.

- **Crisis-Stabilization Foster Care:** Provides short-term (30-180 days) intensive treatment to stabilize behavior and return the child/youth home or to a less restrictive placement.

- **Fast-Track Family Reunification or Permanency Placement:** Provides a fairly short term (6-9 months) intensive treatment program to return a child/youth to a family placement or other permanent placement.

- **Multidimensional Therapeutic Foster Care:** An "evidence-based" TFC model designed for treating juvenile delinquent male youth returning from, or in lieu of, group home placement.

How Children are Referred to Therapeutic Foster Care

Children/youth are referred to TFC by a County placement agency, usually the Social/Human Services Department in concert with Mental Health, and in some counties, the Probation Department. Placements are made through a Team Decision Making model; in many counties, there is an Interagency Placement Committee (IPC). This committee is made up of representatives from Social Services, Mental Health, Probation, County Schools and private providers.

When the Foster Care Provider receives a referral from the referring agency, every effort is made to place the child in a family where there is a good match. Placement considerations include the child's treatment needs, family strengths, family composition, proximity to child's family and community, cultural considerations, school needs and foster family interests.

"It does not matter how much money a family has. If there is a lot of love in a home, that family is richer than any millionaire could ever be."

–Youth age 16

Chapter 3

Essential Elements Of Therapeutic Foster Care

Natural Supports: Services and supports reflect a balance of formal and informal family and community supports, rather than a reliance on formal professional services.

Voice and Choice: Foster families and the child's family (whenever possible) must be full and active partners at every level of the process. Foster parents coordinate with the Foster Care Provider's Social Worker and placing agency to arrange activities and short-term respite options for the child. Foster parents should select rules and behavioral incentive systems that they feel comfortable using.

Child & Family Teams (CFT): Each foster family and child are assisted by the provider in creating a CFT which becomes a micro–community of key players who will have a role in developing and implementing the child's treatment/case plan. The CFT consists of the foster child/youth, TFC parents, Foster Care Provider staff assigned to the child, adjunct agency staff such as a county social worker, probation officer or non-agency therapist, and individuals deemed important by the child and foster family. This team could also include a friend, neighbor, relative or pastor, and, depending on the circumstances, the child's biological family. The CFT should meet regularly at times convenient to the foster family and child. Most notably, however, is that the foster family and child/youth are placed center stage by the CFT, becoming the hub of the process.

Community-Based Services and Supports: Services and support that the child, foster family and child's family receive should be based in their community.

Stability and Support: In a crisis, services and supports should be added rather than moving the child from placement to placement (whenever possible).

Collaboration: The team coordinates services and supports so they appear seamless rather than disjointed to the foster family, child and his/her family. The team should strive to reach consensus.

Cultural Competence: The team is respectful of the foster family's culture, and the child's beliefs and traditions (as well as the beliefs and traditions of the child's family). The team actively seeks to understand every person's unique perspectives, solutions and needs in order to integrate them into the team planning process.

Individualized Services: Services and supports are tailored to the unique situations, strengths and needs of each individual. The team will create a specific plan to meet the foster child's and family's goals, as well as a safety plan to manage potential emergencies at the foster home or when the child is on home visits, respite, etcetera.

Flexible Resources: Successful teams are creative in their approach to acquiring services and resources to implement the Child & Family plan.

Persistence: Despite challenges, the team persists in working towards the goals included in the Child & Family plan, with a positive attitude and a solution-focused approach.

Outcome-Based Services: Specific, measurable outcomes are monitored to assess the child's (and his/her family's) and the foster family's progress toward goals.

Strength-Based Services: The focus of the team should be on what is working and going well for the family, and should capitalize on each person's positive abilities and characteristics, integrating court ordered requirements. Goals may be created based on the needs of the foster family, child and his/her family.

Essential Elements Of Therapeutic Foster Parenting

CHAPTER 3

Provide Extensive Support and Guidance: TFC foster parents should be provided extensive support, guidance, assistance, and 24/7 access to social work and IHC support and assistance.

Professional Therapeutic Foster Parents: TFC foster parents are to be considered "professional" therapeutic parents, and be afforded the respect due them for the challenging, and sometimes daunting work, they engage in while parenting high-needs, emotionally disturbed children/youth.

TFC Foster Parents are Highly Skilled and Capable: TFC foster parents should be properly trained prior to accepting care and supervision responsibilities, as well as on a continual basis, in the skills and techniques necessary to foster parent high-needs, at-risk children and youth. TFC foster parents should maintain a high level of skill, have the ability to work with severely emotionally disturbed children and deal with crisis situations. TFC parents should also be sensitive and responsive to each child/youth's unique background and culture.

Sufficient Reimbursement: TFC foster parents receive "difficulty of care" reimbursement sufficient to support their elevated care and supervision responsibilities, and to maintain one full-time parent within the home.

Ensure Effective Communication: Effective communication between the Foster Care Provider and TFC foster parent is critical to ensure that Safety Plans and Child & Family Plans are properly developed, implemented and monitored; and that the foster child/youth's conduct is observed and properly reported to the child's county Social Worker and other CFT members.

Promote Child & Family Team Participation: A Foster Parent participation on the Child & Family Team is vital. The team provides the foster parent a forum for communicating insights and needs, and contributing to the development of their foster child's Child & Family Plan. Foster parents should also attend treatment team meetings, medical appointments and mental health evaluations to provide insight and advocacy to ensure that the child/youth's needs are being addressed.

TFC Foster Parents Maintain Safe Home and Up-to-Date Records: TFC foster parents must maintain a safe, well maintained home; along with excellent records, notes and files, in order to meet all licensing and case reporting requirements

Implement Plan and Activities: It is essential for TFC foster parents to carefully follow through with the prescribed activities included in the Child & Family Plan and implement therapeutic techniques, methods and interventions as may be required.

TFC Foster Parents Stay Connected as a Resource Post Permanency: Foster parents can play an important role in the successful transition of the foster child to their biological family or other permanent placement by maintaining a connection to the child and his/her family, providing additional support and guidance.

Therapeutic Foster Parent Responsibilities

The following list serves like a "Job Description" for Therapeutic Foster Parents.

- Provide basic parenting (food, clothing, shelter, educational support, meet medical needs and provide transportation to community activities, and support the child's spiritual/religious beliefs, etcetera).

- Teaching or reinforcing home and community-based, age-appropriate life skills; including, but not limited to: social skills; basic life skills; household management; nutrition; physical; behavioral and emotional health; time management; school and/or work attendance; money management; independent living skills; and self-care techniques.

- Provide day-to-day coordination of the child's service, such as taking the child to necessary service appointments, medical appointments, and extra-curricular recreational and social development activities.

- Assist in the development and implementation of the foster child's/youth's Safety Plan, including crisis-stabilization services as detailed in the plan.

- Assist in the development and implementation of the foster child's service delivery and treatment plans.

- Provide basic "care and maintenance" case management (in contrast to the case management functions provided by the Foster Care Provider), such as arranging and taking the child to required service appointments, school functions and/or supervised visits.

- Provide recreation and social activities which are meaningful and purposefully support positive behavior opportunities.

- Provide a stable environment and role modeling in which family interactions and activities present opportunities for the foster child/youth to learn and practice age-appropriate behaviors and skills, as well as the opportunity to live in a family and community-based setting. This TFC environment should also address cultural issues and include positive behavior supports.

- Provide intensive supervision, including keeping the child safe and minimizing association with peers who may present a negative influence.

- Provide behavioral interventions; supervision and training on anger management; stress reduction; conflict resolution; self-esteem; parent-child interactions; peer relations; drug and alcohol awareness; management of physical and behavioral health symptoms; and other behavioral issues.

Basic Expectations for TFC Foster Parents

- Best Practice stipulates that a foster home provides at least one full-time TFC parent;

- TFC parents must participate in training and support groups;

- TFC parents must demonstrate a higher level of skill and ability to work with Severely Emotionally Disturbed (SED) or behaviorally challenged children, and provide de-escalation techniques;

- TFC parents must adapt their home environment to mitigate triggers for maladaptive behavior;

- TFC parents must fully participate in the Child & Family or treatment team process and carry out activities necessary for fulfilling the client's needs and services plan;

- TFC parents must implement and maintain an in-home Behavioral Management System;

- TFC parents must support the child's understanding and development related to life traumas (such as abuse, neglect, loss and multiple placement moves);

- TFC parents must maintain detailed case notes and records as required by the program;

- TFC parents must fully comply with all state and agency regulations/requirements for foster parenting;

- TFC parents must fully comply with all state regulations and agency policies regarding the reporting of unusual incidents;

- TFC parents must work collaboratively with the Foster Care Provider staff, placement workers and adjunct agency staff;

- TFC parents must diligently apply treatment and therapeutic techniques, methods and interventions which are prescribed for the management, growth and wellbeing of TFC foster children.

Primary Staff Positions in TFC

- **Social Worker:** The Social Worker provides a key, pivotal position in the TFC program. They coordinate services; facilitate Child & Family Team meetings; interface with County representatives; create safety and treatment plans, sometimes provide mental health services; consult with and train TFC foster parents; supervise and coordinate In-Home Support staff; and provide crisis counseling and intervention to foster youth and TFC parents.

- **Mental Health Staffing:** As stated earlier, TFC is a "medically-necessary treatment service." This definition means that the foster child/youth must receive the mental health services s/he needs, as prescribed by a medical doctor and authorized through a county/state approved process. The following are the mental health services staff commonly found in TFC:
  - **Psychiatrist:** Responsible for determining "medical necessity" and prescribing/monitoring medications
  - **Clinical Psychologist:** Usually provides specialized assessments and interventions, but may also provide individual and family counseling
  - **Therapist:** Provides individual and/or family counseling; collateral and crisis intervention; develops and monitors client treatment plans; and participates in the Child & Family Team process
  - **Rehabilitation Specialist:** Provides individual and group rehabilitation; collateral and crisis intervention; Therapeutic Behavioral Services (TBS); life-skill development/support; and skills transfer to TFC parents, in addition to participating on the Child & Family Team, and contributing to the assessment, monitoring and updating process

- **In-Home Support Counselor/Behavioral Specialist/Coach (IHC):** Provides augmented care and supervision, as well as behavioral support and guidance. This could include: assisting foster parents with supervision during critical times, (i.e. morning, dinner and bedtime); shadowing the foster child at school or engaging in other social activities; and providing transportation and supervised visits. IHCs also provide TBS and rehabilitation under the mental health services component of TFC.

- **Therapeutic Foster Family Recruiter/Trainer (FFRT):** FFRT are responsible for recruiting, screening, training and certifying TFC parents. They conduct comprehensive home inspections for initial and annual certification; and they provide ongoing support, assistance and guidance to therapeutic foster parents. FFRTs serve a critical role in recruiting and maintaining a sufficient number of quality TFC families.

- **Family/Parent Partner:** A Family/Parent Partner is a current and/or former TFC Foster Parent who is available to provide one-on-one support, training/education and guidance to TFC Foster Parents. This is an essential peer support/training role, which helps foster parents "navigate the system" and execute the foster child/youth's case plan.

- **Administrative Support:** Every TFC program is required to have a Program Administrator and a Supervising Social Worker. Additionally, there will be agency support staff that maintain/manage TFC foster family and foster child/youth files.

- **Volunteer:** Many Foster Care Providers incorporate volunteers into their program model. Community volunteers can serve in a variety of capacities and provide very important adjunct services. Volunteers may include:
    - **Mentors:** Provide a positive adult role model and hopefully become a lifelong support
    - **Interns:** Can perform like a mentor or someone who can help with transportation, childcare, as well as other supports to the TFC foster parents
    - **Tutors:** Assist foster children/youth in improving their academic performance

Tips for Success

Providing Therapeutic Foster Care requires a great commitment to the foster child's/youth's success in the face of many obstacles and challenges. The ability to have a clear sense of purpose and vision, and keeping the "big picture" in focus is essential! Here are some tips to help the TFC foster parent succeed.

- Have a strong support network, including other seasoned foster parents and dependable friends

- Take care of yourselves by maintaining a healthy lifestyle which includes exercise, recreation and regularly planned respite

- Take advantage of the support available through your Foster Care Provider. They have a responsibility and obligation to make sure you succeed. Your success means foster child/youth success!

- Ask for help any time you are unsure of a situation or what you should do. Collaboration and team decision-making works. And don't allow the Foster Care Provider you work with to neglect their responsibilities! If you need to, become a "squeaky wheel."

- Be constantly learning, taking advantage of every opportunity to learn new skills, techniques and methods

- Model integrity, acceptance, compassion, patience and empathy

- Project hope—focus on the child's potential and not their deficits; their strengths and not their weaknesses; and teach your foster children/youth to become resilient and solution-focused

- Become well organized and prepared to handle the increased paperwork and responsibilities associated with providing TFC

- Learn to "neutralize risk" by planning in advance to prevent problems. Here is a great definition of "risk" that you should become familiar with:

  · "Risk is a probability or threat of a damage, injury, liability, loss, or other negative occurrence that is caused by external or internal conditions, events or vulnerabilities, and that may be neutralized through preemptive action."

- Provide a warm, nurturing, peaceful home environment—a place where healing and restoration occur!

- Act like a professional therapeutic foster parent—because that is what you are!

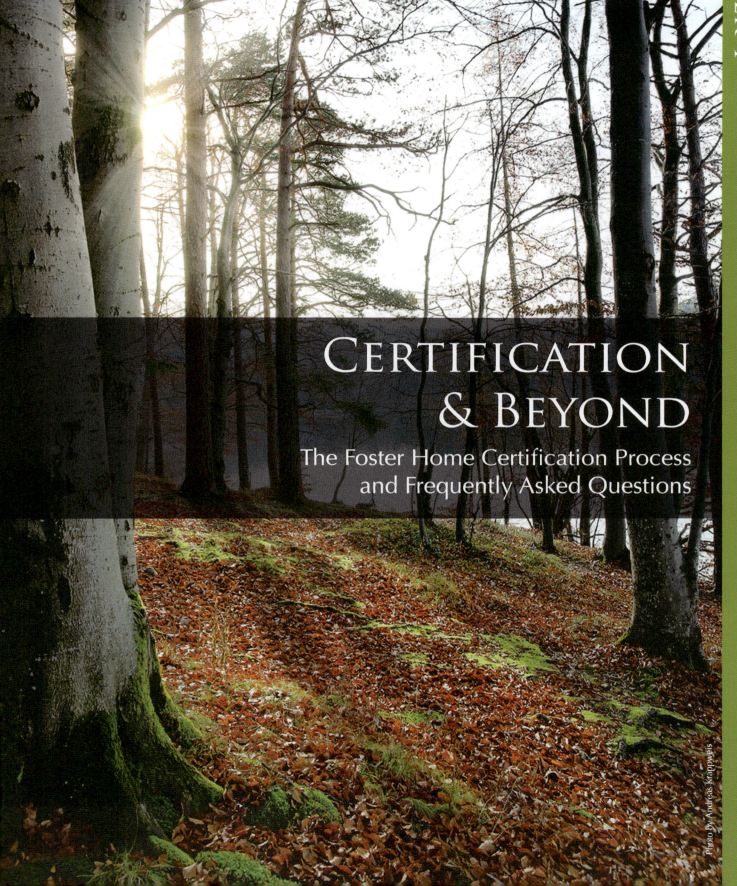

CHAPTER 4

Certification & Beyond

The Foster Home Certification Process and Frequently Asked Questions

Chapter 4

Certification & Beyond
The Foster Home Certification Process and Frequently Asked Questions

Making the decision to become a foster parent is an important one, and has the potential to bring much joy and meaning to your life and, more importantly, to the lives of the children with whom you will share your home.

The Certification Process

Before you can become a foster parent and begin working with children in your home, you must be certified. The certification process can take anywhere from 60 to 180 days. While in the process of becoming certified, you can begin to prepare for when your first foster child arrives. Here is a brief overview of the Certification Process:

- The certification process begins by a Foster Family Development Specialist or Recruiter conducting an **orientation** with you to discuss the certification process, foster care regulations and the requirements that your home must meet. This is your opportunity to ask as many questions as you can in order to make an informed decision on becoming a therapeutic foster parent.

- Following the orientation, if you decide to go forward with the process, you will then complete an application and return it the Foster Care Provider. Some agencies have multiple forms to complete and submit, while others offer an online application process. Either way, be prepared to take the time to thoroughly complete the Provider's application.

- Once the agency has received your application, there are numerous tasks which must be completed, e.g., checking your references, verifying your information and initiating all background checks.

- One of the most important tasks for you to complete is to have your fingerprints submitted for clearance by the FBI/DOJ/Child Abuse Central Index (CACI). This process can take up to two months, so it is suggested that you do this as soon as possible. A livescan form will be provided to you and you will be given instructions on where to go to complete this important step.

- Each foster parent will also be asked to complete precertification training. In California, TFC foster parents are required to complete at least seventy-two (72) hours of training in the care of emotionally disturbed or behaviorally challenged children/youth within their first year; 40 hours prior to receiving their first placement and 32 hours of annual training thereafter. In two-parent homes, placement may be made after one parent has completed 40 hours of training, provided that an additional 20 hours of ongoing in-service training are completed within 12 months after becoming a TFC foster parent, and that the second parent has completed 40 hours of training and completes an additional 20 hours of training within the first six months of certification. Training should include, but not be limited to, the following:
    - Effective communications and relationship building techniques;
    - Introduction to Therapeutic Foster Parenting;
    - Working with abused, neglected and/or delinquent children;
    - Trauma Informed Care
    - Developmental stages and age appropriate interventions;
    - First Aid and CPR;
    - De-escalation techniques;
    - Alternative forms of discipline;

- Child growth and development;
- Behavior Management Technique, including using a Behavioral Management Point/Level system;
- Differential treatment of children;
- Understanding and monitoring psychotropic medications

- The next step in the process is the **Home Study**. A Social Worker from the Foster Care Provider will contact you to set up times and dates to meet with you and all members of your family. You should anticipate meeting on two or three separate occasions at least one week apart for three-hours each time. This time frame will allow the Social Worker to obtain all necessary and pertinent background information. You may be asked to provide documents, including birth certificates, marriage license (if applicable), health records and personal references. You will also be asked to provide written information about yourselves, your family and your life experiences. At this point in the process, you will discuss with a Social Worker from your Provider what types of children you feel you can best parent and accept into your family and home.

- The final step before certification is the **Home Inspection**. The Foster Family Development Specialist or Recruiter will conduct a "walk-through" using a Home Inspection Checklist. They will do a thorough inspection of your home, looking for any health and safety concerns while making sure that the home is compliant with state licensing regulations. Typically, you will be given 30 days to make any necessary corrections; however, a child cannot be placed in your home until all corrections are made. The home inspection process will include:
    - A comprehensive interior/exterior health and safety inspection, and a review of licensing requirements and planned activities, including:
        - Buildings and grounds
        - Living areas including kitchen, bedrooms and bathrooms
        - Medication and hazardous material storage, including weapons
        - Plan to "risk-proof" the home and grounds
        - Supervision requirements
        - Foster child/youth personal rights
        - Confidentiality and record storage
        - A written report citing deficiencies (if any) and a plan of correction with a timeline signed by the prospective foster parents
        - A final approval with no remaining deficiencies

After these seven steps are completed and all required paperwork and clearances are obtained, a Certification Team will assess the readiness of the foster family and make a certification recommendation. This recommendation will include:
- Whether or not the foster home should be certified and why
- The number of children/youth to be served
- The type of children/youth to be served
- Any limitations and/or restrictions
- Additional training and/or skill building deemed necessary

Once you are certified, you will receive a Certificate of Approval and a **Certification/Foster Parenting Agreement** to sign. A Foster Family File will be prepared for you and will include copies of the documents you submitted. You will also receive training on how to maintain your files, as well as those of the foster children placed with you, and how to keep them confidentially secured.

Becoming a foster parent is a team process! You will be assisted every step of the way and you are encouraged to ask for clarification and help whenever needed.

Chapter 4

Ongoing and Annual Evaluation and Recertification Process

Foster Care Providers must conduct ongoing monitoring of TFC foster parent performance in addition to conducting a required annual recertification. Essential practices include:

- A strength-based, solution-focused evaluation and recertification process focusing on skill-building, performance-improvement and celebrating success.

- A "team-driven" process which relies on input from the Child & Family Team members working with the TFC foster family.

- An evaluation of the foster parent's role and performance as a "Therapeutic Change Agent," and as an integral part of the therapeutic process, not focused on just your regulatory compliance and health and safety issues.

- Annual Recertification should be a natural extension of the ongoing, interactive TFC foster parent evaluation process, eliminating "surprises."

- TFC foster parents should be provided the opportunity to annually submit a self-evaluation on a form prepared by their Foster Care Provider.

Once the Annual Recertification process is complete, the foster family will be given documentation showing that the process is complete and that they remain a legally certified foster home.

> Since your home is always in use as a foster home, you should always be prepared for an inspection. Your State Licensing Provider, the Department of Social/Human Services or your Foster Care Provider can come into your home at any time—sometimes with little or no notice.

Reporting Changes in Your Household

Every time a person moves into your home, even for a short time, you need to report it to your Foster Care Provider. Here are the basic rules:

- If a relative or anyone 18 years or older moves into your home (or turns 18 while still living at home) they must be fingerprinted and cleared before they can live with you.

- If your child turns 18 while you have a foster child in your care, s/he must be fingerprinted within five days of his/her birthday. If they are unable to receive a clearance, they will not be allowed to reside in your home as long as you are foster parenting.

- An adult can be a guest in your home for up to 30 days without requiring fingerprinting clearance, but your Foster Care Provider still needs to be informed of their presence in your home, and per state regulations, your foster child(ren) must never be left alone with your adult house guest(s).

- Your Foster Care Provider needs to know if anyone moves out of your home as well. Job changes, health issues, etcetera, are all important changes that need to be reported.

- You must inform your Foster Care Provider when changes are made to your home, such as the addition of a swimming pool, spa, fountain, a room addition or a trampoline.

- Any change that could directly effect the safety or wellbeing of your family or foster child(ren) placed in your home must be reported. This also includes the addition of any lethal weapons. If you have questions, call your Foster Care Provider for clarification.

- If you anticipate any changes as described above, plan these changes with your Foster Care Provider staff. They will help you make sure there are no regulation or policy violations.

- The Foster Care Provider is responsible to Community Care Licensing (CCL) for any changes in your home and would prefer to hear about them from you, rather than from a complaint filed with CCL.

"I never thought my life could get better until you guys (my foster parents) came along."

–Youth age 12

Foster Family Support

Your Foster Care Provider has the legal responsibility to support you, train you and provide 24/7 assistance to you and all foster children placed in your home. It is perfectly okay for you to be assertive in communicating your needs and in requesting guidance and assistance.

Foster Care Providers must provide ongoing training and foster parent support groups. It is the foster parent's responsibility to participate and take advantage of every opportunity to improve skills to be more successful.

Foster Parent Training and Skill Building

Foster Care Providers offer many opportunities for you to develop your skills as a TFC Foster Parent. In addition to the training offered by your agency, there are many ways you can receive additional education and training. Here are a few suggestions:

· Reading books about working with and raising children
· Researching and learning about your child's diagnosis and medications
· Watching programs on television about parenting issues
· Taking parenting or foster parenting courses from your local community college
· Researching online and taking approved courses from foster parenting websites
· Meeting with Social Workers to develop specific skills for working with your foster child's specific needs

Again, the "Best Practice" is for you to actively seek training and opportunities to improve your foster parenting skills, and to be assertive with your Foster Care Provider by communicating your training needs.

Additionally, the most effective Foster Care Providers offer "Parent" or "Family" Partners or Foster Parent Mentors to support their foster parents. Take advantage of these services, and consider becoming a Family Partner, mentor or trainer yourself.

Chapter 4

FAQ: Certification

What kind of person makes a good foster parent?

A good foster parent:
- Cares deeply about children
- Is consistent and understands that routine helps children feel secure, but also remains flexible and is able to adjust to unexpected events
- Is able to respond to a child from a place of balance and calmness
- Takes care of themselves by taking time to release their own stress in healthy ways
- Is willing to learn new parenting techniques
- Understands the child's bond with his/her biological family, and is willing to work with biological parents in the reunification process and/or towards permanency
- Is able to accept the child as they are, and offer unconditional love and approval necessary for a child's healthy development
- Has a willingness to participate in on-going training with a goal of developing therapeutic foster parenting skills
- Is sensitive to spiritual values, truths and relationships
- Has a willingness to learn and understand different cultural values and customs
- Is a team player who will work closely with staff in carrying out the child's treatment plan
- Has a willingness to work with a wide range of behaviors, in a positive, constructive manner
- Is organized but flexible
- Is responsive to administrative requirements and committed to thorough recordkeeping

What is required to become a foster parent?
- Ability to provide adult supervision for the child in your care
- Owning/renting a home that offers adequate living space and a bed for each person living in the home
- Passing a criminal history background check
- Emotional stability, free of drug or alcohol problems
- Passing a medical screening and tuberculosis (TB) test
- A valid driver's license
- A currently registered and insured vehicle to provide transportation
- Able to provide normal transportation for health care, school functions, clothes shopping, etcetera
- An existing income that adequately meets the needs of your family
- Completion of the application and certification process
- Completion of training requirements
- Home inspection, home study and interviews conducted by the Foster Care Provider staff

How long does the Certification process take?

If you are conscientious about completing the application process and attending the training, you could be certified in as little as eight weeks. The best way to speed up the process is to get the Livescan of your fingerprints done as soon as possible. Completing the health screening/TB test, providing proof of auto registration and insurance, and a DMV printout are also requirements that can be taken care of early on in the process.

What if I work out of the home?

Most foster parents are employed outside of the home and are responsible to coordinate with other caregivers to ensure that a foster child has proper supervision.

Does a foster parent need to be married or have prior child care experience?

Marriage or prior experience with children is not a prerequisite to become a foster parent. What is required is the desire and ability to work with a foster child; and to be culturally sensitive, adaptive and diverse. It is essential that you be open to learning new skills and working with a team. Foster Care Providers cannot discriminate based on race, religion, color, national origin, marital status, medical condition, political affiliation, military status, perceived gender, sexual orientation, age or any other legally protected classification.

Do I need to provide the child with his/her own bedroom?

Yes, but it can be shared with another foster or biological child/youth. Most state regulations require that no more than two children occupy one room. Once five years of age, only children of the same gender may share a room. Each child needs his/her own bed and sufficient closet and dresser space. Neither a biological child nor a foster child may share a room with someone who is 18 years or older. Infants may stay in the foster parent's bedroom until they turn three years old.

Is there any financial assistance or compensation available?

Foster parents are considered "Independent Contractors" and receive reimbursement for meeting the needs of foster children/youth. The amount received is set by the state and will be based on the type of care that is provided and the age of the child placed in the home. Families providing Therapeutic Foster Care also receive a "difficulty of care" payment. These funds are generally tax exempt, and after six months, a child in care may be considered a dependent on the foster parent's tax return (check with your tax preparer for more information). The funds are for "care and maintenance" expenses such as food; clothing; personal hygiene supplies; allowance; school supplies; childcare (including supervision for teens); recreation; transportation; housing; utilities; etcetera. Generally, foster parents are not required to maintain detailed receipts/records of their expenditures, but it is strongly recommended that you do so since you are an independent contractor.

What about medical and dental care?

Foster parents are responsible for ensuring that all necessary first aid, medical and dental services are provided to the foster children in their care, but are not responsible for paying for it. Foster children receive state medical insurance sufficient to cover the cost for all medical, dental treatment, medications or other health-care needs.

What kind of support does the Foster Care Provider offer me?

Quality Foster Care Providers offer excellent training and ongoing support to foster parents, providing them with skills and resources necessary to be the best foster parents they can be. There should be frequent contact with your Foster Care Provider's Social Workers, 24/7 emergency assistance, ongoing training and support, and an effort to provide the tools and help to make your foster home environment successful and your foster care experience rewarding.

What is "Therapeutic Foster Care" (TFC)?

Therapeutic Foster Care is a medically necessary treatment service for foster children and youth with special medical, psychological, emotional and social needs who can accept and respond to the close relationships within a family setting and require intensive therapeutic services. TFC is distinguished from "traditional" foster care, "kinship" foster care, and "specialized" foster care, where the fundamental need is for placement. TFC is the integration of foster care with mental health therapeutic services delivered through a single provider, supported by a collaborative, team-driven process.

What is different about being a TFC foster parent?

TFC foster parents provide much more than basic "care and supervision"; they are part of a treatment process. TFC foster parents are "therapeutic change agents," providing one of the most important relationships in the healing process of foster children and youth. Plus, TFC foster parents are an important member of the treatment team process. They are "Professional Foster Parents."

Who are foster children and how are they referred to Foster Care Providers?

Children who are referred to a Foster Care Provider can be from 0 to 18 years of age and come from diverse backgrounds with varying needs. All children referred to foster care have experienced some form of trauma in their lives. Just the experience of being separated from their families, no matter the circumstances, is extremely traumatic for a child. These emotionally, fragile children may experience stress from even the simplest activities and environments. Their behaviors, especially those that appear negative, are indicative of the stress they are experiencing.

Please refer to the Common Characteristics of Traumatized, Emotionally Fragile Children section located in Chapter 2.

Will I receive any information regarding the child's past history and current needs?

Foster Care Providers encourage open and honest communication at all times, wanting foster parents to be well equipped. It is a best practice for the Foster Care Provider to supply as much information as possible about a child to a foster parent so that they have a better understanding of the child's needs. As an informed foster parent, ask your Foster Care Provider about:

- Allergies, medical issues, medications and physical limitations
- Any history of mental health issues or suicidal tendencies, and about any therapy/treatment the child may have or are currently receiving
- Behavioral problems, sexual acting out or violent behaviors
- History of trauma such as physical or sexual abuse, or severe neglect
- Family relationships, siblings and extended family
- Educational needs and learning disabilities

Do I have any choice regarding who is placed in our home?

Absolutely! One of the underlying core principles of effective Therapeutic Foster Care is that foster parents have "voice, choice & preference." Throughout the certification process you will be provided ample opportunity to communicate your placement preferences. Once certified, you will always be included in the decision-making process as a member of the team.

> It is important that when a child is accepted in the foster home that their needs be met. Thus, foster parents need to make an informed decision on which placements they accept based on the best information available.

What if we want children to attend religious services with us?

Many foster families participate in some type of faith or religious activity. This is great and is in no way discouraged. However, foster children have certain rights in this regard. In essence, they have the right to attend religious services of their own choice and cannot be forced to participate in your religious activities. Efforts will be made by our staff to place children in homes compatible with their belief system. It's okay to share family beliefs, but it is not okay to force them upon a foster child. It is better to model your beliefs by your support and nurturing, and by accepting them no matter what they believe.

Can a foster child go on vacation or trips with the foster family?

Foster families are encouraged to accept a foster child as one of the family, and trips are excellent experiences for foster children. However, such plans need to be worked out in advance with the Department of Social/Human Services' Social Worker or probation officer, and Foster Care Provider staff. Additionally, any travel out of state requires a court order.

Do foster children visit with their parents or relatives?

Yes, whenever it is possible. Both Federal and State law require that foster children be reunified with family or placed in some other permanent family placement as soon as is possible. Foster children who are not able to be reunified with biological family are most often placed with and/or adopted by extended family. It is in the best interest of foster children and youth to maintain "essential, lifelong, connections," especially with relatives.

What is a "Foster Parent or Family Partner"?

A Foster Parent Partner is a mentoring foster parent. These are seasoned foster parents who make themselves available to other foster parents for help and guidance. Most of the time, a Foster Parent Partner will be able to provide the direction and answers needed. Having another experienced foster parent to call upon is one of the most important and outstanding aspects of any TFC program—foster parents willingly helping other foster parents!

What if there is an emergency concerning our foster child?

Your Foster Care Provider has a legal responsibility to provide 24/7 emergency services which include staff who can immediately take your call and respond accordingly, face-to-face if needed. TFC foster parents must be provided with current contact information and an emergency response plan. Foster parents should always call 911 for any incident involving the health and safety of the foster child/youth or other members of the household.

What length of commitment is required?

The length of time in which a foster child is placed in a home may vary with each child's individual circumstances. Some may only need temporary emergency shelter while others may need a longer-term home to provide for their needs, stabilize behavior and fulfill Juvenile Court orders. The basic rule of thumb, foster care should only be a "short term intervention" designed to facilitate a foster child's reunification or move to a permanent family. In most cases, a three to nine month placement is common.

Is adoption a possibility?

Yes, and it is an important consideration. "Permanency" is the primary goal of both federal and state law. A foster child/youth should never linger within the foster care system. If a foster child/youth cannot be reunified with biological family, adoption is the next best permanent alternative. Foster parents are a natural choice for adoption because they are familiar with the foster child/youth and it prevents another traumatic disruption. The child's Foster Care Provider's Social Worker works closely with Department of Social Services/Child Welfare Services in securing a permanent placement. Additionally, many Foster Care Providers are also licensed adoption agencies, and are therefore trained and able to facilitate adoptions.

What if a placement is not successful?

Placement decisions are made carefully to reduce the traumatizing effects of moving foster children from home to home. However, there are times when the child's needs cannot be fully or properly met, or when health and safety issues emerge. When this occurs, your Foster Care Provider's Social Worker will initiate a Child & Family Team meeting to determine if there are any interventions available to preserve the placement. In the event of a safety concern where there is imminent danger to the child and/or family, an emergency meeting will be held to address the immediate needs of the child/family.

Therapeutic Foster Care is a very successful program. Unfortunately, it is not perfect. When a placement does not work out, it presents a good opportunity for you to dialogue with your Foster Care Provider's staff to determine what might have been done differently, if anything, to prevent the disruption. The best practice is to always be solution-focused and learn from each placement experience.

CHAPTER 5

HOME & SELF CARE

How to Effectively Manage Your Foster
Home and Take Care of Yourself

CHAPTER 5

HOME & SELF CARE
How to Effectively Manage Your Foster Home and Take Care of Yourself

Managing Your Foster Home

Changes to your Home

Foster Parenting will change the dynamics of your household and it will be helpful if you anticipate some of these changes so that your family and your home is prepared to welcome foster children. Some of the things that may change when you become a Foster Parent are:

Relationships
- There will be a greater need to reserve time alone for you and your spouse/partner.
- If there are other children in the home, there may be competition for your love and attention.
- Often children will go through a process of establishing a "pecking order" and you may find it challenging to maintain consistent treatment of foster children and your children.

Budgeting Time, Money & Resources
Anticipate increased laundry, bigger grocery bills and more transportation needs. Family activities can become more complicated and more expensive as well, so the need to budget expenses will increase.

Communication
Communication is very important. If you have biological children you have a history of relating to one another and your communication style is well established. This will not be the case with newly placed foster children.

Personal Space/Time
Everyone's personal space may change; with family members possibly requiring some sort of schedule for bathroom, computer and telephone time. There will also be numerous outside agencies that will be in your home from time to time offering assistance, which can sometimes seem overwhelming. You can see why effective management of your foster home is essential.

Stress Levels
Without a doubt, everyone's stress levels will go up and down a lot more!

Management Tools

To effectively deal with these changes and successfully manage your home you will need:

Good Communication
We start with this one because it is the foundation for making your foster care experience successful.

Preparation
Planning ahead and anticipating the needs of all members of your family is essential.

Active Listening
Learn the skills of really listening, avoiding the need to always give advice. Be attentive, be present and be quiet. Listening is much more effective than lecturing!

Respond Instead of React
Don't overreact or personalize what you are hearing and seeing. If you feel your emotions catching fire, here is a great, very effective technique:

- STOP – Stop the interaction;

- DROP – Take some deep, calming breaths. Walk away for 10 or 15 minutes to regain your balance and then

- ROLL – Roll back into the conversation.

In most instances, you do not need to respond immediately, if at all. Your role is to help the child first to adjust and then to encourage them to solve their own problems, not to do it for them! Let them own their problems.

Clarity
Make messages understandable, specific and consistent. Your foster child's emotional state may prevent him or her from hearing or possibly remembering what you tell him/her. Writing things down can be very helpful.

Flexibility and Acceptance
Learn to have a high level of tolerance and not overreact to behaviors of the child; remember that negative behavior is the effect of emotional stress. Underneath the behavior is usually fear and when that fear is relieved, the behaviors will lessen. In two-parent homes, the parents must communicate with each other and help each other to stay balanced, which helps to provide clarity and consistency for the child.

A Calm Home Environment
Many foster children have experienced chaos and unpredictability in their previous home lives. Their five senses may be extremely sensitive to things such as light, smells, sounds and even the touch of different textures. Create a home environment that is "Slow and Low." Consider decorating with soft neutral colors, lower the volume of TV and radios, and use soft lighting when possible. The subtle fragrance of lavender or vanilla can have a very calming effect on the whole family.

Family Meetings
Schedule a consistent family meeting time. Sit down together as a group and encourage all family members to participate in a discussion about the upcoming week's activities, family member's successes and challenges, and any other issues in the home. Don't forget to use the communication tips mentioned above or feel free to ask the child's Social Worker for assistance, advice or participation. If things come up in the family meeting that are critical and tense, make sure the Social Worker is informed and request their help.

Family Routines
Every family has routines and rules that are spoken and unspoken. We suggest that you sit down and identify your family's routines and rules; write them down so that a foster child will know what to expect. Things like:

- Wake up time
- Morning hygiene
- Bathroom use
- Computer and cell phone use
- Dinner time
- Curfew
- What is allowable to watch on TV and when
- Breakfast time and how it's served
- Homework
- Discuss how the family handles chores
- Evening activities
- Bed time

CHAPTER 5

BASIC FAMILY RULES AND EXPECTATIONS

It's a given that foster children arrive with a different set of expectations and practices based on their culture and life experiences. It is not uncommon for their practices to be in direct conflict with yours, creating a "Cultural Conflict." Before introducing a lot of structure and rules, make every effort to understand who your foster child is and his/her "unique culture." Here are some good practices to follow:

- Strive to develop a relationship of safety, trust and mutual respect with the child. Remember: "rules without relationship = rebellion."

- Whenever possible, emphasize safety and your overall concern for your foster child's wellbeing.

- Explain the reasoning behind a particular rule. Never say "Because I said so" as it only creates a power struggle.

- When rules are broken, first consider the possible reasons for the child's behavior. S/he may be reacting to past trauma and what appears to you to be a disregard of the rules is really their way of managing their fear. Use these opportunities to talk and listen to the child. You might learn that a certain family routine, such as everyone sitting down together at the dinner table is an emotional trigger for the child. Talk with the child about possible alternatives that would work for everyone.

- Calm conversation with a child when a rule is broken can be a "teachable moment" where life lessons are learned.

- Never use guilt, fear, shame or blame to get a child to follow the rules. This is not only a bad practice; it is a violation of their personal rights.

"You should always listen to older people. They are like living history books and can teach you so much."

–Youth age 13

The following are basic guidelines for setting rules and expectations with foster children:

Curfew
The first step in setting curfews is knowing whether the child already has an existing court-ordered curfew or imposed time limitations set by probation terms. It is also important to know what curfew expectation a child's placement worker and Social Worker may have. The second step is understanding that curfew times should be age appropriate.

Smoking
Unfortunately, there will be youth in foster care who smoke. Legally, foster families may not allow foster children to smoke within the home environment. A foster parent may not give permission for a foster child to smoke, nor may they purchase cigarettes for foster children. Two important suggestions for dealing with smoking are: don't power struggle over the issue and work closely with the child's Social Worker to make sure it is addressed in his/her Child & Family Plan.

Dating and Relationships
Interest in dating and sexuality is part of every teen's normal development. If you have an adolescent foster child, the subject will undoubtedly come up. This is a subject that must be addressed by the Child & Family Team in order to create the guidelines for dating activities if appropriate. Other points to consider are: legal restrictions, (i.e. probation terms; input from the child's placement worker and Social Worker; the child's age, maturity, behaviors, etcetera). Foster parents might also treat dating/sexuality discussions as opportunities to discuss self-care, safety and respect with their foster children.

Homework

Foster parents need to set clear guidelines and expectations regarding when, where and how homework should be completed. Remember, many children in foster care have missed school and may, therefore, be behind in academic skills and/or have learning disabilities. Your child's Social Worker can help arrange tutoring or other assistance if your child is struggling with schoolwork.

Basic Chores and Duties

It is expected that foster children/youth assume household responsibilities as would any other child. Age, capability and equity between foster and other children in the family are issues to consider. Household chores may never be imposed as a consequence or punishment. Rather, it is a way to include the foster child in family routines and an opportunity for them to learn new skills. Don't ever assume a child or youth knows the correct way to complete a chore—always take the time necessary to demonstrate your expectations.

Equipment Use

Foster children, like most children, enjoy watching TV, using computers, game machines, bicycles and other family-used equipment. Foster care regulations encourage normal family activity, accompanied with proper instruction and parameters for use. Make sure to carefully supervise your foster child's use of the internet and always have "parental controls" functioning on your browser. Always remember that there must be equity of use between foster and other children in the home, and consult with the child's Social Worker if there are any questions or problems. To show differential treatment may be a violation of a child's personal rights.

Dress Codes

How a foster child/youth dresses should not become a major point of contention or struggle between the foster family and children/youth. It is suggested that you allow children to wear what they choose unless it is dirty, torn, ripped or in ill repair; it is sexually inappropriate and revealing; or if it shows disrespect to others (i.e., t-shirts with inappropriate or offensive slogans or sayings.) Again, foster parents need to consult closely with the child's Social Worker regarding dress code issues.

Laundry

It is suggested that foster parents not require foster children to do their own laundry, but instead offer to teach them this basic life skill. There are times when this is essential, such as when a foster youth is preparing for independent living. When it is the family's age-appropriate practice for children to do their own laundry, foster children should be treated like the other children in the home. Please make sure that they are given very clear instructions and close supervision until you are confident they can do this task properly.

Other Rules and Behaviors

Again, foster families are encouraged to share their family culture and daily routine with foster children upon placement. Be careful not to impose too many rules or expectations which can become overwhelming for a child and cause resistance. It is strongly recommended that foster families include the child/youth in the process of creating rules and behavior expectations. The Child & Family Team can help with this process.

> Foster children will most likely come from a family with a distinctly different culture than yours. This can create conflict, as well as "teachable moment" opportunities. Be open minded and have reasonable expectations. Always be as preventative as possible and be sensitive to the child's ability to understand and comply. Accept the child "where they are," knowing that as your relationship deepens with them, their ability to meet your expectations will improve.

Family Activities

Foster parents should plan activities involving the entire family, including foster children. Family activities help to facilitate a feeling of togetherness and closeness among the whole group. These activities include: camping; watching movies; playing board or card games; having picnics; going on walks and bike rides; reading books; telling stories; playing musical instruments; baking (especially during holiday seasons); visiting the library; sewing; holding traditional holiday activities; and celebrating birthdays and other special occasions. NEVER treat a foster child/youth differently than other children in your home. They need to feel like they belong and they won't if they perceive that they are somehow not a "real" member of the family. Also, try to engage in cultural activities which are comfortable and familiar to your foster child/youth.

Foster Children/Your Children

It is normal to have different feelings toward your children than toward foster children, but that shouldn't make you less effective as a parent. Try not to show favoritism or act more positively toward your own children. Foster children are quick to sense these differences and can feel rejected. If over time you continue to struggle with this issue, work with the Child & Family Team to resolve the matter, or consider taking some time off from being a foster parent. Many wait to foster parent until after their own children are grown and out of the home.

In any family it is normal for there to be some kind of sibling rivalry. Be prepared to deal with conflict and jealousy between other children in the home and foster children. Biological and foster siblings will be very similar to natural siblings in this respect!

Helpful guidelines to follow:

- Make sure your foster child feels like a full member of the family.
- Be very respectful of his or her culture and family background.
- Be consistent in rewards and consequences.
- What's good for one is good for another.
- Make special time for each child. Take time to listen to their needs and feelings.
- Be sure to include foster children in all significant family activities.
- Use family meetings as a forum to talk about concerns or particular needs.
- Be proactive and look for solutions that have the best outcome for all involved.
- Teach each child to respect others' personal belongings, individual privacy, opinions and feelings.
- Discourage sharing or borrowing of clothes or other belongings that would hurt a relationship if lost or damaged.

> Sibling rivalry is normal and to be expected, so don't overreact! Always ask for help when needed.

Appropriate Touching

The law is very clear: laying your hands on a child as a form of discipline is not appropriate; but touching is normal and essential for human beings. With foster children, though, what you consider "normal" touching, such as hugs, pats, etcetera, may not be okay. For instance, with children who have been victims of physical or sexual abuse, a hug may trigger a negative reaction or be perceived as sexual in nature.

Helpful guidelines to follow:

- Always talk to the child's Social Worker to get specific information and advice. Be mindful of the fact that every child is different, and his/her need for human contact will vary depending on past experiences.
- Never approach a child quickly or unexpectedly. For example: do not rush up behind them to give them a hug.
- Avoid frontal hugs, especially male to female. This may be okay with younger children, but please talk with your agency's Social Worker first. It is recommended that foster parents use side-by-side hugs or gentle squeezes.
- Ask permission. For example, ask "Can I give you a hug? Is it okay if I pat your shoulder?" Don't make assumptions that this kind of affection is okay.
- Think before you touch. Anticipate how the child may react or interpret your action.
- Respect the child's boundaries—don't make them feel bad if they reject your affections.
- Always accept a small child's hugs if they are offered to you. If an older child wants a hug, turn your body and give them a side hug.
- Never slap or touch a child's buttocks.
- Avoid wrestling, rough tickling or similar activity.
- Only young children should be allowed to sit on your lap. Sitting side by side can be just as affectionate.
- Don't ever make suggestive comments or jokes in the presence of a foster child/youth!
- The basic rule to follow is to make sure nothing you do can be misinterpreted as a sexual or threatening gesture. Touching must be viewed as though through the eyes of the foster child, and not necessarily what is normal for your family.
- Make sure that other children in your home understand the necessity of being sensitive to and following these guidelines.

Foster Children and Their Families

Most foster children have some connection with their biological family. Many are in the process of family reunification and have court ordered visits with parents or relatives. Reunification can be one of the most difficult situations for foster parents to accept, especially if the biological parents have been abusive. Nonetheless, it is not only the law, but research has demonstrated that it is in the best interest of foster children/youth to be in permanent families, even where prior abuse has occurred.

A Few Points to Remember

- The Juvenile Court must attempt reunification or pursue a permanent family.

- Even when a child has been abused by his/her parent, s/he is still that parent's child. It is normal for the child to be protective of an abusive parent and even deny the abuse to others.

- Since it is the primary goal of the foster care system to reunite families whenever possible, or to place children in permanent families, foster parents play a critical role towards this end, with many even becoming adoptive or guardianship families.

Family Visits are scheduled with biological parents or relatives in order to comply with court ordered case plans. These visits will be coordinated by the child's Social Worker in conjunction and cooperation with the placement agency. Always request a written schedule of planned visits to ensure that they are not missed. Visits may include different individuals that provide transportation and/or supervise the visit. This can include agency staff as well as representatives from the county placement agency and even the foster parents.

It is important to remember that the foster family cannot change or stop visitation from occurring without a court order. Obviously, when the child is sick the child's Social Worker needs to be immediately contacted. If the child's safety is in question, then the visit may be cancelled but only by the child/youth's county placement worker.

Here are some ways that you as a foster parent can help make family visits go more smoothly:

- Keep a family calendar for special events, visitations, birthdays, etcetera, and make sure that everyone updates their PDA's, computer calendars, etcetera.

- Be sure to schedule family activities with your foster children that do not conflict with their visitation. As a side note, when your foster child is on a visitation, it can provide you with an excellent opportunity to have one-on-one time with your own children.

- Be supportive and encourage children before and after visits.

- After family visits, it is not unusual for foster children/youth to act out their feelings. It is at these times that you may notice a difference in their behavior. Be understanding and most important, listen! You do not need to provide solutions, but providing them a listening ear can help them process their feelings and come up with solutions on their own.

- It is important to make it a habit to keep notes in their file that describe their behavior and/or mood and attitude before and after these visits.

SPEAK UP

Finally, with all the additional activity going on in your home, the presence of social workers, probation officers, in-home support counselors, etcetera, it is easy to forget that it is your home. Your home is the "nest" where your family feels safe, and you should take the steps necessary to keep it that way. Speak up! If there is something going on with your foster child that disturbs you, whether it is a behavior, reaction to visits with bio family, treatment (or lack thereof), talk to someone. That "someone" might be the child's Social Worker, a foster parent partner, the child's therapist or the Child & Family Team, the point is that you need to identify your concerns and create a plan to resolve them. Letting concerns or negative feelings fester is not good for you and ultimately may be very detrimental to your family and your foster child. Foster parents are not expected to surrender their home to frightening or extremely disturbing experiences. If you feel uncomfortable or unsafe, you must speak up and resolve the issues in order to restore the safety and security of your "nest."

Learning To Care For Yourself

"Whenever I tell someone I'm a foster parent of teen boys, they tell me I must be a saint. But, you know, I get as much out of the experience as the foster kids. People have a hard time believing this, but it is absolutely true for me. As I watch the boys start to do better in school, or get their first job, or graduate from high school, I feel a sense of pride and satisfaction that no job has ever come close to providing me." -Foster Parent of 16 years

Foster parents have the most impact on the healing of traumatized children. There is no doubt that foster parenting is one of the most fulfilling and rewarding endeavors a person can undergo. But, the rewards and benefits can also come at a cost to your privacy and peace of mind. In this chapter we will discuss some proven strategies for making sure that you are able to be the best foster parent possible by taking good care of yourself.

It goes without saying that when a foster child thrives under your care, your feelings of satisfaction and sense of pride will grow. However, success for a foster child can look a lot differently than success for your own children or even yourself. For a child that has been absent from school for long periods of time, just going to school every day is a huge accomplishment. A child that has a tantrum every night about going to bed has made great progress if they can calmly go to bed one or two nights a week. Successes for foster children often come in small increments and take a lot more time than you might imagine to achieve.

When you stick with the child through all the good and bad times, the rewards are great. Not only will the child's life be impacted for the better, but so will yours. Take a moment and reflect on what inspired you to become a foster parent in the first place, because these motivating factors can have a positive effect on your experience as a foster parent.

Healthy Motivators
· Do you believe foster parenting is your life's purpose?
· Do you like children and feel like you have an abundance of love to give?
· Do you feel like you can help your community by fostering parenting?
· Did you become a foster parent to help a particular child or family?
· Do you believe that you are a good parent to your own children, so you will be a good foster parent?

Motivators That Can Lead to Disappointment
· Do you need the financial benefits to maintain your current lifestyle?
· Were you lonely and looking for companionship?
· Were you looking for a companion/playmate for your own child?

Whatever your inspiration, just know that things may not go the way you have envisioned, so you need to be open to different outcomes. Sometimes the biggest rewards come in ways you would never have expected.

The success of a foster child/youth depends very much on the balance and self-discipline of the foster parents and the home. Unfortunately, in day-to-day life we often put our own self-care as our lowest priority.

A Few Points to Remember

- Learn how to take care of yourself. This is an important skill you can develop as a caregiver.

- Model how you take care of yourself to help your foster children learn how to take better care of themselves.

- Maintain good physical and mental health.

- Parenting any child is a demanding and stressful job. For many foster parents, the day to day stress of caring for a high-needs child or children takes an emotional and physical toll.

- You need to have a plan to take care of your physical, mental and emotional needs on a regular basis in order to avoid getting burned out.

FIRST, TAKE CARE OF YOURSELF

Anyone who has ever flown on an airplane has heard the flight attendant say, "In the event of loss of cabin pressure oxygen masks will deploy. Be sure to place the mask on yourself before placing the mask on your child." In other words, in order for you to take the best care of your child, you need to first take care of yourself.

Schedule "You-Time"
Everyone needs their own space and quiet time, so schedule this for yourself and let everyone know. Whether it's reading, painting, walking, meditation or prayer—whatever you need to recharge your batteries—do it!

Sanctuary
Create a sanctuary for quiet and reflection. It could be a place outside in your garden or it could be at your desk or in your bedroom—it could even be in your bathroom if that's the only place you can get some peace and quiet. Select some peaceful music that you can listen to. Make this a daily practice, not just something you only do when you are in a state of stress or are upset.

Learn to STOP, DROP AND ROLL

- STOP – Stop the interaction;

- DROP – Take some deep, calming breaths. Walk away for 10 or 15 minutes to regain your balance and then

- ROLL – Roll back into the conversation.

Prepare
Prepare for tomorrow the night before so you don't get stressed or hurried. Begin each day with a clear intention for smooth sailing. Don't rely on your memory for important things; instead utilize a master calendar, write notes and lists—whatever you can do to take the burden off yourself of having to remember every little thing. Sometimes you will need to relax your standards and "go with the flow." Always have a plan B, C and even a D for when things don't go as you had planned. And don't forget to BREATHE!

Finding balance is a learning process and it takes time. Learn how to say "No" when you need to!

Manage your Physical Health
Don't discount the importance of good physical health management.

- Eat a healthy, balanced diet, including breakfast. Try to avoid eating on the run, at your desk or in the car.

- Limit your caffeine and alcohol intake.

- Exercise regularly.

- Develop a consistent sleep schedule that includes an adequate amount of rest.

- Take regular breaks from stressful activities—find a way, every day, to have at least a few minutes to yourself.

- Have regular doctor checkups and when you do get sick take the necessary steps to get better—don't try to tough it out!

- Express yourself. If you're feeling frustrated, sad or angry, be honest about your emotions before they get out of control. Express the positive as well by making time to do something you love, such as a craft, game, writing, painting, sports, etcetera.

- Let someone else do something to take care of you.

- Laughter really is good medicine, so keep a good sense of humor and be sure to laugh often.

Discover Your Strengths

The "Best Practice" of an effective Foster Care Provider is to focus on "Strength-Based" methods and solutions. Likewise, it is important for you as a foster parent to discover your own strengths and learn to identify the strengths in your foster child.

- One way to do this is to ask your best friend or spouse to list your strengths. Often we are hesitant to name our own strengths, yet our closest friends have no trouble creating a long list.

- If you are in a relationship, talk with your partner about the strengths you see in each other. Then develop strategies that utilize your strengths and your partner's strengths as a team.

- Establish your roles with each new placement as you may need to change your roll depending on the personality, interests and needs of each child. Maintain flexibility and don't set yourself up for situations where you know you will not be at your best.

COUPLES

Good relationships don't just happen; they take effort on the part of both partners.

- Make sure you schedule regular "date nights" and practice good communication by taking the time to talk with each other and share experiences daily.

- Don't "dump" on each other as soon as one of you walks in the door at the end of the day. Give each other time to wind down and change gears.

- Consider attending couple's retreats, classes, seminars, etcetera, taking the opportunity to help re-focus on each other's needs and to strengthen your "team."

- At times when you experience differences or disagreements, be sure to model appropriate conflict resolution. Talk it out. Avoid shouting or dramatic, manipulative behaviors.

You must learn to manage your own behavior before you can effectively manage a child's behavior! The healthier your relationship is, the healthier your family is, which means less stress and turmoil.

> Most foster children don't know what healthy relationships look like or what is normal. You are modeling healthy behavior and showing your foster child that you can have your needs heard or met without emotional outbursts or loss of control. To the extent that you are able to do this, it may very well "break the pattern of abuse" for your foster child, teaching them to treat others in their lives as you do—with patience and respect.

SINGLE PARENTS

Fostering as a single parent presents some unique demands and needs. It is important not to become so involved in parenting that you forget yourself. You need regular adult contact and relationships.

- Be sure to have a friend, possibly another foster parent who you are able to call when you feel you need another's feedback or a listening ear.

- Just as with couples who are foster parents, it is very important to schedule time for outside social activities away from children.

- For a single foster parent it is essential to have a few approved caregivers who you can call in an emergency, as well as to give you regular time out. Work closely with your Foster Care Provider to help arrange for temporary care.

YOUR FAMILY'S NEEDS

While you are expected to include foster children in most family events, there are times when you may need to do things with just your own family. It's not uncommon for your biological children to feel like they are not getting the same kind of attention they used to get before the foster child arrived, and to some extent, they may be right! Be sure to have individual one-on-one time with each child when possible. A good opportunity to do something special with your child is when a foster child is on a home visit or attending an activity. The key is to do things in such a manner as to not have the foster child feel intentionally left out or rejected. For example, it would be a terrible message if the family goes to an amusement park and doesn't include the foster child.

ASK FOR HELP

Foster parents are professionals and, like all successful professionals, they need to seek guidance and assistance to be successful.

- You are part of a team, so use the team to help relieve pressure and diffuse problems.

- Know when to ask for help and advice, and do it often.

- The importance of clear communication cannot be stressed enough. One of the "Core Principles" in effective foster parenting is to ensure that foster parents, as well as clients, have "Voice, Choice and Preference," which means your needs, opinions and preferences are very important, and should be addressed by your Foster Care Provider.

- Do not believe that you have to sacrifice your life to give to others.

> In the event you disagree with the foster child/youth's Child & Family Plan, or experience a disagreement with someone involved with the child, learn the proper way to communicate your feelings. You should discuss your concerns with the child's Foster Care Provider's Social Worker. If, after discussing the situation with the Social Worker, you still feel that your voice is not being heard, ask to speak with your Foster Care Provider's Supervising Social Worker or Manager. You need to feel that you can express your opinions and concerns freely, but always appropriately. Never express your frustration or concerns to your foster child.

Time Out

Every foster parent needs a short break once in a while. It's not a sign of weakness or failure; it's the right thing to do given the amount of energy, time and attention it takes to parent a high-needs child. Ask the agency to arrange to have the child/youth spend a few days in another home in order to give you a break. Who knows, you may be called on to give another foster parent a respite break!

> **It is very important that you have an approved Temporary Care Provider (as you know, even foster teens need to be supervised by an adult while in your home). Be sure to complete a Temporary Care Provider request form and submit it to your child's Social Worker at least two weeks before you need your foster child to be in someone else's care. Approvals and clearances need to be obtained.**

Have a Good Support Group

One of the best ways to be an effective foster parent is to be connected with another foster parent or parents in general. You need a place to share ideas, feelings, frustrations and techniques. Just remember not to breach confidentiality by talking about a specific child's problems, background, etcetera; instead, talk in generalities focusing on managing behaviors, solutions, best practices and lessons learned.

Foster parent training and support meetings are invaluable. You may believe that the subject matter doesn't pertain to you but the questions and comments from other foster parents can be very enlightening and they provide you with another way to develop your network of support. Other foster parents, sharing from their own experiences, will teach you patterns to anticipate and offer practical solutions to some typical behaviors of both biological and foster children. The lessons learned from seasoned foster parents can help you to respond like a veteran yourself.

Attend meetings concerning your foster child because important decisions are going to be made whether you're there or not. You can prevent frustration by attending these meetings and advocating for the specific needs of the child. After all, you know the subtle details, the likes, dislikes and personality traits of your particular foster child. Make every effort to participate and share pertinent information that could affect decisions made on his/her behalf. Your attendance at these meetings also keeps you informed of schedule changes and new appointments which can greatly reduce confusion and, in turn, your own stress levels.

> **Whether you participate in foster parent support groups, retreats, church groups, social or service clubs, the point is to make foster parenting a part of your life; just don't make it your whole life! Have a solid plan for meeting your needs and you will find that you are better able to meet the needs of those who depend on you.**

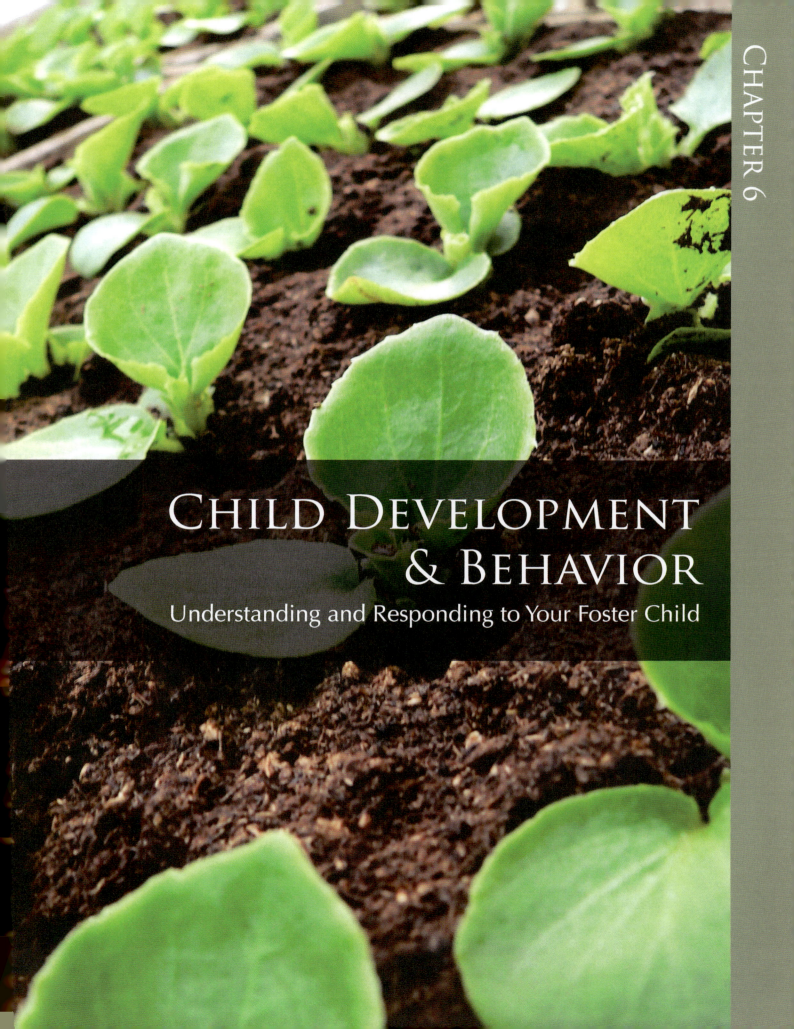

Chapter 6

Child Development & Behavior
Understanding and Responding to Your Foster Child

In this chapter you are presented with a basic overview of a child's stages of development and are introduced to some of the most innovative and effective methods for understanding and responding to children's behaviors. Also included in this chapter are the teachings and concepts of Parent Effectiveness Training by Dr. Thomas Gordon, Active Parenting by Dr. Michael Popkin, as well as the work on trauma by Dr. Bruce Perry and Juli Alvarado. These authorities support the basic belief that children and youth are resilient and are able to develop solutions to meet their needs with the proper support and guidance. They also support a philosophy that the relationship between foster parents and children is "therapeutic" and is instrumental in the development of resiliency, self-respect and the promotion of healing from severe trauma and critical life crises.

Child Development

Much research has been devoted to the study of the growth and development of human beings during the first 18 years of life, and to identify ways to encourage positive development at certain life stages. This information is especially useful when working with children and youth who have experienced trauma, abuse and neglect as it gives us insight into specific needs and challenges they may present.

Abuse and neglect literally changes the way the brain operates and affects the "typical" development of a child in many ways. Foster Parents play an important role in helping a child by providing a genuine, loving, supportive relationship that encourages healthy physical, emotional and social development.

Infancy (ages birth to 2)

- This is the most important growth time for a human being as this is when vital connections are being made in the brain.

- All the senses are developing and the need for safety and nurturing is paramount as the child is basically helpless.

- Experience, especially interactions with parents or other care givers, determines the growth and pattern of brain development. The more an experience is repeated (such as repeating a word or phrase to a baby) the stronger the brain connections become.

- It is during this stage of development that the child bonds or attaches to a parent figure who is ensuring that all their basic needs are met.

- A baby who has experienced trauma will develop a brain that is "wired" for survival, causing the child to be on constant alert for danger.

- Foster parents can fulfill the attachment and safety needs so that the infant will understand how to bond later to others.

Early Childhood (Ages 2-6)

- Early childhood is a time of social development and discovering identity and personality.

- Children in this stage tend to observe adults and imitate what they do to assist them in learning about their own identity and skills.

- In this stage, children who are victims of abuse and neglect are also victims of poorly modeled behaviors. These children are not given the opportunity to observe healthy behaviors and roles and, therefore, what they consider normal may fall far outside the boundaries of what society considers "normal."

- Anticipated Stages of Development
    - Emphasis on self—view themselves as the "center of the universe"
    - Identification with own gender
    - Enjoyment in group play
    - Attachment to their primary caregiver
    - Need for secure environment
    - Learning and understanding emotional cues
    - Processing what they see and hear

- Ways to Encourage Growth
    - Build self-esteem and pro-social development
    - Emphasize positive caring
    - Teach and practice good health
    - Model appropriate behavior to help them re-learn what is appropriate

Middle Childhood (Ages 6-12)

- During this stage, children begin to understand logical systems, and their new level of thinking gives them more advanced problem solving skills.

- Children at this stage are also able to think about how others perceive them, and they understand that a person is capable of feeling one way and acting another.

- These new understandings make rules and "fairness" very important.

- As children become rule focused, they begin to judge behaviors and they tend to believe that there should be consequences for breaking the rules.

- Anticipated Stages of Development
    - Oriented to parents and teachers
    - Focused attention on learning and solving problems
    - Enjoys group play with peers of same gender
    - Often competitive
    - Manages fears, anxieties and aggression
    - Impressed by older role models
    - Learns behavior from parents, peers, TV, role models
    - May begin to experiment with drugs—more concerned with physical effects than social

- Ways to Encourage Growth
    - Teaching coping skills.
    - Involving the child in setting up expectations, rules and consequences before problems arise
    - Providing feedback on behavior
    - Using peer assistance and positive role models (limit negative influences)
    - Helping them to become competent at making good decisions/choices
    - Promoting healthy eating habits

Adolescence & Emerging Adulthood (ages 13-18)

- Ask almost anyone about typical adolescent behavior and they will mention how much time adolescents want to spend alone in their room or plugged into music.

- They may also mention the amount of time an adolescent prefers to spend with friends instead of family.

- These behaviors are developmentally appropriate as youth in this stage are developing their individualization—their sense of self—and this takes a lot of reflection and processing.

- It is important to foster an adolescent's self-esteem and problem solving skills by pointing out strengths and encouraging the possibility for change, especially when confronting a negative situation or choice.

- Anticipated Stages of Development
    - Focused on the present rather than future
    - Preoccupied with self-presentation and acceptance of peers
    - Beginning of sexual exploration
    - Seeking opportunities for independent moral judgment
    - Feeling unsure and awkward in social skills
    - Motivated by peer pressure regarding drug use more than the physical effects
    - Critical Thinking skills are developing with practice

- Ways to Encourage Growth
    - Promoting leadership skills and identifying the consequences of their choices regarding drug and alcohol use
    - Focusing on self-respect
    - Encouraging goals
    - Valuing and knowing their friends
    - Opening lines of communication

The Effects of Trauma on Children

Every child who comes into foster care has experienced some kind of trauma in their lives, whether it be physical, mental or both. Just being removed from their families is traumatic, but many have also experienced horrible traumatic events that resulted in their being placed into care. This trauma can be attributed to one single event lasting for a limited amount of time (Acute Trauma) or from Chronic Trauma in which recurrent traumatic events occur over a long period of time.

Examples of **Acute Trauma**
- Being in a car accident
- Witnessing (or being a victim of) an act of violence or crime
- Physical or sexual assault
- Witnessing a loved one die

Examples of **Chronic Trauma**
- Long-term traumatic events of the same kind (such as physical or sexual abuse)
- The experience of many traumatic events such as witnessing their parents fight and experiencing physical abuse
- Being hurt in a violent incident and having to undergo weeks/months of medical treatments and/or physical therapy.

Complex Trauma occurs when a child experiences continued traumatic events from a very young age (usually age 5 and under) **as a result of actions by their parents or other significant adults who should have been caring for them and protecting them**. Repeated physical and sexual abuse, combined with prolonged neglect, is an example of Complex Trauma.

According to mental health experts, traumatic events differ from run-of-the-mill, stressful or upsetting events in a number of ways:

- First, it threatens the life or physical integrity of the child or of someone critically important to the child (parent, sibling, etc.)

- Second, it causes an overwhelming sense of terror, helplessness and horror

- Third, the body reacts automatically by releasing stress hormones which cause an increased heart rate, shaking, dizziness or faintness, rapid breathing, possible loss of bowel or bladder control.

The physical responses to trauma can be terrifying in and of themselves. Feeling that their body is out of control adds to the child's feelings of helplessness and panic. It can feel like the danger is both outside them and inside their bodies at the same time.

CHANGES IN DEVELOPMENT DUE TO TRAUMA

While it is important to know the basics of child development, it is even more important for Therapeutic Foster Parents to know how children with mental health needs or children who have been abused and neglected may vary from these expectations.

Trauma effects the normal development of the brain and changes the way the brain functions.

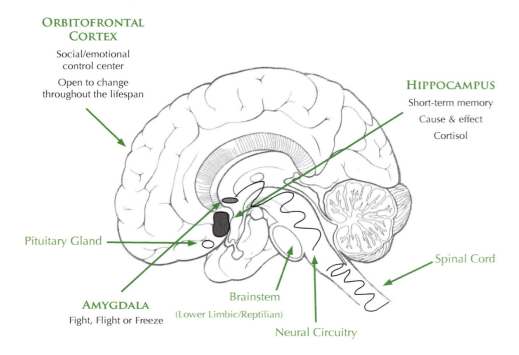

A part of the brain called the Amygdala responds to real or perceived threats by sending a message to other parts of the brain to release hormones that assists the **"fight, flight or freeze"** response. One of these hormones is **Adrenaline**, which causes the body to prepare for fight or flight by increasing the heart and breath rate, diverting blood flow to the muscles and heart (away from the brain and other organs such as the skin).

Cortisol is another stress response hormone which is released by the part of the brain called the hippocampus. Cortisol gives the body a quick burst of energy, lowers sensitivity to pain and helps restore calm and balance. These hormones are meant to provide short-term relief from stress, and subside when external relief is received, such as when a baby is crying because she is hungry and Mom arrives with food and a warm, loving touch.

For those who have experienced long periods of traumatic events without the external interventions that tell the brain that everything is now safe, the stress hormones will continue to flood the brain and normal functioning is impaired. **Basically, the brain becomes damaged.** These children may show one or more of the following characteristics:

Observable Behaviors

- Traumatic play in which a child acts out the story of the trauma. They might even take on the role of the abuser or they might become a superhero flying in to the rescue
- Trouble going to sleep or staying asleep
- Sudden, dramatic mood swings

- The child may not "act their age," instead behaving like a much younger child
- Difficulty with school such as truancy, poor performance, behavior issues
- Delinquent, anti-social behavior
- Reckless, risky behavior such as running away, sexual promiscuity, disregard for personal safety
- Rage or anger
- Crying and overly emotional
- Food related issues such as hoarding or eating disorders
- Hyper sensitivity to sounds, textures, light
- Suicidal or self-destructive tendencies
- Limited or negative interactions with parents or other adults
- Drug or alcohol use

Thoughts and Feelings
- Feels unloved or uncared for, has a very low self-image
- Doesn't have a sense of belonging
- Feels no control over their life or over personal situations
- Lacks a sense of any personal power
- Can't see a positive future for themselves
- Distrusts adults
- Lacks self-control
- Lacks goals or dreams
- Confused about their feelings
- Feels like a victim
- Has no support system (friends or family) or has a negative support system (gang)
- Lacks decision-making and problem solving skills

THE BRAIN IS THE BOSS OF BEHAVIOR

Repeated traumatic experiences alter critical pathways in the developing brain. A child who has been traumatized over and over again may not react normally to even minor, every day stresses. Behaviors that happen under stress are responses to the stress and not usually a choice. The brain is calling the shots and the child is probably incapable of doing anything different at that moment.

It is important that you be observant and aware of any abrupt changes in a child's behavior and record your observations so that you can share this information with the child's Social Worker, doctor, etc.

The good news is that children and youth whose development has been affected by trauma can learn new ways of thinking, relating and responding emotionally. In fact, the part of the brain that is associated with reason and analysis (Orbitofrontal Cortex) continues to develop throughout adolescence and into adulthood.

By providing new, positive experiences and examples, we can help traumatized children and youth build new brain connections and by-pass old ones. The healing process of unlearning and rebuilding takes time and patience, but foster parents should always remember that there is hope and the potential for change.

"Life is filled with ups and downs but most of the time I'm going sideways."

—Youth age 11

Chapter 6

Creating Safety for a Tramatized Child

Physical safety is not always the same as psychological safety. A person can be physically safe and not feel safe. Additionally, a child's definition of safety will probably not be the same as yours.

Children who have experienced trauma may get great comfort and a sense of safety from things we take for granted, like having heat in every room of the house or food in the refrigerator. On the other hand, actions and activities that we consider comforting, such as a pat on the shoulder or a warm bath, may have dangerous overtones to a child who has been physically or sexually abused.

Children who have been through trauma may need more control, more reassurance and more information to feel psychologically and physically safe. There are several ways you can help create a feeling of safety in your foster child:

- The most important thing you can do is know yourself. Learn what increases your stress level and ways to maintain emotional regulation and balance. The ways that you model emotional self-control will be an invaluable lesson for the children in your care.

- Create a home environment that is **"Slow and Low."** This means soft neutral colors, low lighting, and low sound volume. Even something as simple as a calming fragrance such as lavender or vanilla will create a sense of peaceful calm in your home.

- **"Slow and Low"** also applies to your interactions with the child. Keeping your body at the child's level (or even lower) and keeping your tone soft and low will send a message to the child that you are not a threat and that they are safe with you.

- Help them become familiar with your home and neighborhood so these places feel less foreign.

- Give the child choices and responsibilities so they can experience a sense of control over their day-to-day lives.

- Provide consistent, predictable routines and patterns for the day, and when the day includes new or different activities, tell the child beforehand. It is important for traumatized children to know that their caretakers are "in control."

- Set limits so they don't feel overwhelmed or responsible for more than they can handle.

- Don't hesitate to cut short or stop activities which are upsetting or re-traumatizing for the child. If you observe increased symptoms in a child that occur in a certain situation or following exposure to certain movies, activities, etcetera, avoid these activities. Teach your entire family to STOP, DROP AND ROLL. This means when things start to become stressful or behaviors escalate: STOP the interaction or communication; DROP into calm deep breathing; ROLL back into the interaction once calm and balance have been restored.

- Give them some idea of what is going to happen in their future. Children will feel safe if they understand how decisions affecting them will be made. How much specific information you provide will depend on the age of the child.

- See and appreciate each child as a unique and special person. Provide opportunities for children to express themselves freely. The more a child feels "known" and understood by the people around them, the less they will feel like a stranger among strangers.

- Don't be afraid to talk about the traumatic event or experience. Children do not benefit from "not thinking about it" or "putting it out of their minds." **Don't bring it up on your own**, but when the child brings it up, don't avoid discussion.

- Listen to the child, answer questions, and provide comfort and support. Listening and not offering solutions or overreacting to the subject, but instead offering empathy and comfort will have a long-lasting positive effect. **Someone in emotional pain doesn't need you to fix anything; they just want to be heard.** Words such as, "That must feel so bad"; "I can see how hurt you are right now"; "That must have been so hard for you" will offer the empathy the child needs in the moment.

- Help your foster child maintain a sense of continuity with their culture and their past.

Managing Emotional "Hot Spots"

Some situations may be particularly difficult for children who have experienced trauma and may trigger a child to act out, struggle over control or become emotionally upset. Some of these "hot spots" include:

Mealtimes or other situations that involve food:

- Be aware of your foster child's history. In their past, food may have been scarce or it may have been the only source of comfort. Mealtimes may have been unpredictable—at times peaceful and at other times filled with conflict and chaos. Never force a child to sit at the table with the family or to eat foods that s/he does not want to eat. Instead, work on creating a feeling of safety around mealtimes and you will probably find that the child will begin to join the family at mealtimes and even try foods they have never tried before.

- When possible, try to accommodate your child's food preferences. Foods that a child equates with safety and comfort may seem foreign or even unhealthy to you, but if you make sure that at least some of them are available, you will be sending a powerful message of safety to your child.

- For children who have experienced scarcity and lack, providing an abundance of their favorite foods when in the first few weeks of placement will show them that there will always be plenty of food.

- Involve the child in planning and preparing meals, keeping the child's history in mind. While having a say in the menu can be empowering, for a child who may have had to fend for themselves, helping to prepare a meal can be more of a trauma reminder than a comfort. Tailor your actions to the needs and history of your child.

- Always keep mealtimes calm and supportive. Make mealtimes a time when family members come together to enjoy each other and share positive experiences.

Bedtime, including getting to sleep, staying asleep and being awakened in the morning:

- Encourage a sense of control and ownership by letting the child make choices about the look and feel of the bedroom space.

- Understand that some children have heightened sensitivity to textures, such as the feel of fabric. Never force a child to sleep between the bed sheets or tucked in tight. This may trigger past stressful memories, so allow the child to sleep the way they feel most comfortable.

- Respect and protect the child's privacy and make sure other family members do the same. For example, always ask permission before sitting on a child's bed.

- Acknowledge and respect your foster child's fears, be willing to repeatedly check under the bed, in the closet

or show that the window is locked. Provide a nightlight and reassure the child that you will protect them against any threat.

- Set consistent times for going to bed and waking in the morning. Establish a regular, calming routine. Let the child decide how to be awakened, as an alarm clock might be too jarring for a child who is always on the alert for danger; maybe a clock radio tuned to a favorite station would be better. Creating dependable routines will help your child start and end the day feeling safe.

- If your child experiences great difficulty with bedtime and sleep, you should contact the child's Foster Care Provider's Social Worker as more therapeutic interventions may be needed.

Anything that involves physical boundaries, including baths, personal grooming, nudity, privacy issues, or medical exams/procedures that expose or invade the body:

Some children who come into foster care may arrive with teeth that are in desperate need of cleaning, or hair so tangled it's hard to get a brush through it. They may be resistant to grooming or bathing or anything that involves seeing or touching their bodies. Children who have been abused and neglected may never have learned that their bodies should be cared for and protected. Some ways you can help children feel more comfortable and safe within their bodies include:

- Respect the child's physical boundaries. Physical contact is important for all human beings to thrive, however, children who have experienced trauma may associate physical intimacy or contact with confusion, pain, fear and abandonment. Providing hugs and other physical comfort to younger children is very important, however, don't assume the child wants to be hugged, take cues from the child before initiating physical contact. Never demand that a child give you a hug or kiss, but instead allow them to initiate such affection.

- Make the bathroom a safe zone: introduce older children to all the workings of the bathroom, and make it clear that their time in the bathroom is private, and that no one will be walking in on them during bath time.

- When helping to bathe younger children, be careful to ask permission before touching and be clear about exactly why, how and where you will be touching them.

- Introduce an element of fun! Provide fun bath toys for younger children and make a game out of bath time by finding ways to encourage older children to bathe, such as an incentive chart. One creative foster mom would draw funny pictures with non-toxic washable markers on her 10 year old child's arms, face and legs and then challenge her to show that they were all gone when her bath was over. This turned a traumatic power struggle into a fun activity that the child couldn't wait to do!

Successful Approaches To Working With High-Needs Children

Therapeutic foster parents have learned that communication and relationship skills are essential to working with high-needs children. These skills help children to grow, learn to solve problems, become responsible and psychologically healthy; and helps them to reach their fullest potential. Foster parents can directly impact and help break the abuse cycle that affects most foster children.

Negative behavior is the effect of underlying stress. When children are given unconditional love and support, their stress levels reduce and negative behaviors subside. The key to healing trauma is RELATIONSHIP.

The following techniques and skills are proven and effective ways of strengthening relationships:

THE BEST PRACTICES APPROACH

"Best Practices" is a phrase used within most industries to describe the most effective methods for achieving a goal, accomplishing a task and/or getting a job done. Human Services has defined its "Best Practices" as well, and, in many states, such as California, Best Practices have been established through legislation. Though there are some variations in the Best Practices for Human Services, the basics are the same. Best Practices include services that are:

- Family-Centered
- Needs-Driven
- Strength-Based
- Solution-Focused
- Community-Based

So, what does "Best Practices" mean to you as a foster parent? First off, it helps to create a foundation for success. See the examples below:

- **Family-Centered:** Children need families and this is why Foster Care Providers have created therapeutic foster care programs.

- **Needs-Driven:** For decades the Human/Social Services industry focused on finding "problems" and attempting to "fix" them. Research has clearly demonstrated that "problems" are really coping behaviors or the way a person tries to solve their problems and, in essence, symptoms of unmet needs. Who better to know what their unmet needs are than the child?

    A primary skill for a therapeutic foster parent is to discern what a child/youth's needs are, assist them (when age-appropriate) to identify and verbalize their needs, and guide them towards finding solutions and meeting these needs. Needs-driven means that the individual's personal needs determine a course of action. It is not about telling someone the problem, i.e. what is wrong with them and then attempting to "fix" them. Needs-driven services are therapeutic, healthy and productive, while problem-driven services can be condescending, non-therapeutic and counterproductive.

- **Strength-Based:** A "Strength-Based" approach goes hand-in-hand with "needs-driven" services. Focusing on strengths rather than problems builds self-esteem and confidence. Everyone has strengths, or assets, to build upon. Thus, the skilled therapeutic foster parent knows how to identify the child's strengths, help them see their personal strengths and nurture and develop these positive attributes. "Strength-Based" means finding the best in a child or youth and developing those strengths. It is the most positive, character building, and healthy way to raise a child.

    Another way to view the strength-based approach is called "Asset Development." The Search Institute of Minneapolis, Minnesota has developed wonderful tools for Asset Development. Your Foster Care Provider's Social Worker may be able to provide these materials to you at your request.

    There are six premises to Asset Development which apply to you as a therapeutic foster parent:
    - Everyone can build assets
    - All young people need assets
    - Relationships are the key to building assets
    - Asset building is an ongoing process
    - Consistent messages are necessary for proper asset development
    - Assets and strengths must be continually reinforced

- **Solution-Focused:** Many times people seem to focus on problems rather than seeking the solutions to the problems. Too often our first reaction is to criticize and tell someone what they have done wrong, and not really mention what was done right. It is very important for the therapeutic foster parent to learn to be solution-focused, always helping the child find solutions to unmet needs.

> While a focus on problems and deficits, may resolve behaviors for the short term, but does not heal trauma. But a focus on needs, strengths and Solutions, provides healing and allows children long-term strategies for success that will last their whole lifetime.

- **Community-Based:** Common sense tells us that it is better to serve someone in need within his or her own community. This is especially true for foster children. Being removed from family is difficult enough, let alone being taken away from friends, neighbors and all that is familiar to them. This is why the Foster Care Provider makes every effort to place foster children within their community.

From a therapeutic perspective "Community" has a much deeper and more profound meaning. Individuals, including foster children and families are better served through a collaborative, team approach, in essence a micro-community. Additionally, "Community" means resources. The more clearly defined one's community is, the more visible and connected they are with resources.

Thus, it is a goal of the Foster Care Provider to assist each therapeutic foster family in developing their clearly defined "Community" and the resources that come with it. The use of a "Child & Family Team" serves this purpose. Additionally, a skilled therapeutic foster parent knows how to assist a foster child or youth in creating their own "Community of Resources."

> The most effective foster family is one that is well linked to a community of resources.

THE THERAPEUTIC FOSTER CARE APPROACH

The "Therapeutic Foster Care" approach is another remarkably effective method for promoting positive change in children, youth, individuals and families. In fact, research has demonstrated that the Therapeutic Foster Care approach is the most effective alternative to institutional care.

Therapeutic Foster Care is a process of surrounding an individual or family with a community of resources to assist them in finding solutions to meet needs and build on strengths.

The Therapeutic Foster Care (TFC) approach is based on 10 key components:

- It fully integrates medically necessary mental health services.

- TFC is a short-term intervention, designed to quickly achieve permanency for the foster child/youth.

- TFC emphasizes foster family participation, voice, choice and preference.

- It is a "team-driven" process, including the foster child, foster family, natural supports and other significant stakeholders involved in the life of the child.

- It builds on strengths to meet needs and achieve outcomes.

- TFC utilizes a team-created, comprehensive case plan to coordinate services in all areas of life.

- It focuses on developing formal and informal, community-based services and supports.

- Services are individualized to best fit unique culture and preferences.
- TFC is an outcomes-based service using observable and measurable indicators to track foster child progress.
- TFC provides unconditional "whatever it takes" commitment to success.

Therapeutic Foster Care is very beneficial for a foster family. Here are just a few of its many benefits:

- It works, producing great results.
- It helps to ensure that the foster family's needs are being met.
- It makes sure that they are given voice, choice and preference.
- It provides ongoing support and encouragement to the foster family.
- It provides open and effective channels of communication.
- TFC ensures that the foster children's needs are being met.
- It creates a structure to make sure everyone is working together to accomplish the same goals. This is especially important with multiagency involvement.
- It provides greater input in creating solutions.
- TFC teaches foster families effective, therapeutic skills to help traumatized foster children heal.
- Therapeutic Foster Care brings greater resources to the family and foster child/youth.

Under the Therapeutic Foster Care model, the foster family and child/youth are assisted in creating a **Child & Family Team**. This team becomes a micro–community of key players who will have a role in developing and implementing the child's case plan. The Child-Parent Team will consist of the FFA staff assigned to the child, placing agency staff such as a county social worker or probation officer. It could also include the child's therapist and other individuals important to the child and foster family. This could include a friend, neighbor, relative or pastor and, whenever possible, the child/youth's biological family. This team meets regularly at times most convenient to the foster family and child/youth. Most importantly, the foster family and child/youth are placed center stage, becoming the hub of the process.

Developing Effective Relationships and Communications

Acceptance

Learning the "language of acceptance" is a necessary ingredient for an effective helping relationship. The language of acceptance gives foster children the message that it is OK to share their feelings and needs, which can be a very powerful force in building relationships. Conversely, un-acceptance can make them feel defensive, uncomfortable, and afraid or even unloved. To feel accepted is to feel loved.

It is important to remember that all parents have human faults, limitations and real feelings. Parents can readily accept some of a child's behaviors, while other behaviors are unacceptable. Unfortunately, a person's acceptance or non-acceptance of a behavior can get misinterpreted as acceptance or non-acceptance of the person. Thus, we emphasize the need to be skilled in the "language of acceptance." Develop the ability to respond to unacceptable behavior and still communicate personal acceptance of the child.

The degree of acceptance that a parent has for a child is influenced by:
- Personal values and beliefs
- Expectations of the parent
- Personality of the parent
- Personality and behaviors of the child
- Parent's level of energy and patience in a given situation
- Parent's level of stress at any given moment

It is important to understand and be aware of your own areas of acceptance and non-acceptance, and what "acceptance" message you project to a foster child.

It is not necessary to pretend to be accepting or to be unconditionally accepting. The key to success is the depth of the parent-child relationship. Children want to be accepted and they can handle their parents' un-acceptance when it is focused on their behavior, not themselves, and it is clearly and honestly communicated in a supportive way.

Healthy Communications

Your acceptance of a foster child should be clearly felt by him/her. It must be actively communicated. Therapists and counselors undergo extensive training and experience in order to acquire skills in communicating acceptance. Parents must ask themselves, "Are we talking and communicating with our children in constructive and helpful ways?"

Communication can be **Therapeutic** (helpful) or **Nontherapeutic** (destructive).

- **Therapeutic Communication:** makes the child feel better, encourages them to share feelings and talk, fosters feelings of worth and self-esteem, reduces threat or fear, and facilitates growth and healing.

- **Non-therapeutic Communication:** makes the child feel judged or guilty, restricts expression of honest feelings, threatens and instills fear, fosters feelings of unworthiness or low self-esteem, blocks growth and healing.

Points to Remember

- Communication involves talking and listening; both are equally important.

- Relationships are formed by actively communicating. Timing is essential.

- How and when parents talk to children is most important. Talk can be constructive (therapeutic) to the child and to their relationship, or it can be destructive (non-therapeutic).

- Constructive talk happens when everyone's stress levels are reduced and parents are able to respond to the child in a balanced way. This may mean waiting to talk until this can occur.

- Destructive talk happens when stress levels are high and parents are reacting to a child's behavior, usually by yelling, lecturing or threatening punishment.

It's important to understand that in any communication between two people, there will be differences in expectations and perceptions. For example, you might think that when you ask your foster child to complete a chore, like taking out the trash, s/he will complete all the steps that you expect to be done (emptying wastebaskets, replacing the trash bag in the kitchen, taking the can out to the curb, etcetera). However, your child may perceive that all they need to do is take the trash can out to the curb. Differing expectations and perceptions can cause a breakdown in communication, causing disappointment and frustration for everyone.

Roadblocks to Communication

We begin with certain types of non-therapeutic forms called "roadblocks" of communication that parents too often use with children, usually when under stress and incapable of a balanced response.

- **Directing, Ordering and Commanding:** These messages produce fright, resistance, defensiveness and arouse retaliation, revenge and/or rebellion. Examples:
    - "Don't talk to me that way!"
    - "Stop complaining and take out the trash!"
    - "Get out there and do the dishes!"

- **Threatening, Warning and Punishing:** These messages invite testing and sabotage, while producing anger, resentment and resistance. Examples:
    - "If you say anything, you'll be sorry!"
    - "One more word and you'll have to go to your room!"
    - "You'd better not do that if you know what's good for you!"

- **Moralizing, Preaching and Obliging:** These messages induce guilt, reduce self-esteem and build generalized resistance to authority. Examples:
    - "You shouldn't act like that."
    - "You should not talk back to your parents."
    - "You ought to stay away from him next time."

- **Advising, Recommending, Providing Answers or Solutions:** Statements of this nature imply superiority, deprive the listener of the esteem building experience of solving their own problems and may encourage dependency. Examples:
    - "I suggest that you forget about her and make a new friend!"
    - "You need to stop arguing with your teacher!"
    - "If you put your things away next time you won't lose them!"

- **Lecturing, Persuading with Logic, Arguing and Instructing:** These invite counter arguments, imply that you're right and the listener is wrong, increase defensiveness and reduce openness. Examples:
    - "When I was your age, I had a lot more chores."
    - "Children these days do not know how to save money."
    - "You children must learn to get along with each other."

- **Criticizing, Name Calling, Blaming, Evaluating, Labeling:** These messages lower self-esteem, induce guilt feelings, reduce openness, and arouse resentment and retaliation. They can also be violations of a child's rights! Examples:
    - "You're not using your head."
    - "You're lazy."
    - "Okay, little baby."
    - "Look here, smart mouth."
    - "You teenagers are all alike."

- **Kidding, Teasing, Making Light Of, Using Sarcasm:** These messages may arouse feelings of rejection, resentment, humiliation and hostility. Examples:
    - "You think you know it all."
    - "Why don't you burn down the school?"
    - "When did you last read a newspaper?"
    - "Did you get up on the wrong side of the bed?"

- **Over Praising, Judging Positively and Approving:** These messages are usually well intended when they are not manipulative. However, when they are misused, they imply that the speaker is in a position to judge the other person's performance. That may imply that the next performance may be disapproved. Also, the listener may receive overly generalized praise as phony or fake. Examples:
    - "You are the best student in your school."
    - "Well, I think you're the smartest."
    - "You were a good boy today."

- **Diagnosing, Analyzing, Interpreting and Reading-in:** These messages are received as threatening to privacy and rejecting the listener's self-perception, arousing anger and defensiveness, and possibly causing serious insecurity. Examples:
    - "You're only saying that to make me angry."
    - "You don't really mean that."
    - "You're just trying to get attention."
    - "What's wrong with you is…"

- **Reassuring, Consoling, Excusing and Sympathizing:** This approach is usually an attempt to reduce the other's pain by trying to talk them out of their feelings, make their feelings go away, or deny the strength of their feelings. These types of messages often have the opposite effect because they do not convey an understanding or empathy for the pain the person is experiencing. Examples:
    - "Forget about it, you'll feel better tomorrow."
    - "All teenagers go through this sometime."
    - "Don't worry, things will work out."

- **Cross Examining, Interrogating, Questioning, Probing and Prying:** These messages may show interest in what the person is saying, but actually, they ignore the other person's feelings and may communicate distrust. The listener may feel like they are being subjected to the "third degree." Examples:
    - "What gave you that idea?"
    - "When are you going to…?"
    - "What did you do to make that person say that?"

- **Withdrawing, Diverting, Avoiding, Digressing and Shifting:** This approach communicates a lack of respect towards the listener and produces anxiety in the speaker. The "Silent Treatment" has a punishing effect. Examples:
    - "We've been through this before and I don't want to hear about it."
    - "Just forget about it."
    - "Let's not talk about it now."

Responding to your children in these ways will discourage them from continuing to talk about their experiences, problems and feelings. These types of statements can "shut down" positive communications and become "destructive" and "non-therapeutic."

Opening the Door to Communication

These are statements inviting the child to say more and share their own ideas, feelings, thoughts and solutions. They convey acceptance of the child and respect for them as persons. Some examples of "door-openers" are:

- "Really?"
- "Interesting."
- "I'd like to hear about it."
- "Would you like to talk about it?"
- "This sounds important."
- "Is that so?"
- "Tell me about it."
- "Tell me more."
- "Let's hear what you have to say."

Active Listening

Acceptance of a foster child can be communicated by listening. Two powerful ways to listen are:

- **Passive Listening:** The listener stays silent and does not talk. This is a time to learn important information about the speaker.

- **Active Listening:** The listener uses statements that prompt the speaker to talk. The listener gives feedback and acknowledges what the speaker has said by repeating their statements back to them. This is a tool to use when the speaker clearly has a problem. Listen with a goal to encourage the speaker to explore solutions to the problem.

In **Active Listening** the parent tries to understand what the child is saying and the meaning in their statement. The parent simply decodes the child's message and feeds it back to them in a "reflective" statement.

For example:

Child: "I hate school and I have a lousy teacher. I don't like her, she's mean."

Parent: "Sounds like you dislike school and you are really disappointed with your teacher. You really hate school."

Child: "That's right. I hate the homework, I hate the classes and I hate my teacher."

Parent: "You just hate everything about school."

These responses may seem awkward and uncomfortable at first. Parents are used to telling, questioning, judging, warning, threatening or reassuring, especially reassuring. It is natural for us to want to make the child feel better. This does not allow the child to learn to solve his/her own problems and resolve his/her own conflicts.

Active listening helps children express their feelings about a situation and feel more accepted. It provides parents with a way of engagement that allows the child to define their needs themselves and begin the process of developing solutions.

MEETING UNMET NEEDS

Parents are inclined to focus on the child's negative behaviors and want to fix them, **ignoring the unmet needs** that contributed to the problem. By doing so, they cause themselves unnecessary grief, anxiety, worry, anger and frustration. Furthermore, it damages their relationship with the child. They miss opportunities to enable a child to solve his or her own problems and meet their own needs.

Effective parenting is learning to discern who had unmet needs. All children have circumstances in their lives that produce disappointment, frustration or pain. These circumstances include a disrupted family; a conflict with friends, siblings, teachers, parents; or any number of issues which signify that a child has an unmet need.

Active listening is used when the child has an unmet need. A clue for parents is to listen to the child when s/he is expressing his or her feelings. Parents must tune into hearing "I've got a problem/need" kind of expressions. This can come from spoken and unspoken cues and clues. Parents who understand that children have unmet needs can learn to assist the child in finding solutions, not just solve their problems for them, allowing the child to draw upon inner resources and build on personal strengths to problem solve.

In the above example when the child states "I hate school and I have a lousy teacher. I don't like her, she's mean." The child definitely has an unmet need, they want to have a good school experience and they aren't. This is an opportunity for the parent to help the child think of ways to solve their problem without offering solutions.

Try asking the child why they think their teacher is mean, and then ask if they can think of ways to help the teacher with whatever they think is making them act "mean."

Children are surprisingly insightful and they will usually come up with a great solution on their own. Parents initially find it hard to understand the idea of empowering a child to meet their own needs. It is common to think in terms of having a "problem child" that "needs to be fixed." But keep in mind the basic belief that children and youth are resilient and are able to develop solutions and meet needs with proper guidance.

When a parent has unmet needs in a parent-child relationship, it can show up as un-acceptance, frustration, annoyance, resentment or anger. As your stress level increases, you may find yourself becoming dis-regulated and unable to communicate therapeutically. It is at this time that the parent needs to learn ways to meet their own needs and not transfer their frustration to the child.

When emotions run too high in a conversation with your child, remember to STOP, DROP AND ROLL: STOP the interaction or communication, DROP into deep, calming breathing and, when calm is restored, ROLL back into the communication.

"I" MESSAGES AND "YOU" MESSAGES

The needs of parents are best resolved through genuine and strategic "I" messages and natural supports. This includes healthy relationships, good friends, a support group or expressing your needs at a Child & Family Team meeting.

Non-therapeutic messages usually start with the word "You" or contain that word. They are often vague and general, focusing on the person and not the person's choices or behavior. For example:
- "You stop that."
- "You shouldn't do that."
- "Don't you ever talk to me that way!"
- "You are acting like a baby."
- "You should know better."

Therapeutic messages are relationship focused and tell the child how the unacceptable behavior is making the parent feel and usually include the word "I". These messages are specific and focus on an action or behavior, not on the person. For example:

- "I get discouraged when I have to keep cleaning your room."
- "I need to get some sleep. We'll talk in the morning."
- "I can't let you get hurt. I have to keep you safe."
- "I am worried when I don't hear from you."

"I" messages are more effective in influencing a child to change unacceptable behavior and are healthier for the child and the parent-child relationship. "I" messages are much less likely to produce power struggles because they express how the speaker is feeling and it's hard to argue about how someone feels. "I" messages are also helpful in setting limits because you are focused on what you need rather than what the child needs to do.

> Use "I" messages to convey positive and loving feelings to your children as well as negative feelings. Sending positive "I" messages first makes a huge difference in the child's ability to accept a parent's negative or disappointing feelings.

A warning about ANGER!

The feeling of anger is nearly always directed at another person. "I am angry" usually means, "I am angry at you" or "You made me angry." So, angry expressions are really a "You" message, not an "I" message. These messages feel like "You" messages to children. They think they are to blame and are responsible for causing the parent's anger. They then feel put down, blamed, guilty, shameful, hurt, rejected, etcetera.

Anger is a secondary feeling that comes after first experiencing a primary feeling such as hurt, fear, disappointment, worry or embarrassment. For example:

- The child acts up at the grocery store and starts to throw a tantrum by crying and screaming. The parent's primary feeling is embarrassment. The secondary feeling is anger: "You're acting like a two-year old."

- The child starts yelling and talking back to the parent and says, "I hate you, you aren't my mother and you can't tell me what to do." The parent's primary feeling is hurt and frustration. The secondary feeling is anger: "Don't talk to me that way, you really make me angry."

As a secondary feeling, **anger** then becomes a "You" message that blames, judges, punishes and is an attempt to teach the child a lesson that s/he shouldn't do that again. Parents must learn to **STOP, DROP AND ROLL** in order to regain emotional balance and control. Then, send primary feeling messages—"I" messages—and avoid sending angry "You" messages to children. For example:

- "I feel embarrassed when this happens at the grocery store."
- "I feel hurt and frustrated when I hear that."

Resolving Conflict

Most people hate to experience conflict and don't know how to handle it constructively. Conflict is a reality of any relationship; it is normal and therefore not necessarily bad. Conflict in families, openly accepted and expressed, is healthy for children and parents. Children need to learn how to cope with conflict so they will be better prepared to deal with it throughout their lives.

Therapeutic foster parents can model appropriate conflict resolution in their spousal relationships. It is very healthy for children to observe adults work out a problem constructively. Proper conflict resolution is probably the most critical factor in parent-child relationships.

The **Win-Lose Method** of conflict resolution is often seen in terms of "someone has to win and someone has to lose." Parents can get locked into this when they see the problem of discipline as a matter of being strict or lenient, tough or soft, authoritarian or permissive. The relationship becomes a power struggle, a contest of wills, and a fight to see who wins. Some parents try to resolve conflict in their favor so that the parent wins and the child loses. Other parents give in to avoid conflict, resulting in both the child wins and the parents losing.

The Win-Win Method: Here, the parent and the child experience working with each other, not against one another on a common task: the solution of a problem. This method of conflict resolution and problem solving is a process that creates compromise and is therapeutic. The Child & Family Team is an excellent forum for resolving conflict and developing Win-Win solutions. This process gives the parent and child additional input and removes the one-on-one confrontational dynamic of a conflict.

The Win-Win method involves seven separate steps:
1. Identify and define conflict
2. List possible alternative solutions
3. Evaluate the alternative solutions
4. Decide on best acceptable solution
5. Work out ways to implement solution
6. Evaluate how solution worked
7. Stay solution-focused to prevent further conflicts

During the Win-Win process, parents must do a lot of active listening, send clear "I" messages and avoid non-therapeutic "You" messages.

Reasons why the Win-Win method works:

- Foster children/youth participate in decisions and solutions. This method empowers them to have a say in the decision, causing the child to be more motivated to carry out a decision that s/he has participated in making, rather than in a decision that has been imposed upon them by a parent.

- The solution(s) and decisions will likely be more creative, innovative and individualized to the issue at hand, meeting the needs of both the foster parent and the child.

- Foster children/youth are required to think and reason to come up with a workable solution. It becomes a challenge and requires a team (parent/child) effort to figure out solutions.

- The relationship between a foster child/youth and foster parent is strengthened and both come away feeling good. The child feels listened to, respected and valued, and the foster parent feels satisfied, appreciated and helpful.

- Power struggles are prevented as the foster child/youth and the foster parent work with each other rather than against each other, resulting in a win-win.

Responding to a Crisis or "Meltdown"

Foster Parents should be prepared for times when a foster child/youth enters into a crisis or "meltdown" mode of behavior. These events are normal for children at different stages of development and can be handled best with understanding and preparation.

The most critical element of your response to a foster child/youth who is heading towards a crisis is **self-control**. It is a fact that as a foster child/youth's behavior escalates, your stress levels elevates. If you are feeling dis-regulated and out of control, it will be impossible for you to help your foster child/youth re-gain and maintain control.

Children will take their cues from you, so modeling self-control is essential. A foster child/youth's crisis usually follows a distinct pattern of progressive steps or phases. If you are able to intervene at an early stage of the crisis, you will most likely prevent it from escalating.

The Triggering Event
This is any event that triggers responses in the foster child/youth that could lead to the escalation of problem behaviors. The event can be external and observable, such as a disturbing conversation with a parent, a provocation by a peer, being told "No," etcetera. Or it can be internal, such as a memory, thought or reaction to medication.

> **Reasonable Expectations:** The foster child/youth is still close to their "normal, regulated state" or baseline, meaning that their hearing is still intact, impulse control is still fairly good, etcetera.
>
> **Suggested Interventions:** During this phase, ask yourself, "What will happen if I do nothing?" Give the foster child/youth a chance to de-escalate her/himself. At this stage, making an attempt to talk or offering an alternative is more likely to work. Tell the child your expectation for their self-control and state those expectations briefly, simply and calmly. Try using a diversion or distraction to re-direct the child's attention.

Escalation
The foster child/youth will appear to be less and less in control of his/her words or actions. Their behaviors increasingly put themselves and others at risk of harm. Often the foster child/youth will exhibit repetitive behaviors (that we have seen before when the child was headed into crisis). For example, the child/youth may start pacing followed by raising his/her tone of voice, which then leads to banging on walls and increasing volume of voice.

> **Reasonable Expectations:** As the crisis escalates, the foster child/youth's hearing starts to diminish rapidly as well as their reasoning skills. When you look at the diagram on the following page, you will see that the child's ability to process information mirror's their behavior level. Your response must adjust to match the developmental level presented, meaning your words should be simple and brief.
>
> **Suggested Interventions:** At this stage, you must assess for risks. The goal is to de-escalate, to assist the foster child/youth to regain self-control. Keep it Low and Slow. If possible, get down to the foster child/youth's level and lower the tone of your voice. Make clear and simple statements and requests. Offer the child minimal options, give them permission to take his/her space. Avoid a power struggle and be patient. Statements such as, "Because I said so" or "You will do what I say" will only lead to power struggles.

Crisis
The foster child/youth "explodes" and his/her behavior increases the possibility of injury to themselves or others. The behavior could be in the form of hitting, kicking, throwing objects, yelling or running away. Remember, a crisis cannot last forever and, eventually a crisis ends, however, the timeframe will vary depending on your responses and the individual in crisis.

> **Reasonable Expectations:** As seen in the diagram on the following page, the foster child/youth is at the lowest point in their ability to think clearly and rationally.
>
> **Suggested Interventions:** At the height of a foster child/youth's crisis, it is imperative that you assess for risks. Again, keep it Low and Slow—communication with the foster child/youth should be kept short and simple. Give clear directions without lectures or discussing consequences. Keep communicating to the foster

child/youth that you are there to keep them safe. Protect yourself from physical attacks and call 911 or the Mental Health Crisis Unit if there is any possibility of the child or others being injured. Notify the child's Foster Care Provider's Social Worker or on-call social worker.

Recovery
The foster child/youth regains a measure of self-control and composure. They are extremely vulnerable to re-escalate during this phase.

Reasonable Expectations: For many children, a reasonable expectation would be for them to voluntarily take some space and time to be alone. However, note that their cognitive ability is still severely hampered (see diagram below). As they are still far from baseline, this is not the time for discussing consequences, engaging in lengthy conversations, lecturing, or other strategies that don't allow the foster child/youth to continue the de-escalation of their behavior.

Suggested Interventions: Give the foster child/youth time and space to recover while continuing risk assessment and providing supervision.

Post-Crisis Depression
The foster child/youth appears physically and emotionally fatigued and or depressed. They may cry, hide, sleep or self-blame.

Reasonable Expectations: At this point the child's energy should be spent and they will have a heightened sense of remorse and will acknowledge what they did (as noted in the diagram below). It is important for the child to be allowed to express their feelings.

Suggested Interventions: Use active listening and unconditional positive regard. This is NOT the time to determine blame or provide consequences. Continue the risk assessment, especially for suicide statements or other risk factors. Provide hope and present the future in a positive light.

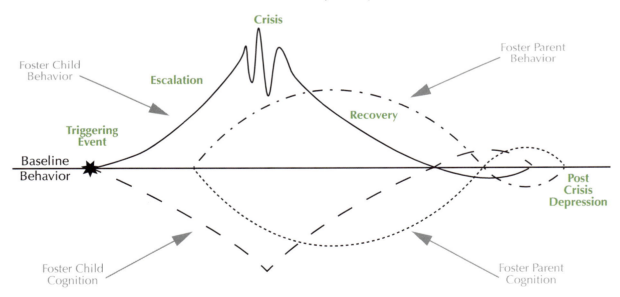

> The best time for a foster child/youth to understand the consequences of their choices and actions is when they are at baseline. Even though it may seem like a long time before you and the child/youth can finally deal with the issue, it is best to wait until their reasoning and rational skills are at their best. And your response to the child's crisis is key to a successful de-escalation of their behavior, so be prepared when a crisis happens.

Maintaining Your Self-Control

Again, we cannot stress enough the importance of exercising your own self-control when a foster child/youth is in crisis. One of the most successful therapeutic tools you can use in a crisis is to model self-control. This is often challenging because it is normal to feel anxiety when another is in crisis. Here are some helpful guidelines:

- Have a self-control plan that includes self-assessment and take a moment to check your own physical and emotional state.

- Know your limits! Be aware when you are approaching the limits of your own self-control and take specific steps to regain balance and regulation.

- STOP, DROP AND ROLL—STOP the interaction or communication, DROP into deep, calming breathing and when calm is restored, ROLL back into the communication.

- Give yourself space and time to respond and delay giving consequences until you are fully recovered.

- Take care of yourself. Crisis situations create emotional stress, so plan ways to restore your own emotional balance after a crisis situation. Develop a list of things to do to make yourself feel better after a stressful incident.

Encouragement

All children need to be encouraged to develop their strengths and individual personalities, thus boosting their self-esteem. Encouraging a foster child/youth is therapeutic and extremely critical in their healthy development. Two ways to encourage children are to show confidence in them and build on their strengths.

Ways to encourage a child's develpment include:

Give Responsibilities
Showing confidence in the foster child/youth's ability allows the child to discover their own strengths and talents. Giving a child/youth responsibility is a non-verbal way of expressing confidence; a way of saying, "I know that you can do this."

Parents must select and assign responsibilities that are in-line with a child's abilities, age and level of development. This is important for them to experience success and gain confidence. An example of giving responsibility in a way that demonstrates confidence would be to say, "I think that you did well in getting yourself up this morning and getting ready for school, so I think that you have shown me that you can handle staying up until 9:30 p.m. What do you think?"

Ask for Advice/Their Opinion
Asking your foster child/youth's advice from time to time also gives a message that you value their opinion. Ask them to teach you certain things they know how to do. When you do this, you are communicating with them that you have confidence in their skills and knowledge. Examples of seeking their advice might include asking them, "Which way do you think is the best way to the grocery store?" or "Would you teach me how to play that game?"

Allow Them to Problem Solve
Allowing foster children/youth to complete difficult tasks or solve problems when they are discouraged shows them that you have confidence in their abilities. Avoid the temptation to rescue. Try not to do for a foster child/youth what s/he can do independently. Rescuing a foster child/youth gives the message that you do not have confidence in him/her. The foster child/youth will learn to give up and not tolerate frustration. By building on a foster child/youth's strengths, you are encouraging them to continue to develop abilities in other areas and points out the things they are doing right.

Acknowledge Their Strengths and Skills

Acknowledging a foster child/youth's strengths and the things they do well, shows that you notice their positive traits and good behaviors. Expressing appreciation for help with tasks is a way to acknowledge them. Some examples are: "It was great the way you shared your toys with Tommy today", "It sure is fun to play with you", "Thanks for your help with the dinner dishes tonight. You did very well and you knew exactly where all the dishes belong", or "I appreciate your playing quietly while Billy was taking a nap this afternoon."

Acknowledge Their Improvements/Development

Encouraging and concentrating on a foster child/youth's improvement without expecting perfection is supportive and builds confidence. Recognize the child/youth's efforts and their resolve to improve or attain a goal. Give positive comments on each success. Some examples are: "You are really improving your reading. I can hear the difference", "You really did well with feeding the cat and giving her water today", "I can see all the effort that you put into that."

SPECIAL TIME

All the children/youth in your care, including your own, need a certain amount of individual, one-on-one time with parents. During this time, the child/youth should decide the type of activity and play, giving them a sense of control over the environment. This is time for relationship bonding and is essential for creating a sense of safety and belonging for the child.

"Special Time" spent with children is the time for the parent to give his/her undivided attention and conveys the message: "I'm here, I hear you, I care, I understand."

During "Special Time," **DO**:
- Let the foster child decide on the play and lead in the play—enter the child's world.
- Allow the foster child/youth to make the choices, with the parent being accepting and empathic in responding.
- Set limits that the activities be safe and able to be completed within the time available.
- Give the foster child your undivided attention.
- Observe and track behavior.
- Match the foster child's attitude and behaviors.
- Acknowledge the foster child's efforts.
- Join in the play as a follower (within limits).
- Be verbally engaged.
- Schedule and always follow through with your commitment to "Special Time."

During "Special Time," **DON'T**:
- Criticize any behavior or exhibit anger.
- Overly or inappropriately praise the child.
- Ask leading questions.
- Allow interruptions.
- Offer to help or teach.
- Initiate or direct new activities.
- Be passive or quiet.
- "Special Time" should never be taken away as a punishment or consequence.

Contributing to the Success of Your Foster Child

It is very important for foster parents to understand that success for a foster child/youth will look very different from child to child. It's important to understand what success would be for each individual foster child and not relative to your expectations (or society's in general). You have the opportunity to model a healthy lifestyle and attitudes that the child will always take with her/him wherever they go no matter how short their stay with you.

A whole different framework from which to define "success" is needed for a foster child. Consider the following:

- For a foster child, the smallest bit of progress can be a great success; even just establishing some consistency in their lives can be major accomplishment.

- You, as a foster parent, cannot measure success by your own or even traditional standards.

- Practicing affirmation, acceptance, tolerance and encouragement of the child will go much further in helping them than a self-generated code of behavior.

- You and the foster child/youth's Foster Care Provider's Social Worker may collaborate to define reasonable goals; including the foster child if s/he is old enough.

- Little, step-by-step goals should be defined first so that the foster child/youth can manage the overall challenge.
    · Consider a reward system to reinforce the steps in the process.

- It is important that you don't try to accomplish too much, too fast, as it takes time to develop the kind of relationship to actually ignite a child's desire to earn your approval and praise.

- Try to catch your foster child doing something positive that you can acknowledge her/him for, and take the time to tell her/him what s/he did right.

- Take the time to analyze your own frame of mind about life. It is difficult to produce positive life changes in an emotionally fragile foster child/youth if your outlook is less than positive. Teens, especially, may not be open to "parents" in the traditional sense, and they may be much more responsive to positive adults who are able to show understanding and respect for their individual needs.

- Your attitude towards the foster child/youth is key to her/him developing a positive outlook towards her/his own abilities. Your attitude will be reflected in the words you use, your treatment of the child and the quality of relationship you develop with her/him. Accepting a foster child for who they are and not what they do will help build their self-esteem.

Proactive Parenting

Proactive Parenting is "parenting smart!" It is the process of anticipating all the possibilities or situations that might occur while parenting a foster child/youth, and putting a plan in place to respond appropriately. Proactive Parenting is about understanding your role as a therapeutic foster parent, and being fully prepared and equipped to fulfill that responsibility. Proactive Parenting consists of:

- Being prepared
- Relationship building
- Creating mutual respect
- Maintaining positive and open communication
- Being mindful of self-disclosure
- Building trust
- Maintaining a child-friendly home
- Being a good teacher
- Being a role model

Be Prepared
A reasonable person would not attempt to fly an airplane without much training and preparation! The same applies to our approach in therapeutic foster parenting.

- Expect the unexpected
- Be prepared for any situation you can imagine

Relationship Building
The key to success in any human service endeavor is the quality of relationships. The more effort you put into relationship building, the more effective you will be as a parent. Make an effort to thoroughly understand the child or youth. Be aware of their culture, past trauma, family history, personality, strengths, likes, dislikes, etcetera; in essence, "know what makes them tick." Spend individual one-on-one time with your child or youth, and plan for and routinely engage in relationship building activities.

Create Mutual Respect
Learning to be respectful of others is not necessarily something that is "taught" but rather "caught!" Respect is learned by seeing it in others and experiencing it yourself.

- Model respect in every relationship
- Make respect an unshakable family value and expectation
- Maintain a positive, warm and healthy family environment

Maintaining Positive and Open Communication
We cannot emphasize enough the importance of good communication between the foster parent and the foster child/youth. This also applies to communications within the foster child/youth's Child & Family Team.

Be Mindful of Self Disclosure
Sharing stories from your personal life can be very therapeutic, however any time you choose to share such stories it should always be for the sole purpose of benefitting the foster child/youth.

When self-disclosure is well timed and utilized properly, it can assist in building rapport, establishing trust, and providing an example to the foster child/youth that they are not alone in experiencing a challenge or obstacle in life. The secret is to have excellent professional "boundaries." Some guidelines to follow when sharing your life stories are:

- Only share your personal experience when it is clear that the purpose is to benefit the foster child/youth. It is never appropriate to process your own feelings of grief, anger, etcetera, with your foster child.

- Always consider the timing of the self-disclosure and the amount of information that is necessary to accomplish your goal.

- Only share what information you are comfortable sharing, it is always OK to say that you're not comfortable sharing an aspect of your personal life when questioned by a child/youth.

- Be proactive, think about the kinds of questions you may be asked and how you will answer them. ("Have you ever used drugs?" "How did you do in school?" "Did you ever disobey your parents", etcetera.) A good rule of thumb is to give generalized answers to specific questions. For example, if a youth asks you if you have ever gotten into trouble as a teen, you might respond by saying, "I was a teen once and some of the choices I made had negative consequences."

- Less is more; it is usually advisable to disclose less personal information rather than more. Sometimes sharing too much may block the child/youth from sharing their own story.

- Be aware that what you share with a foster child/youth will be shared with others. It is not reasonable to expect a child to keep anything you tell them confidential.

Building Trust
It goes without saying that some foster children and youth have learned not to trust adults, or anyone for that matter. Thus, a major task for every skilled foster parent is to help foster children and youth develop the ability to know who is safe to trust and to give them the tools to be able to trust themselves.

- Model trusting relationships within the family and with agency staff, community partners, or even the child's or youth's biological family.

- Take the risk of extending your trust to a foster child or youth.

- Be trustworthy yourself. There is nothing more damaging than for a parent, especially a foster parent, to violate the child's trust.

- Be patient and do not give up on a foster child or youth who violates your trust. Remember, they will most likely test you to see if you are truly genuine. At the first opportunity, give them a chance to once again prove they are trustworthy. Trust building is a process of time, so give it enough!

Maintaining a Child-Friendly Home
Nothing can be more uncomfortable for a foster child or youth than to arrive at a home where they do not feel welcome. Make it your goal to have a warm "Low and Slow" home environment. This means soft neutral colors, low lighting and low sound volume. Even something as simple as a calming fragrance such as lavender or vanilla will create a sense of peaceful calm in your home.

Try not to create "off limits" living areas of your house, except for your own personal space. Make sure that foster children or youth have a living area they feel comfortable hanging out in. Understand that all children can be hard on furniture and household items, so don't overreact to accidental messes or incidents.

Become a Teacher
One of the most important roles of a parent, especially a therapeutic foster parent is that of a teacher.

- Don't assume that your foster child knows what you want them to do, or has the same base of understanding as your own child.

- Be prepared to teach the basics of life (e.g. social skills, grooming, etiquette, etcetera).

- Be very observant of a foster child/youth's behavior, so that you know how to instruct.

- Do not be critical—be instructive.

- Look for creative opportunities to be instructive, without being intrusive.

- Help the foster child/youth learn how their behavior affects their life and the quality of their relationships. When a child is in calm state they are able to understand cause and effect—this is when teachable moments are most effective.

Role Modeling
As we have said, values and behaviors are not necessarily "taught" but rather they are "caught." All children learn by observing and emulating what they see. So, model the behavior that you want your foster child or youth to emulate.

- Be aware of your own weaknesses and triggers, and learn ways to reduce your stress and maintain balance.

- Be consistent in your conduct and behavior, but also be open and honest about your mistakes. No one is perfect. There will be times when you make a mistake, saying or doing something that you may later regret. When that happens, acknowledge it and make amends. One of the most powerful experiences for a foster child/youth is when an adult acknowledges that they made a mistake and offers an apology. This strengthens the parent-child bond making the child feel respected and valued. It also lets them know that even grown-ups make mistakes and that no one is expected to be perfect—what a relief!

CHAPTER 7

Ready, Set, Go!
Welcoming Foster Children into Your Home

Ready, Set, Go!
Welcoming Foster Children into Your Home

Your First Meeting

Foster parents and prospective foster children may meet each other for the first time in a variety of ways—in a Social Worker's office, in a park, in some neutral location or even in Juvenile Hall. In every situation, the foster parent must be sensitive to the feelings the foster child/youth may be experiencing given the timing and circumstances occurring in the child's life.

A foster child/youth who has just been removed from their home or who has been in a group home or Juvenile Hall will be experiencing many emotions that may affect your first meeting. Sometimes a pre-placement visit is scheduled to allow both the foster parent and child to get to know each other before placement; however, this is not the norm.

Regardless of whether there is a pre-placement visit, make sure to obtain as much information ahead of time about the child's past history and exposure to trauma. Your sensitivity to a particular foster child/youth's needs, concerns and fears will make her/him feel comfortable and welcomed into your home.

Welcoming a Foster Child/Youth Into Your Home

- Sit down and have a snack together, make the child/youth feel welcomed!

- Introduce family members and tell the foster child/youth a little about the family, (e.g., discuss the other children in your family, what pets you might have, what you do for a living, interests and hobbies, etcetera).

- Share with the foster child/youth why you have chosen to be a foster parent, keeping your statement brief and welcoming, such as, "I want to help you succeed" or "We really enjoy helping young people accomplish their goals."

- Show the foster child/youth around your home, making sure to pay special attention to their bedroom with its freshly made bed, and empty dresser drawers and closet all set for them to move in.

- While showing them around, point out areas where it's OK to be and not OK to be. Introduce basic house rules.

- Show them the kitchen, and explain how your meal routine works and what is available for snacks. Ask the foster child/youth what they do and don't like to eat, and assure them that there will always be plenty of food available to them.

- Explain what your family likes to do (hobbies, activities) and ask them what they like to do.

- Get the foster child/youth interested in doing something as this helps the child when their Social Worker leaves. Get other children/youth in the home to help with welcoming them (i.e., games, treats, snacks).

- Be prepared—have a plan! Make sure the first day is not rushed.

- If the foster child/youth leaves with the Social Worker, let the child know that you look forward to him/her coming back.

- If the foster child/youth stays, help him/her to assimilate into your normal family routine. Don't let s/he become isolated; rather, make an effort to include him/her. Avoid asking a lot of questions, but encourage the child to ask any and all questions s/he may have.

- Have a welcome kit with toiletries, a small journal and pen, or maybe a coloring book and crayons for younger children. Do something to make their arrival at your home special.

UNDERSTANDING YOUR FOSTER CHILD'S INITIAL EMOTIONAL NEEDS

Once a foster child/youth is placed in your home, the most important thing you can do is to be patient and understanding. **Don't set high expectations which may set them up for failure.** Chances are they are not going to act as you want them to, and for good reason.

Foster children who have experienced loss are naturally fearful about further loss. They may challenge or test you to see if you are going to reject them. They have learned that it's less painful to be rejected before they develop a bond.

> Remember that a foster child is just that—a child, no matter their age. Furthermore, a foster child is most likely traumatized, frightened, often coming from a very challenging home environment or abusive situation, and/or having moved from foster home to foster home or even from a group home.

The following are some very real feeling statements your foster child may be experiencing. Getting in touch with these will help you to be empathetic and "see things through the eyes of that child."

- "I want to go home to my mom, and I don't understand why I can't live with her right now."
- "I've been removed from those I love the most. It's my fault, it must have been something I did and now I'm being punished."
- "I've learned not to trust adults very much, especially social workers and police officers because they've taken me from my family."
- "I'm scared and angry, and I don't know what's going to happen next. I wonder if I'll be safe in this home."
- "This is just another foster home and I haven't had very good experiences in the other ones."
- "I must be a bad child and it's probably only a matter of time before they take me away from this home as well."
- "I don't like it here and I'm going to try to leave as soon as I can."
- "I don't want to get too close because I don't want to be hurt again."
- "I'm not sure that you won't do the same thing to me that my parents did."
- "I'm afraid that the other kids in your home will pick on me and that the foster parents will always believe them."
- "I don't need your help, I can do it myself."
- "I'm afraid I won't get enough to eat."

HOW TO MEET YOUR FOSTER CHILD'S EMOTIONAL NEEDS

Foster children may arrive at your home in the state of **"separation trauma,"** experiencing shock and denial. They are usually fearful, and this may be expressed as hurt and anger.

Good communications is the key:

- Go **"Slow and Low"**— get down to the child's eye level and use a soft tone of voice, using words appropriate to their age.

- Let them know you're glad they are in your home.

- Let the child know your home is a safe place where no one will hurt them and that you understand how hard it is to be away from their family.

- Keep lighting soft and sounds low. Avoid raising your voice or yelling at/or around them.
- It is okay to let them know that it is not their fault they are in a new placement without blaming anyone.
- Above all, take time and listen without asking a lot of questions. Expect to see anger or sadness whether spoken or acted out in negative behaviors because they've been separated from their family. This is a normal reaction to separation and loss.

If a foster child/youth does share their fears or worries with you, **take them seriously**, even if they seem exaggerated or unrealistic.

IMPORTANT TIPS FOR SUCCESS

- Acknowledge that the child's feelings make sense in light of their past experiences, communicating to him/her that all fears and concerns are mentionable in your household. This can go a long way towards helping the child feel more "normal" and less bound by secrecy.
- Be reassuring but also be realistic about the limitations of your own power.
- Don't promise more than you can deliver.
- Don't engage in negative talk regarding the child's biological family or previous foster family; listen, but don't agree or add to the conversation.
- Be honest about what you do and do not know, and, if necessary, help the child to make a list of concerns for their Social Worker or other members of the team. Sometimes just writing down a fear can help a child feel more in control.
- Initially, because s/he will not know what to expect, the foster child/youth will be fearful and anxious about what happens in your home. Their senses are heightened and even simple things, such as the feel of bed sheets on their skin, can be irritating and upsetting.
- Keep sounds and lighting soft, use calming scents such as vanilla and lavender candles or air fresheners.
- It's important to explain (and repeat often) daily routines, expectations and home rules, and to communicate this information gradually over time as the child is able to take it in. This approach will help them learn and understand what you expect of them.
- It is a good idea to ask the foster child/youth how things were done in his/her home (what kind of foods did s/he eat, when did s/he eat supper, who did dishes, etcetera). You might choose to incorporate some of these routines into your home, as well as explain why your expectations may be different.

Be sensitive to each child's background, experiences and personal perspectives. Foster children are dealing with separation as well as adjusting to your home. Your job will be to calm their "separation trauma" and this will take time.

BASIC STRATEGIES FOR WELCOMING FOSTER CHILDREN

Things you should always do:

- Be patient, be patient and continue to be patient! Changes take time—give them that time!
- Be there for them—do lots of listening.
- Know the foster child/youth's history and case plan.

- Treat them with respect.

- Explain normal family routines and don't explain everything all at once. Start with the things they need to know right away and then explain others as the need arises.

- Explain family rules and the "why" behind them. Children respond better when they understand the reason for a particular rule.

- Be flexible even as you set limits. Keep in mind that a foster child/youth coming from a neglectful or abusive home may be unfamiliar with the concept of consistent rules. Let the child/youth know you are willing to listen and help if they have trouble understanding or following the rules.

- Be willing to modify the rules in response to a foster child/youth's need for comfort and security. For example, allowing a light to be left on if a child/youth is fearful of the dark, or allowing extra snacks to a child/youth who has been deprived of regular meals until s/he feels secure that there will always be enough food for everyone.

- When rules are broken, use the opportunity to teach life lessons; remember, rules without relationship = rebellion.

- Establish individual space for each foster child/youth.

- Respect unique culture, individuality and privacy.

- Play or spend time with them for a period of time each day. Show you are interested in what is important to them – find out what kind of music they like or what movies, games or sports they enjoy. This sends the message, "I am interested in you."

- If the foster child/youth is young, read a story to them at bedtime. Let them know where you are sleeping in case they need to wake you during the night.

- Leave a night light on in their room and in the hallway and bathroom. It may be helpful to provide younger children with a flashlight and a stuffed animal to have in bed.

- Give the child a photo album or inexpensive digital camera, and a special box or container to collect "things." These things will provide familiarity, constancy, anchors, memories and a sense of identity and belonging.

- Know that they may eat a lot of food or even horde food at first because they fear scarcity and that is an area where they can exercise control.

Things you must never do:

- Judge the foster child/youth or their past history (family). Don't say anything bad about their biological parents or family.

- Push affection. Always use appropriate touching and allow the child to be the first to initiate it.

- Kiss a foster child/youth on their lips or mouth.

- Assume the foster child/youth knows things (even basic/common things).

- Push belief systems of any kind on the foster child/youth.

- Threaten the foster child/youth with removal from the foster home.

- Ask a lot of questions.

- Insist they call you Mom or Dad.

- Yell, curse or threaten them.

Chapter 7

Remember the Basics

- Review the information in the foster child/youth's file with his/her Social Worker, and make sure you are aware of any dangerous propensities, paying particular attention to behaviors reported by others, some of which will be normal for this child and some which may require specific interventions.

- Be sure to complete an inventory of the foster child/youth's belongings on the personal property inventory form. If the child/youth arrives with anything that might be dangerous to them or other family members, you must place these items in a secure place until you can speak with the child's Social Worker. Additionally, clothing that is gang related (or otherwise inappropriate) should also be secured, as well as large sums of money, unauthorized cell phone, etcetera. Simply explain to the child that you are not confiscating the items from them, but that you need to talk to their Social Worker before they can have possession of them.

- Every school age foster child/youth must be given an age appropriate orientation to their personal rights and foster parents must address the child's questions and concerns.

- Inform the foster child/youth of how you provide for allowances and clothing. Let them know how they can use these funds. Ask the child's Social Worker if the foster child/youth can manage his/her own money. Talk to your Social Worker if you need assistance with this.

- Conduct a disaster drill with the foster child/youth **on the first day** and then every six months, maintaining a written record of these events.

- Review any contact restrictions that the foster child/youth may have and discuss this with the child/youth, preferably in the presence of his/her Social Worker.

- If the foster child/youth arrives with prescription medications, make sure you understand how to administer the medications and be sure to fill out the appropriate logs in the child/youth's file. If the foster child/youth becomes ill or injured before they have had their initial doctor visit, remember that you cannot administer any over-the-counter medications without written instructions from the doctor. Utilize home remedies such as bed rest, water, chicken soup, ginger ale, etcetera, or take the child to the emergency room if medication or professional treatment is necessary. Be sure to call your Foster Care Provider if you are unsure what to do.

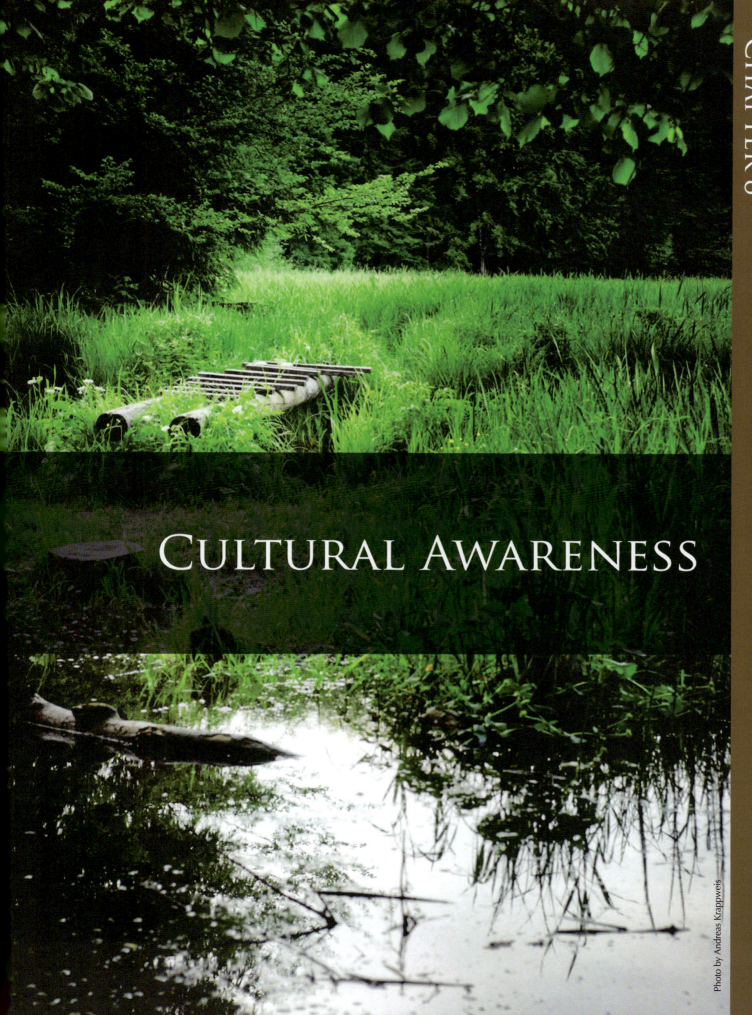

CHAPTER 8

Cultural Awareness

CHAPTER 8

CULTURAL AWARENESS

THE IMPORTANCE OF UNDERSTANDING CULTURE

Culture has always played a role in the relationships of people. Human beings seem to be drawn to "sameness," people thinking, acting and looking like themselves. Consequently, human history is a story of cultural conflict and the attempt to impose one culture upon another. As the cultural landscape of America has become unbelievably diverse, the need for learning to respect and live with cultural differences is more important than ever.

Foster parenting is inherently and dramatically a cross-cultural experience. Every foster family has its own distinct, unique culture as does every foster child/youth. Every time a child or youth enters into your home they are crossing your cultural barrier, as well as introducing you to the culture of their family. Obviously, this can create a very distinct cultural conflict. Thus, proactive planning and cross-cultural skill building are essential.

Effective foster parents learn everything they can about their foster child/youth and his/her family culture in order to properly and effectively meet his/her needs. Perhaps even more importantly, foster parents must know and understand their own cultural insensitivities, biases and relationship roadblocks, and initiate changes. It has been said that diversity has a way of introducing us to ourselves.

 Understanding the culture of a foster child or youth is essential to becoming an effective therapeutic foster parent.

DEFINITION OF CULTURE

By **culture**, we do not just mean "ethnicity," rather the definition is much broader and deeper than simply this. Within ethnic groups there can exist many cultures and subcultures. There are two basic definitions of culture.

First, **culture** is a system of shared values, styles, perspectives, beliefs, history, background and behaviors.

Examples include:
- Age and generations (i.e., children, adolescents, elders)
- Developmental and acquired disabilities (Downs Syndrome, Cerebral Palsy, blindness)
- Religious and spiritual beliefs
- Ethnicity (Asian, Hispanic, African-American, Japanese, Mexican, etcetera)
- Socioeconomic status (middle class, educational level, homeless, rural or urban)
- Sexual orientation
- National origin (refugee, immigrant)
- Gender

Second, **culture** is also any group that one identifies with. There are thousands of such identities, ranging from ethnic subcultures, to social clubs, (e.g., the Elk's Lodge, religious groups, hobby or sports groups, counter-cultural groups [such as gangs, hate-groups], etcetera). There is probably a group of people who identify with almost anything you can think of.

Today, many youth are attracted to different alternative **cultures**, (such as punk, gothic, skater, etcetera), and identify themselves with that culture. They may have symbols that reflect this cultural affiliation such as gang tattoos/clothing, anarchy symbols or specific jewelry. A foster parent who is unaware of the symbols associated with a particular culture may find them offensive or judge the youth unfairly, creating barriers to a healthy relationship.

The Value of Knowing a Foster Child's Culture

- You cannot effectively meet the needs of a foster child or youth without understanding who they are and their particular culture. Learn to appropriately explore a foster child or youth's cultural uniqueness.

- As you learn the child's culture, you also must know and understand your own culture (values and biases) in order to effectively bridge cultural gaps.

- Being aware of cultural differences does not mean having to give up or compromise your culture. Instead, it enables you to create bridges and find similarities on which to build relationship.

- Being aware of cultural differences enables you to be more proactive in preventing cultural conflicts, but more importantly, in creating solutions.

- In knowing the child or youth's culture, you can avoid negative consequences from inadvertently misinterpreting their conduct, appearance or actions.

- It provides you a significant lense for viewing and understanding the child's or youth's worldview, life experiences and factors that have influenced his or her development.

- It provides you a new set of "cultural tools" to help you achieve case and treatment plan goals. Using cultural-based activities is a great way to co-opt the foster child/youth into the treatment process.

- You can avoid offending or hurting a child by being aware and informed of cultural differences.

Children may react differently to things such as eye contact, personal space and food depending on their culture; it is important that you as a foster parent work with your foster children's Social Workers in order to understand and deal with these differences appropriately.

- Your cultural awareness of a foster child or youth sends a message that you are interested in his or her life, which helps build relationship and trust.

A Word About Poverty

Across the country, poverty rates are higher for children under the age of 18 than for adults aged 18 to 64. In California as of 2007, the poverty rate for children was 17% versus 11% for adults and a shocking 43% of children from single parent homes lived in poverty. In 2012, the California poverty rate has jumped to 23% for children and 17% for adults, with the single parent household rate remaining over 40%.

Many of the children/youth who enter foster care come from a standard of living that could be defined as "poor." While our society has agreed upon a certain statistic which we label as the "poverty line," a person's experience of poverty is relative. Making assumptions about a person because you perceive them as poor is just as damaging as being prejudiced toward a person's skin color. Aspects of a person's life that might seem like poverty to you (such as the kinds of foods they eat, their living conditions, the amount or condition of their possessions) can seem like abundance to someone who has even less.

A foster child or youth will often have very fond feelings about the life they lived before coming to your home, no matter how hard a life it may seem to you. It is important to show respect toward the child's past living conditions and to try to see it through their eyes so that you can appreciate what they value about it. American culture often errantly depicts poor people as lazy, uneducated and unmotivated, but the reality is that people who live in poverty can be extremely resourceful and have strong coping/survival skills. Children and youth raised in poverty often have a maturity beyond their years and possess many strengths gleaned from having to survive with less. Some of these children will actually need to learn how to be a child (and not an adult); learning how to relax and let the parents be the adults.

Culture Shock

When people suddenly find themselves in a different or unknown culture, feelings of anxiety and surprise, disorientation, uncertainty, confusion, etcetera, may be experienced. Culture shock is a subcategory of a more universal phenomenon and is often called **transition shock**. Transition shock is a state of loss and disorientation brought on by a change in one's familiar environment.

There are many symptoms of transition shock, including the following:

- Excessive concern over cleanliness and health
- Feelings of helplessness and withdrawal
- Irritability
- Glazed stare
- Desire for home and old friends
- Physiological stress reactions
- Homesickness
- Boredom
- Withdrawing
- Getting "stuck" on one thing
- Excessive sleep
- Compulsive eating/drinking/weight gain
- Stereotyping foster family
- Hostility towards authority figures

Culture shock usually progresses in stages, starting with the period when the differences between one's own culture and new culture are seen as wonderful and new. During the first few weeks, most people are fascinated by the new culture. This period is full of observations and new discoveries. After some time (usually weeks), differences between one's own culture and the new culture become apparent and may create anxiety. The initial sense of excitement will eventually give way to feelings of frustration and anger as the person continues to have encounters that seem strange, offensive, and unacceptable. One may long for foods they were used to, or for comfortable routines from their previous culture. This stage is where excitement turns to disappointment and more and more differences start to emerge. Anger or mood swings as well as depression are not uncommon.

The final stage of culture shock typically happens after six to 12 months. Finally, one grows used to the new culture and develops routines. One knows what to expect in most situations and the new culture no longer feels all that new. The culture begins to make sense, and negative reactions and responses to the new culture are reduced.

THE IMPORTANCE OF CULTURAL SENSITIVITY

To a degree, everyone is culturally insensitive, but most of the time it's due to lack of knowledge. In the extreme, cultural insensitivity breeds resentment, hate and hostility. The consequences of this extreme are obvious.

The following are some excellent questions for self-examination:

- Have you thought about your own personal prejudices? Is there a group of people for which you harbor negative feelings or thoughts?
- Have you been discriminated against? If so, how did that make you feel?
- Do you inadvertently or overtly discriminate against anyone?
- Have you ever felt superior or inferior to others, or have you looked upon the wealthy, poor, mentally ill, less educated or homeless with disdain?
- Have you ever made a racial slur, joke or derogatory comment?
- Have you ever engaged in "gay" bashing?
- Is there a religious group or movement that offends you or makes you angry?

Every honest person will have some "yes" answers to these questions. It is an unfortunate side of human nature. The critical question is "what are we willing to do about it?" Positive change always starts with a willingness to improve and grow more accepting!

Some important points to keep in mind:

- Cultural insensitivity will prevent effective foster parenting.
- Cultural insensitivity can be extremely damaging and harmful to a foster child or youth.
- Beware of stereotyping. Often a child, especially a teenager, will identify with a group more as a fad rather than a deep-seated conviction.
- Everyone has the need to belong and have an identity. Emotionally damaged or victimized children or youth very often associate with counter-cultural groups. Rejecting a child or youth because of their counter-cultural identity will deny them the opportunity to develop a positive identity through relationship and trust building.
- Foster parents cannot ignore cultural differences and expect that everything will be just fine.
- A foster parent's ability to positively integrate cultures will be directly related to their ability to positively influence the life of a child or youth.

WAYS TO DETERMINE A FOSTER CHILD'S CULTURAL INFLUENCES

- TALK to THEM! Ask how they do things. Ask what they like and dislike. Ask them what is different about your family from theirs. Ask them what would make them more comfortable in your home.
- Learn new skills on how to explore the child's cultural background without seeming intrusive, nosy or offensive.
- Show that you are interested in finding out about their history and background. Talk to them about their biological family, family history and people they admire and respect.
- Involve yourself in their lives, know their friends, likes and dislikes, music, hobbies; whatever will help you to see and understand their world.
- Be informed and aware. Ask for every piece of information you can get about a foster child or youth, even before they arrive.
- Be willing to learn. Attend cultural training, visit the library and talk to your Foster Care Provider's Social Worker.

- Don't be afraid to learn from the foster child/youth.

- Find out what traditions and holidays are important to your foster child and incorporate them into your life. Invite the child to participate in your family traditions, holidays or activities you routinely engage in, but be respectful and understanding if the child does not want to join in. Also, if your family does not celebrate holidays, you may want to accommodate your foster child and find a way to allow them to have holiday experiences that they are used to (birthdays, etcetera).

- Understand the child or youth's cultural language style and attempt to incorporate it into the way you communicate with the child.

- Ask them what culturally-related things you can do to make them more comfortable in your home, (i.e., preparing certain foods, listening to specific music, celebrating certain events, etcetera). Ask them to teach you how to prepare special foods they'll enjoy, if they don't know how, you can research it together.

- If appropriate, find out about the child or youth's parents, how their parenting style was different, and determine if there is something you can appropriately change to accommodate them.

- Be instructive about your culture, pointing out similarities as well as distinct differences. Educating your foster child about your family culture is just as important as understanding theirs. Be open to answer questions your foster child/youth may have about your culture without becoming defensive. Don't assume that a foster child/youth knows even the basics about your culture.

- Share your differences in a positive way, so that a range of views can be presented. In this way, the child learns more about you and you will both find similarities in each of your worlds.

- Live by example. Be proud of your culture and model acceptance and understanding of others.

Incorporating cultural issues into daily life will make the child's foster care experience more valuable

Some Suggestions For Avoiding or Resolving "Cultural Conflicts"

- Choose your battles. Sometimes allowing the child to dress a certain way or listen to their favorite music will go a long way towards making them feel comfortable and adjust better to their new environment. However, if what is causing the conflict is intolerable, seek a compromise so both parties feel validated.

- Never discard a child's belongings no matter what you may think about their condition. Items such as clothing, blankets, books, even small scraps of paper, may be extremely important and in many cases may be all that a child has left to remind them of their previous culture, their family or their history. Always consult the child/youth if you think something should be discarded and make sure they agree.

- Get outside help whenever there appears to be a clear impasse. Utilize the foster child/youth's Foster Care Provider's Social Worker, the Child & Family Team or any positive community resource. There are many cultural resources available to foster families.

- Communicate openly about culture, cultural differences and similarities, and the need to create bridges to cultural differences.

- Be honest and acknowledge your own feelings to allow the child to do the same.

Unique Challenges of Children & Youth in Foster Care

CHAPTER 9

Unique Challenges of Children & Youth in Foster Care

Chapter 9

Most children experience some bumps along the way from infancy to adolescence. Children and youth who are referred to foster care have many strengths but also some unique challenges. Most have experienced emotional trauma resulting in feelings or behaviors that cause problems in their lives and the lives of those around them. These children may have feelings of abandonment, shame, hopelessness, rejection, grief and loss. Often they may face multiple challenges that include mental health issues and physical disabilities requiring special assistance, training, counseling or intervention.

An important component of every foster child and youth's Child & Family Plan will be a Safety Plan which will address any special needs the foster child/youth may have. The safety plan will be developed by the Child & Family Team (CFT) and will contain strategies to ensure that the foster child/youth is given the support they need to be successful. It is very important that foster parents continue to be observant of the foster child/youth's behavior and report any new behaviors that may arise to the team.

In this chapter, we will highlight some common special needs and provide suggestions for meeting these needs. This chapter and the chapter entitled, "Child Development and Behavior," are important references for every foster parent regardless of the program in which they are participating.

> Often the special needs of a child may be undiscovered so it's important for foster parents to rely on their own observations and intuition. Always discuss in detail the child's needs and behaviors with his/her Foster Care Provider's Social Worker.

Learning Disabilities

National studies conclude that as many as 15% of Americans have a learning disability. Unfortunately, the rate amongst foster children and youth is substantially higher, some estimates being as high as 70-80%. Children with learning disabilities usually have a normal range of intelligence, and they try very hard to follow instructions, concentrate, and "be good" at home and in school. Yet despite their best efforts, these children/youth have trouble mastering school tasks and may fall behind. There are many types of learning disabilities and they manifest in different ways, affecting each child uniquely.

Learning disability indicators:
- Extreme frustration with and failure to master a core subject (reading, writing and/or math)
- School avoidance
- Procrastination in completing homework and preparing for projects/tests
- Anger at self; refers to self as "stupid"
- Inattentive, hyperactive, impulsive
- Difficulty understanding and following directions
- Difficulty remembering instructions
- Easily confused; misplaces important items like homework
- Handwriting that is slow, hard to read and does not improve

If you suspect your foster child has a learning disability, here are some helpful strategies:

- As a first step, make an appointment with the child's doctor to rule out a sight or hearing challenge.
- Be sure to find out who has educational rights for the child—it may be a biological parent, Court Appointed Special Advocate (CASA) or another individual. This information is important because the person who holds rights will need to approve any special education services.
- Keep a calm demeanor—even if you feel frustrated and don't understand how your foster child is reacting to his/her academic challenges.
- Keep a log, document your observations.
- Talk to the child's teacher(s) and ask if they notice similar difficulties or behaviors. Make requests to teachers and other school/social work staff in writing (letter form).
- Ask the teacher or school counselor if the child has ever had an open Individualized Education Plan (IEP). If the child has an open IEP, ask the child's teacher or counselor to go over it with you and provide you a copy.
- Become a strong, tenacious advocate for the child/youth's educational rights with their school, being mindful not to let school personnel minimize their responsibilities to provide your foster child/youth with a proper education.
- Keep the child's Social Worker informed of recurring difficulties. They should know who has educational rights over the child (the person who has the authority to request an education assessment that would detect a learning disability).
- Do homework/read with your foster child to discover if s/he is having any difficulties.
- Research learning disabilities—there are great websites and books with excellent information that your Social Worker may be able to direct you to.
- Encourage your foster child in both strengths and areas of needed growth.
- Notice the things that your foster child does correctly and recognize his/her achievements.
- Believe that your foster child can overcome his/her obstacles.
- Get resources. Many Foster Care Providers can match your foster child/youth with a tutor, mentor, reading teacher, etcetera; you must advocate for your foster child/youth to ensure that their needs are being met!

"I feel important when people look up to me. I feel significant when my parents ask me to do something hard."

-Youth age 10

In dealing with academic challenges, it's important to keep the following in mind:

- Be patient with your foster child/youth if s/he is having real difficulties completing assignments, following directions, remembering instructions, etcetera.
- Don't assume that your foster child/youth is being lazy or not trying. Telling a child to "try harder" when s/he is already doing the best s/he can is frustrating for them and may cause them to give up.
- Avoid stereotypes, such as labeling a foster child/youth as uneducated, incompetent or simply unmotivated.

For more in-depth information about learning disabilities and how school systems serve learning disabled students, **please review the Education Section of this handbook on page 179.**

> Often, children and youth who have experienced trauma, neglect, have lived in extreme poverty or have moved many times, will have learning challenges. They may not be performing at their grade level or may experience behavioral or social difficulties at school. While they may not have a "traditional" learning disability, they may still display many of the same characteristics of a learning disabled child. You will want to follow many of the same guidelines listed above to give them the support they need. For many of these children/youth, once they are in a stable living situation, they will begin to thrive and catch up academically.

Medical and Emotional Issues

Children and youth in foster care have disproportionately high rates of physical, developmental and mental health issues, as well as many unmet medical, dental and mental health needs. Therefore, it is very important for foster parents to make sure that foster child/youth receive regular medical attention and that they follow all doctor recommendations to ensure that the child receives the best care possible. Some children and youth coming into foster care may have undiagnosed physical or mental health needs, making you, the foster parent, a critical source of observation, information and feedback for medical professionals.

If a child has been diagnosed as Developmentally Delayed (DD), there will be an extra layer of services to be coordinated. Children with developmental disabilities may also have difficulty with hearing, sight or speech. Additionally, they may experience emotional and behavioral issues as most children recognize that they are behind other children of their own age. Some may become frustrated, withdrawn, anxious and/or act out to get attention. Others may become depressed and might not have enough language skills to talk about their feelings. Their depression may be reflected in their behavior, sleep or eating issues. It is important that foster parents of developmentally delayed children set appropriate expectations, limits, opportunities to succeed and other measures which will help the child handle the stresses of their circumstances.

Fetal Exposure to Drugs and Alcohol

An unborn baby depends on his/her mother for nourishment. Research demonstrates that when a pregnant woman drinks alcohol, takes drugs or even smokes, she risks seriously damaging her unborn child.

A baby is at risk for many preventable problems if the mother drinks alcohol, including beer and wine, during pregnancy. Babies born to mothers who drink can develop fetal alcohol syndrome, one of three leading causes of physical and mental birth defects. It is uncertain how much alcohol it takes to create a fetal alcohol syndrome infant.

The following symptoms are characteristic of fetal alcohol syndrome:
- Small size, particularly the head
- Club foot, "strawberry" birthmarks or facial deformities
- Mental retardation
- Learning disabilities

- Behavioral problems
- Jittery gait and lack of coordination
- Problems with the liver, kidneys, heart and joints

When there is alcohol in the mother's blood, it is in her unborn baby's blood as well. Many of these babies suffer alcohol withdrawal, which can last from one week up to six months after birth. The signs of withdrawal are agitation, tremors and seizures. The physical damage of alcohol on a developing fetus can last a lifetime, and any alcohol that a mother drinks puts her unborn baby at risk. Even modest alcohol drinkers have more miscarriages and stillborn babies than nondrinkers.

Infants whose mothers took drugs, such as methamphetamines, cocaine or heroin, during their pregnancy may also go through withdrawal at birth. Symptoms may range from mild to severe; and they include: hyperactivity; sleep and feeding problems; a high-pitched cry; fussiness; breathing problems; diarrhea; vomiting; and convulsions. For mild symptoms, treatment may include oxygen for difficulties with breathing; gentle handling; frequent feedings; and quiet, cozy surroundings. Severe symptoms may require drug therapy as well. Infants with drug withdrawal may also be more prone to respiratory distress and sudden infant death syndrome, stressing the importance of watching these infants closely. A baby having been born addicted to a substance may also suffer long-term development issues as well.

Many children/youth entering foster care were exposed to perinatal substance use and abuse. Often, the damage caused by this exposure will manifest in notable behavioral challenges throughout their development. These behaviors are treatable, but it is important for the Foster Care Provider to be fully informed of the child/youth's fetal history, to address behavioral issues within the child/youth treatment planning process, and for the foster parent to have the skills to effectively work with substance exposed foster children and youth.

BEDWETTING (ENURESIS)

Bedwetting is normal for children, with girls often times developing control much earlier than boys. However, it is important that as a foster parent, you take the steps necessary to rule out a medical condition that could be causing your foster child to wet their bed, as some of the other causes can include deep sleep or possible emotional trauma.

If bedwetting occurs:

- Notify the foster child/youth's Foster Care Provider's Social Worker right away. A physical examination by a physician may be required. Bedwetting sometimes is a physical problem and can be aided through medication or other interventions.

- Remember that the foster child/youth may have no control over it.

- Have the foster child/youth assist in changing the bedding and soiled clothing. Obtain and use a rubber sheet to prevent damage to the mattress.

- Give a lot of verbal praise and assurance that bedwetting is something s/he will get help to change.

- Work with the Child & Family Team to develop a behavior incentive plan.

- Restrict liquids before bedtime.

- Establish a routine for going to the bathroom, maybe even set an alarm to wake the foster child/youth up later in the evening to use the bathroom.

- Talk with the foster child/youth's Foster Care Provider's Social Worker for other alternatives to support the child/youth.

It's important that you DON'T:

- Ignore a possible problem.
- Require a foster child/youth to wear training pants or rubberized outerwear.
- Threaten, belittle or embarrass the foster child/youth after a bedwetting incident.
- Punish or give consequences for bedwetting incidents, which not only won't help the problem, but may make it worse. Instead, find incentives for when bedwetting doesn't occur.

And DO:

- Limit the amount of liquids your foster child consumes before bedtime.
- Be supportive if the foster child/youth won't (or can't) wake up to use the bathroom—this process takes time and practice.
- Remember that your foster child/youth is not "bad" for wetting the bed, nor is it an intentional act; they just need to work through the problem, and your patience and acceptance will go a long way toward helping them do this.

Don't give up! Bedwetting will most likely diminish as the child grows or with proper intervention.

SOILING AND BOWEL CONTROL (ENCOPRESIS)

On rare occasions, a foster child/youth will defecate in his/her pants while either awake or asleep. This is a condition that can be treated medically if necessary. If this problem does occur, immediately contact the child's Social Worker and approach the problem as you would bedwetting (please see above). On rarer occasions, a foster child/youth will intentionally act out using feces. If you observe any behavior of this nature, such as "smearing" feces on a wall or defecation on a floor or furniture, **you must notify the Foster Care Provider's Social Worker immediately**. This is an indication of a much deeper emotional issue that must be immediately addressed through the proper interventions as well as presenting a serious health problem.

HEAD LICE

It is not uncommon for a child to get head lice. Having head lice does not necessarily mean that the child comes from a dirty environment or that there is a cleanliness problem with your home. Anyone can get head lice and it can be challenging to get rid of once it is well established.

If you suspect the foster child/youth has lice, we suggest the following:

- Immediately obtain a de-lousing shampoo from the health department, the pharmacy or through your family doctor. Shampooing only kills live bugs and not the eggs, therefore it is necessary to repeat the shampooing process every seven to 10 days.
- A foolproof way to de-lice an individual is to use a temporary, wash-out hair dye. This technique kills the live bugs and eggs. Plus, the hair dye quickly washes out.
- As an alternative, there are several good natural remedies, such as applying Vaseline or mayonnaise on the hair and scalp and covering with a shower cap. These and other natural options can be found on the internet.

- The eggs or "nits" must be removed by hand. They will hatch in about 10 days. "Nits" are located at the bottom of the hair shaft and look like white dots. A "nit" comb can be obtained at a pharmacy.

- Other than hair dye, the only thing that will kill eggs is heat. Clothing, stuffed animals, sheets, towels etcetera, must be washed in HOT water. Objects that cannot be treated by heat can be placed in large plastic (black) bags and placed in the sun for a couple of days.

- If lice is detected and treated early it can be easily gotten rid of. If detected too late it can be very difficult and costly to control and remove.

- **NEVER** use any non-approved chemical or insecticide on a child or animal. These are toxic and very dangerous!

Nightmares

Nightmares can be unconscious feelings and fears or past experiences (such as past abuse) played out in dreams. They can range from a nightmare to a night terror (traumatic experience that interrupts the sleep). Nightmares serve to release children's feelings, fears and anxieties; but they are also traumatic for the foster child/youth and caregivers.

Tips for dealing with nightmares:

- Talk with children about where they're sleeping. Ask them about their room and bed, and whether or not they feel safe.

- Be positive and reassure them that they are safe and that you are close by should they need you (i.e., no one is going to hurt you!).

- Provide a nightlight and remove any objects that may be potentially frightening such as pictures, posters, open closets, objects under bed, etcetera. It may be helpful to provide children with a flashlight.

- Establish a routine to show them around the bedroom.

- Provide a stuffed animal or appropriate object for children to sleep with or have near their bed.

- Spend a few minutes with them in their room and read happy stories to them. These stories and quality time will instill positive, happy thoughts in the child's mind before sleep. You can even make up a story that includes a super hero or a magical ring or magical wand that will always keep them safe.

- Monitor and restrict T.V. shows, books, movies, comic books, video games, etcetera, that may be frightening or violent.

Difficult Behaviors

Tantrums

Tantrums are common behaviors that children have learned to use to get their needs met and express their feelings. This may be a learned behavior that has been incorrectly rewarded by an adult caretaker, which unfortunately only reinforced this behavior.

Points to remember:

- As children develop, they need to learn to delay instant gratification and control their impulses.

- Sometimes, it's appropriate to ignore this behavior and, when possible, allow them to complete the tantrum behavior. Always make sure the foster child is safe from possible injury during a tantrum.

- Once the child/youth has regained their ability to hear you, encourage him/her to talk and verbalize his/her feelings, wants or desires. Attempt to redirect the foster child/youth's attention and tantrum behaviors. Make clear statements to the child/youth that this type of behavior is not appropriate.

- Sometimes it may be appropriate, depending on age level, to comfort children/youth by touching their hand and establishing contact in order to reassure them.

- Don't take the foster child/youth's tantrum personally. Keep your emotions under control and speak in a soft, low tone. Your body posture should be relaxed and non-threatening (body language sends more signals than your words).

- Learn what sets children off and how to prevent a tantrum. For example, if the foster child predictably tantrums at the supermarket in order to get you to buy something, talk with the child prior to going to market. Set the ground rules for a win-win solution so that the child feels there is an incentive to behaving properly. Always follow through and be consistent in doing what you say you will do within the limits you set before going into the store.

HITTING, BITING, KICKING AND AGGRESSIVE BEHAVIORS

Sometimes if a child or youth is unable to identify or express their emotions through words, they may use aggressive behavior as a means of communicating difficult emotions. It is common for children or youth to be physically aggressive with others if they've been around domestic violence.

Tips for dealing with aggressive behaviors:

- Talk to your foster child or youth and explain to them that hitting is not okay, and assure them that they will not be hit by any adults while in your home.

- Provide empathy and let the child or youth know you understand why they might be feeling angry and aggressive. Encourage opportunities to talk about what might be triggering their strong emotions.

- Use a lot of positive reinforcement when a foster child interacts non-aggressively and/or doesn't hit when they are in conflict or angry. For example, "You did a very good job today sharing your toys" or "I really appreciated that you used your words with Johnny today when you were angry."

- Provide the child or youth with a ball to kick or throw (an indoor sponge ball is an excellent choice), or encourage some other type of acceptable physical activity to give them a safe and healthy outlet to release their anger and/or frustration.

- Never physically restrain a child/youth. Remember, it is a violation of their personal rights to take any physical actions which would force a child to do anything.

- Notify the foster child/youth's Foster Care Provider's Social Worker immediately if aggressive behaviors continue or escalate.

BULLYING

Bullying is a common experience for many children and adolescents and is unfortunately increasing, especially within the school environment. Surveys indicate that as many as half of all children are bullied at some time during their school years and at least 10% are bullied on a regular basis. Bullying behavior can be physical or verbal, and can occur face to face, on internet social networking sites or by text messaging.

Foster children and youth who are bullied experience real suffering that can interfere with their social and emotional development, as well as their school performance and attendance. Some victims of bullying have even committed or attempted suicide rather than continue to endure such harassment, threats or fear of harm.

The following are important points about bullying:

- Children and adolescents who bully thrive on controlling or dominating others.
- Bullies have often been victims of physical abuse or bullying themselves.
- Bullies may also be depressed, angry or upset by events at school or home.
- Bullies often target children who are passive, easily intimidated or have few friends.
- Victims of bullies may also be smaller or younger and have a hard time defending themselves.

If you suspect your foster child or youth may be bullying others, contact his or her Social Worker to develop a plan of intervention.

> Without intervention, bullying can lead to serious academic, social, emotional and legal consequences. The child/youth must be helped to understand what is causing the bullying and be supported in stopping this destructive behavior.

If you suspect your child may be the victim of bullying, provide lots of opportunities for them to talk with you openly and honestly. Make sure they know that they are doing the right thing by telling you, and that it's not their fault.

Other suggestions include:

- Ask the child what they think should be done. What have they tried and what worked and didn't work?
- Seek help from the child's teacher, school counselor or administrator. It is important to note that schools serving students in grades 8 through 12 are required to establish programs that promote school safety and emphasize violence prevention.
- Contact your child's school to learn more about programs to combat bullying such as peer mediation, conflict resolution, anger management training and increased adult supervision. Always communicate with the school if you feel that your foster child may be at risk.
- Don't encourage the child to fight back! Instead, suggest that they try walking away or seeking help from a nearby adult.
- Help your child practice being assertive. The simple act of insisting that the bully leave them alone may be surprisingly effective.
- Encourage your child to be with friends when traveling back and forth from school, during shopping trips or on other outings. Bullies are less likely to pick on a child in a group.
- Supervise your child when they are using the computer.

If your child becomes withdrawn, depressed or reluctant to go to school, talk with the child's Foster Care Provider's Social Worker as additional consultation and intervention may be required.

Chapter 9

Self-Destructive Behavior

Self-destructive behaviors include: head banging; scratching; pulling fingernails off; burns; self-inflicted tattoos; cutting of the skin; swallowing dangerous items or materials; fighting; or any form of self-mutilation. Self injury is a complex behavior and results from a variety of factors, including the child merely following a fad to serious psychiatric problems such as depression or Post-Traumatic Stress Disorder.

Some adolescents may self-mutilate to take risks, rebel, reject their parent's values, state their individuality or to merely be accepted. However, others may injure themselves out of desperation, anger, to seek attention, to show their hopelessness and worthlessness, or because they have suicidal thoughts. Children or youth who self-injure are at a higher risk of suicide. Sometimes we will know about a child/youth's tendency toward self-destructive behavior and this will be addressed in the Child & Family Team meetings and a safety plan will be developed.

Here are some important approaches to try:

- Give clear messages about the inappropriateness of the destructive behavior. Use "I" messages; for example, "I don't want you to hurt yourself" or "I can't let you hurt yourself" or "I must keep you safe."

- Use active listening; help the child identify his/her feelings and talk through them rather than act on them. Take every opportunity to build the child's self-esteem and encourage continued expression of feelings.

- Offer ways they can distract themselves from feelings of self-harm; for example, counting to 10; waiting 15 minutes; practicing breathing; journaling; drawing; or using ice or the snap of a rubber band.

- Help the child learn to soothe themselves in a positive, non-injurious way. Teach them how to practice positive stress management.

- Above all, keep the child safe. Take extra steps to remove any objects that the child may be prone to use to hurt themselves and provide extra supervision.

If you observe self-destructive behaviors, immediately notify the child's Social Worker and make sure the issue is addressed in the child's Child & Family Team meetings.

Attachment and Bonding

Children who have experienced trauma early in their life may have difficulty attaching and bonding with others. It is not uncommon to see children in foster care who have experienced this type of early life trauma and, consequently, demonstrate specific behaviors, such as difficulty establishing and keeping relationships, acting withdrawn or excessively wanting to be alone. They may exhibit a lack of conscience or lack of impulse control, and you may notice their inability to give and receive affection in a real way and yet see them show indiscriminate affection with strangers.

We know from current research that trauma experienced in utero and in early life causes damage to the brain. With the right interventions, foster parents can actually help promote healing to important parts of the brain, which in turn improves bonding and attachment.

It's important to note that children with attachment challenges struggle to trust others; they can become oppositional, angry and often dangerous to themselves and others. They are unable to give and receive affection in a healthy way. They lack cause and effect thinking and engage themselves in high risk behaviors.

As a foster parent, your relationship with your foster child/youth is the most important factor in helping the child or youth learn to trust and bond with others. Working hand-in-hand with your Foster Care Provider's staff, you can develop solutions and activities that will support the child to better cope with life's challenges.

Here are some helpful tips:

- Be consistent and provide clear expectations for behavior.
- Minimize the child/youth's stress and reinforce that s/he is safe.
- Help the child to experience and accept loving, nurturing care.
- Validate the child/youth's feelings.
- Encourage appropriate and safe expressions of feelings.
- Encourage and acknowledge appropriate behavior.
- Help the child work through grief and loss issues.
- Increase the child's self-control abilities and develop thoughtful decision making skills.
- Help the child develop a positive sense of identity, thereby enhancing their self-esteem.
- Help the child accept responsibility.

The process of attachment/bonding takes time. Behaviors will vary from child to child, and so will the time it takes for him/her to heal. The key to successful intervention is enhanced skills, patience and consistency!

SEXUALIZED BEHAVIOR

Children are naturally inquisitive and go through developmental stages in which they present some types of sexual acting out. This may range from mimicking what they see at home, on T.V. or in books; to exploring their own body parts and playing doctor or nurse with each other. Foster parents need to learn to distinguish between normal sexual play and sexual acting out. If you observe your foster child or youth exhibiting behaviors that concern or disturb you, talk with the child/youth's Foster Care Provider's Social Worker and the Child & Family Team. It is important to be direct with the child/youth about what they are doing and whether or not it is appropriate, but always convey the message without inducing them to feel shame or guilt.

Children and youth who have been victims of sexual abuse manifest certain behaviors and in fact, it is very common for molest victims to act out and play in sexual ways. We may not know what the child has experienced, so it is imperative that you observe and supervise. If any of the following behaviors are observed, report them to the child/youth's Foster Care Provider's Social Worker.

Some of the signs that a child may have been sexually abused include:

Physical Symptoms
· Genital infection/Vaginal discharge
· Bedwetting or Soiling
· Sexually Transmitted Disease
· Preoccupation with genitals

Emotional Symptoms
· Fantasizes often
· Mood swings
· Poor self-esteem

- Hyper vigilance
- Internalized guilt
- Dissociation
- Depression
- High level of irritability

Behavioral Symptoms
- Bizarre, sophisticated and/or age inappropriate sexual behavior or knowledge
- Hints of sexual activity
- Promiscuity
- Sexual details in art and drawings
- Sexual abuse of other children
- Excessive masturbation

Other Symptoms
- Lack of social skills
- Delinquency or running away
- Withdrawn
- Suicidal
- Secretive behavior
- Fighting
- Fire setting
- Poor peer relationships
- Coercive or manipulative behavior

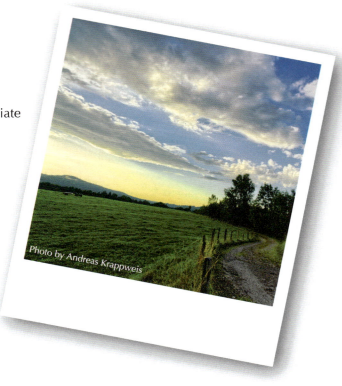

The following are things to be aware of and some suggestions on how you can support children who have been sexually abused:

- Many victims of sexual abuse will act out sexual behavior which is not age appropriate. For example, oral copulation of dolls, masturbation, humping, insertion of objects into body cavities, etcetera. If this behavior is observed, the child/youth's Foster Care Provider's Social Worker should be notified immediately.

- Sexually abused children need to learn the boundaries of appropriate and inappropriate sexual behavior, and Foster parents play a critical role in teaching children/youth the type of touching that is acceptable. Distract children and youth when they are observed masturbating around others, then privately instruct them that they will not be allowed to do this around others in your home. You are teaching boundaries and setting limits.

- Give repeated non-critical messages as to the appropriateness of behavior. Remember, these children and youth have to be re-programmed as to what types of physical affection is acceptable. For example, don't punish or criticize a foster child/youth for showing inappropriate physical affection with a foster parent or other child/youth; rather, carefully explain to them that their behavior is not appropriate and teach them acceptable behaviors instead. The Child & Family Team will develop guidelines and boundaries regarding appropriate physical contact that will support every child's specific needs.

- Foster parents need to be particularly sensitive and aware of the type of physical affection they give and receive. Every foster child/youth has different needs for affection, and you should never assume a child/youth wants to be hugged or shown other types of "normal" parental affection. Always ask the child/youth for permission before showing affection. Foster parents should also avoid **not** allowing for any type of physical affection or, conversely, being overly affectionate. Children need to see the appropriate ways that people show affection.

- Adolescent molest victims are at high risk of sexually acting out. This can include promiscuous, seductive or manipulative behaviors towards adults and other children. There often exists the possibility that they would, under certain circumstances, victimize others in the ways similar to how they were victimized.

DO:

- Teach foster children/youth the importance of appropriate clothing, and set limits for when and how to dress. For example, foster children and youth should not be allowed to run around the house naked or partially clothed.

- Allow for foster children and youth to bathe individually and in private (when age appropriate). Be especially careful in teaching them how to wash themselves. Recognize sex and age difference when supervising baths.

- Foster parents and other children/youth in the home should model appropriate behaviors to teach foster children and youth acceptable boundaries.

- Foster parents should keep their bedroom door closed when changing clothes, and especially, while engaging in sexual activity.

- Teach foster children and youth to close the doors to their room or bathroom when changing clothes or using the bathroom.

- Teach foster children and youth appropriate physical contact and how to give and receive affection by modeling this behavior.

- Kisses, hugs and other types of touching must be appropriate to the age and sex of the foster child/youth.

- Increase supervision at home if you have a foster child or youth that has a history of sexual acting out.

DON'T:

- Get angry, yell, criticize or punish children who may act out sexually. Remember, they have not been taught the correct or appropriate way to behave.

- Allow foster children and youth to bathe with other foster children or your children.

- Walk around the house scantily/partially clothed or inappropriately dressed. Remember, foster children and youth will model foster parent behavior.

- Force children to show physical affection. Don't kiss them on the mouth or lips, don't pat the buttocks, don't tickle them by touching inappropriately, etcetera. Be familiar with what is and what is not appropriate touching.

FIRE SETTING

Just because a child is playing with matches doesn't mean s/he is an arsonist. It could simply just be a childhood fascination and an impulsive curiosity. All children are fascinated by fire. It's important to be able to distinguish whether a child sets a fire intentionally or accidentally.

Look for the following red flags:
- Is there an attempt to hide it or cover up?
- Is fire setting or playing with fire done when the child is very angry or upset?
- Does the child burn significant items such as pictures, letters, documents, etcetera?

Habitual, purposeful fire setting is an indication of deep-seated anger, pain and/or rage. It is not uncommon for severely abused or traumatized children to act out their anger through this type of destructive behavior.

The following are precautions you should take in regards to fire safety:

- Keep your home free from incendiary devices (matches, lighters) or lock them up.
- Teach children about the use and abuse of fire.
- Carefully discuss the implications of fire setting. You may want to involve the fire or police department in helping you educate your foster child.

A child exhibiting this type of destructive behavior needs intensive therapy to deal with his/her rage. Let the child's Foster Care Provider's Social Worker know immediately should any of these behaviors be observed or discovered.

Dishonestly, Exaggeration and Stealing

It's normal for children as they grow up to test limits through dishonesty or taking things that don't belong to them. Although a child may know that dishonesty or stealing is wrong, s/he will do it for a number of reasons, including the following:

- They may have been exposed to dishonesty or manipulation in the past, so this behavior is normal to them
- If the child has been abused or violated, they may have found that dishonesty could be a successful survival skill which helped them to avoid further abuse
- Dishonesty and exaggeration may have served as a coping skill allowing the child to fulfill their needs
- To garner attention from a parent or another authority figure
- To gain power and control when they feel powerless
- Abused and neglected children often "steal" or "hoard" food by hiding it in their rooms because they may be fearful that they will not be fed or nurtured by their caregivers
- For instant gratification—children are still learning to delay gratification and wait for things
- Excitement, adventure or thrill-seeking
- Anger or to "get even"

Tips for dealing with dishonesty or stealing:

- It is important for foster parents to keep valuables and items that cannot be replaced due to sentimental value in a safe, locked place.
- If you notice your foster child continually has new possessions, clothing, electronics, etcetera, that you have never seen before, you should talk with your Foster Care Provider's Social Worker about the possibility that the child may be stealing, and together you can develop a strategy as to how to address this concern.
- If you suspect that your child has been stealing and/or has been dishonest, severe punishment must never be used, nor should you tell them you will not punish them if they simply "own up" and "tell the truth."
- Avoid calling your child a liar, thief or making statements that imply s/he can never be trusted again.
- Never set a child up to lie, especially if you know what they've done ahead of time; or to steal by leaving alcohol, money or other valuables easily accessible.
- When you are certain the child is telling a lie or stealing, you will need to work with the Child & Family Team to develop an appropriate, logical consequence. This could include returning to the store where the item was stolen and returning it, or asking the child/youth to write a letter of apol-

ogy. In some cases, the consequence might even involve law enforcement or probation. Again, the appropriate consequence will be determined by the CFT.

It is normal for children to exaggerate, be dishonest and sometimes to take things that don't belong to them. However, if dishonesty and stealing become habitual behaviors, you will need patience and understanding to help the child break this cycle.

Substance Abuse

Youth are experimenting with and abusing drugs and other substances at an alarming rate. Depending on the circumstances, it could start as early as elementary school. Foster youth often have been exposed to some additional risk factors, ranging from genetic predisposition (family history) to pre-natal exposure to co-existing disorders (substance abuse and other serious emotional disorders such as depression, Post-Traumatic Stress Disorder, Attention Deficit Hyperactive Disorder, etcetera). They may also have an intensified sense of not fitting in socially or feelings of rejection and abandonment related to being displaced from their family. The largest contributing factor to substance use is family environment. As incredible as it may seem, it is estimated that well over 85% of all foster children come from families where substance abuse was an issue.

Some behaviors or indicators of substance abuse include:
- Youth may tell you about their experiences with drugs and alcohol
- Drug paraphernalia, pipes (or items crafted into pipes), cigarette papers, over the counter cough/cold or diet medications, or even prescription medications that were not prescribed to the youth
- Alcohol or drugs hidden in drawers, hampers, etcetera, in the child's room or outside on the property
- Family background and history of substance-related behaviors prior to coming into your home
- Drop in grades and school attendance
- Loss of interest in activities they once enjoyed
- Change in friends
- Change in sleeping and eating habits
- Violating curfew
- Physical signs of use: increased irritability, mood swings, dilated pupils, red and glazed eyes, odor/smell in clothing and on breath
- Shoplifting, items missing from the home

Some of the warning signs listed above can also be signs of other problems. Foster parents may recognize signs of trouble but should not be expected to make a diagnosis. One of the most effective ways for parents to show care and concern is to openly discuss the use and possible abuse of alcohol and other drugs with their child.

Room searches may NOT be conducted without the knowledge and approval of the Foster Care Provider. If you suspect that the youth may have drugs or other contraband hidden in their rooms, address this with the Child & Family Team or immediately contact your Foster Care Provider's Social Worker.

If you know or suspect that substance use is occurring, you should:

- Report concerns to the youth's FFA social worker to explore counseling and initiate an assessment for substance abuse. Remember, there is a big difference between experimental use and actual abuse! Experimental use is very common among adolescents and youth, and can be more readily stopped and corrected.

Chapter 9

Photo by Anita Peppers

- If your foster youth is on probation, review and be familiar with the terms and conditions of their probation related to drug testing, curfew, counseling, non-association, etcetera.

- Continue to be a loving and supportive foster parent, setting firm limits and boundaries related to alcohol and drug use. Be clear on the law, and encourage the youth to follow the law, including not drinking alcohol if under 21 years of age.

- Seek the support of the youth's Child & Family Team for logical consequences to employ.

Always remember that as adults, we are role models. The Foster Care Provider discourages foster parents from consuming alcohol in front of children/youth, and requires that all alcohol in the home be locked up and out of sight. Be aware of your foster child's history and whether alcohol was an issue in their past.

Prescription Drug Abuse

The use and abuse of prescription medications for non-medical reasons is an increasingly alarming trend. Because these medications are prescribed by doctors, they are thought of as safe, but the truth is that the addictive potential for some of these drugs is the same as that of heroin and methamphetamine. The following are some important facts related to prescription drug abuse:

- Prescription drugs, such as pain relievers, tranquilizers, stimulants and sedatives, are among the substances most commonly abused by children, teens and adults in the United States.

- Prescription drugs are readily available and can easily be obtained by those who abuse these drugs to experience a variety of desired effects.

- Often, those who abuse these drugs are unaware of the serious health risks involved in abusing prescription drugs.

- Increasingly, younger adolescents obtain prescription drugs from classmates, friends and family members, or they steal the drugs from school medicine dispensaries and from people for whom the drug had been legitimately prescribed.

- Some of the most frequently abused prescription medications include Oxycontin, Vicodin, Percodan, Valium, Xanax and medications commonly prescribed for ADHD, such as Adderall, Concerta and Ritalin.

- "Pharming Parties" are a new trend among young people in which everyone brings whatever prescription drugs they can get and puts them all together in a bowl. Then each person takes a handful of pills and waits to see what happens.

- Needless to say, emergency rooms across the country have seen a 300% increase (from 1995 to 2002) in patients needing assistance due to prescription medication abuse or overdose.

Cough and Cold Medications

The use of OTC (over the counter) cough and cold medications to get high is also becoming more common among adolescents and youth. Abusers of these medications take large doses in order to experience hallucinations, or to have out-of-body or other unusual experiences. Again, there is a perception that because the medication is available for purchase in retail stores without a prescription, that it is safe. However, an overdose of one of these medications can cause vomiting, uncontrolled violent muscle spasms, irregular heartbeat, delirium and even death.

Inhalant Abuse

A growing trend among youth is the deliberate inhalation or sniffing of fumes, vapors or gases from common household products for the purpose of getting high. Inhalants are often the first drug to be abused and in fact, one in five kids have admitted to abusing a product as an inhalant by the time they reach eight grade.

While it may be difficult for young people to get illegal drugs or alcohol, there are more than 1,400 common items that can be "sniffed" or "huffed," including many that are found in the kitchen, garage or office. Some common products abused are:

- Correction fluid, rubber cement, computer keyboard dust cleaners
- Refrigerant, gasoline, propane, nitrous oxide, butane
- Glue, marking pens, spray paint
- Dusting spray, hairspray, air fresheners, whipped cream and cooking sprays

Many children and youth are unaware of the lethality of inhaling common household products. They believe because it is found in the home and sold in stores that it is safe. It is essential for parents to educate their children about the dangers of inhalant abuse. Along with loss of memory and smell, abusing inhalants can cause brain, liver and kidney damage, and can cause death the very first time it is used to get high. Some warning signs that your child may be abusing inhalants include:

- Coordination difficulties, slurred speech, disorientation or dazed appearance
- Chemical odor on clothes or breath
- Red spots or sores around mouth or nose
- Empty lighters, spray cans, whipped cream containers (the cream will still be in the can, but the gas propellant will be gone), plastic bags, balloons or rags with chemical odors

All prescription and OTC drugs, alcohol, and toxic chemicals must be locked and stored.

If a youth appears to be under the influence or intoxicated at the time of placement, it is the responsibility of the placing agency to have them medically cleared, prior to placement in your home.

If a foster youth comes home intoxicated or under the influence, please do the following:

- Contact the Foster Care Provider's Social Worker assigned to the youth, or the after hours on-call Social Worker.
- Seek medical attention.
- Contact law enforcement if you meet any resistance or inappropriate behavior, or if the youth is on probation.

Self-Choking Game

The self-choking game, or "The Game" as is its slang/street term, involves youth either choking themselves or taking turn choking each other until passing out. Youth use belts, ropes, ties or their own bare hands to deprive their brains of oxygen and achieve a drug-like high. This method of gaining a "high" has become widespread among children as young as nine on up to young adults.

There are two "high" parts to the "choking" experience; first is a feeling of lightheadedness due to reduced blood flow to the brain and second is the rush that comes from removing the pressure on the neck or chest that causes the blood to surge through the carotid arteries into the brain.

Many youth who would not use drugs to get high, try this method because they don't think anything bad could happen. Unfortunately, many have died or developed brain damage from this deadly "game."

GANG AWARENESS

It has been our experience that hardcore gang members do not usually end up in foster care; however, when one looks at adolescent development and the issues facing youth entering foster care, you can see how these youth can be at risk for gang involvement. Young people join gangs for some of the same reasons they join other social groups, such as 4-H, scouting, school related clubs, etcetera. These reasons can vary, such as a search for structure/discipline, a sense of belonging, a need for recognition/power, companionship, excitement, a sense of self-worth/status, a need for protection, and/or family tradition. Parents need to know that prevention is the most important key to minimizing the risk of gang involvement. Understanding the indicators of possible gang involvement will enable you to redirect your child away from harmful involvement.

Signs of Possible Gang Involvement

- Obsession with one particular color of clothing, logo, etcetera
- Changes in hair/dress style or associating with other youths who have the same hair/clothing style. Usually some of the clothing, such as a hat or jacket, will have the gang's initials and/or the child's nickname (street name)
- Withdraws from family and/or longtime friends; secretive about new friends and activities
- Uses hand signals with friends; may practice at home
- Unexplained money, jewelry, expensive clothes
- Peculiar drawings or language on books, notes, etcetera
- Physical injuries in which the child lies about the events surrounding the injuries
- Discipline/attendance problems at school, failing classes
- Change in behavior at home (i.e. talking back, disrespect, verbal abuse)
- Use of a new nickname
- A new "fear" of police
- Graffiti on or around your residence, especially in child's room.
- Tattoos or "branding" with gang-related symbols
- Appears paranoid in public

Ways to Prevent Gang Involvement

- Take the time to get to know your foster youth's background.
- Get to know their friends, invite them to your house; meet their parents.
- Lead by example and avoid power struggles. Always appeal to the concept of respect.
- Invest in your relationship. Your best strategy is always to enhance your relationship.
- Talk with them, not at them.
- Remain solution focused.
- If the Child & Family Team determines that it is in the youth's best interest to go out with friends, always know where they are going, who they will be with, how they are getting there and when they will be home.

- Set rules and limits and enforce them. Young people need structure and limits.
- Assist with problem solving and provide healthy, positive choices and alternatives such as youth groups, music/art, meaningful volunteer work (e.g., working with animals, helping other children, etcetera) and mentors.
- Talk to teachers and counselors at school. Attend school functions.
- If the foster youth is on probation, seek their Probation Officer's assistance in setting limits. Often, probation youth who are gang involved have court ordered terms and conditions related to appropriate clothing, non-association with other gang affiliates, etcetera.

If your foster child is being pressured to join a gang, help them come up with strategies by which they can get out of a situation.

Some examples include:
- If the foster youth finds themselves in a situation where they are being pressured, they can say things such as: "I'm on probation and my 'P.O.' is keeping a close eye on me and I don't want to go back to 'juvie.' That would really hurt my family or my little brother or sister. My brother and sister look up to me, and I don't want to let them down."
- "I am getting drug tested tonight. One more dirty test and I'm back in the 'Hall.'"
- "I can't afford to lose my job. I send money to my grandmother."

If you have concerns that your foster youth may be contemplating gang involvement, talk with his/her Foster Care Provider's Social Worker. Also, be aware of local resources such as youth employment programs, tattoo removal services, etcetera, as these are also key resources in preparing the youth for employment to improve sense of pride and give them necessary life skills to make positive choices.

It is important that you're dedicated and committed to foster parenting, and to providing a healthy loving family environment. Without you, these children may never experience a positive alternative!

"My mom is my hero because every time I have a problem, she always comes and saves me and gets me back on the right road."

—Youth age 13

Guiding Principles

Regulations and Agency Policy

CHAPTER 10

CHAPTER 10

GUIDING PRINCIPLES
Regulations and Agency Policy

One thing that can be said for sure about this business is that it's well regulated; and it's good that it is. Clear regulations and requirements help ensure the safety of children in foster care, enhance the quality of care that children receive and provide state-wide consistency. The importance of knowing the regulations cannot be stressed enough—it is in the child's and your best interest to do so!

The Foster Care Provider is governed by two sets of regulations.

- **Foster Family Agency Regulations (FFA):** These regulations cover the specific details of how an agency's operates, its staff, its files, etcetera, and they oversee the operation of certifying foster homes and the placement of children.

- **Foster Family Homes Regulations (FFH):** These regulations are the ones that govern you as a foster parent and your home. You should be intimately familiar with these regulations. A copy of the full FFH regulations has been included in the Addendum of this handbook. All FFH-Section numbers referenced are from the: *Manual of Policies and Procedures, COMMUNITY CARE LICENSING DIVISION. Title 22, Division 6, Chapter 9.5.*

This chapter covers the main requirements as well as some agency policy and procedures. Requirements have been grouped into three categories:

- Those that pertain to you, the **FOSTER PARENT**
- Those that pertain to your **HOME AND PROPERTY**
- Those that pertain to the **FOSTER CHILD**

THE FOSTER PARENT

REASONABLE AND PRUDENT PARENT STANDARD

One of the most important concepts which have been incorporated into the FFH regulations is the Reasonable and Prudent Parent Standard.

FFH-Section 89377 of the Foster Family Homes Regulations defines the "Reasonable and Prudent Parent Standard" as the standard characterized by careful and sensible parental decisions that maintain the child's health, safety and best interest.

In applying the reasonable and prudent parent standard, the foster parent must consider:

- The age, maturity and developmental level of the child.

- The possible risks of harm; and the best interests of the child based on information known by the foster parent.

- The Prudent Parent Standard should never result in the denial of the rights of a foster child or contradict court orders or the Child & Family Plan identifying the specific needs and services of the child.

- The Reasonable and Prudent Parent Standard applies to many areas of regulations and will be highlighted throughout this chapter.

> We cannot stress enough the importance of proper consideration of all the risk factors involved whenever a decision is made utilizing the Reasonable and Prudent Parent Standard. Foster parents, when necessary, must be prepared to demonstrate the decision making process they employed and the efforts made to determine the appropriateness of their decision.

Licensing

All foster family homes must be certified by an approved licensing agency. One of the conditions for certification is for all persons residing in the foster home who are age 18 or older to submit a set of fingerprint images and related information, and to receive clearance from the Department of Justice, the Federal Bureau of Investigation and the Child Abuse Central Index (FFH-Section 89219). Additionally, the licensing agency shall have the authority to request review of your license (FFH-Section 89209).

Parent Qualification/Training

Any adult shall be permitted to apply for a license or approval to become a foster parent regardless of age, sex, race, religion, color, political affiliation, national origin, disability, marital status, actual or perceived sexual orientation, gender identity, HIV status or ancestry (FFH-Section 89317).

All foster parents must participate in an agency orientation and on-going education/training and professional development (FFH-Sections 89318).

Prior to certification, most Foster Care Providers require prospective foster parents to complete:

- First Aid/CPR training (both parents).
- Community Water Safety
- Introduction to Foster Parenting, a one-on-one orientation to familiarize you with your Foster Care Provider's policies and procedures.
- Communication And Relationship Enhancement training (CARE)
- Professional Assault Crisis training (PRO ACT)
- Intensive Therapeutic Foster Care training
- Program specific training
- Foster Parent Handbook review and review test
- Medications training

Following your first year as a foster parent, your Foster Care Provider must ensure that you participate in a minimum number of training hours per year and provide documentation of such training. 24 hours per year is a common threshold. This requirement may be satisfied in a number of ways:

- Participation in Foster Care Provider-sponsored training and support meetings
- Participation in Community College or Department of Social Services or Child Welfare Services foster parent education workshops
- Participation in any other related class or workshop with prior approval
- Review of approved video or audio tape, and completion of a general test form
- Time spent familiarizing yourself with your child's mental or physical diagnosis and/or medications
- Reading selected books or other written materials from the Foster Care Provider's library with approval
- Be creative—if you have a training idea, call your Foster Care Provider to discuss it

The best training policy is flexibility. You are expected to complete the required training, but there are many ways to accomplish this and meet your family's needs. Work closely with your Foster Care Provider in meeting this requirement.

Chapter 10

Health/Mental Health Status

Foster Parents should be in good physical and mental health. Good health shall be verified by a health screening, including a test for tuberculosis not more than one year old, and performed under the supervision of a physician. The report, signed by the physician, should indicate the presence of any health conditions that would create a hazard to the foster parent or children in their care (FFH-Section 89465(b)).

Reporting Requirements

Foster parents must report to the Foster Care Provider and the agency responsible for placing the child when certain events occur (FFH-Section 89361). This report is to be made by telephone, email or fax **as soon as possible, day or night**. As a foster parent, it is critical that you report incidents to your Foster Care Provider, as they are subjected to reporting requirements as well. Whenever one of the following events occurs, the Foster Care Provider must report it to their state's licensing agency by the next working day:

- Any injury to or illness of any child which required emergency medical treatment or hospitalization
- Any unusual incident or absence of a child which threatens the physical or emotional health and/or safety of the child
- Any suspected physical or psychological abuse of any child
- Communicable disease outbreak as reported to the foster parent by a health professional
- Poisoning
- Any fire or explosion which occurs in or on the premises
- Any incident or event involving the foster child resulting in the police or law enforcement being having been called
- Death of a child from any cause

In the case of an emergency or life threatening situation, always contact 911 Emergency Services first!

Mandated Reporting

Don't forget you are a mandatory child abuse reporter! The California child abuse reporting law requires that child abuse reports be made when mandated reporters observe, have knowledge of or have a reasonable suspicion of child abuse. When mandated reporters have reasonable suspicion they are not required to prove the abuse or collect evidence—that is done by law enforcement. If you suspect your foster child has been abused, you must report it.

Child abuse includes:

- **Physical abuse:** A physical injury which is inflicted by other than accidental means on a child by another person. Corporal punishment is not necessarily child abuse; however, it would be child abuse if the punishment was used with enough force to cause internal or external injuries.

- **Sexual abuse:** This includes sexual assault and sexual exploitation. Sexual assault includes a broad spectrum of hands-on and hands-off behaviors. Sexual abuse also includes lewd and lascivious behavior with a child under age 14 with the intent of arousing or gratifying either person. Sexual exploitation refers to conduct or activities related to the use of children in pornography or prostitution.

- **Willful cruelty or unjustifiable punishment of a child:** If any person willfully causes or permits a child to suffer, or inflicts unjustifiable physical pain or mental suffering on a child, this constitutes willful cruelty.

- **Neglect:** This occurs when parents are unable or unwilling to provide for the basic needs of their children. Basic needs include food, shelter, medical and educational care, etcetera.
- **Mental suffering or endangerment of emotional wellbeing:** This occurs when parents cause or permit children's mental suffering and do not provide the normal experiences which produce feelings of being loved, wanted, secure and worthy.

As way of an example, if your foster child returns to your home from a family visit with suspicious bruises, it is not your responsibility to determine the truth of the matter—that is for experts to determine—it is, however, your responsibility to report that you "suspect" something may have occurred during the visit. The first thing you do is call the child's Foster Care Provider's Social Worker, or the after-hours on-call Social Worker. Your Foster Care Provider will supply you with the required forms and explain the process of reporting your suspicions.

Changes in your Household Composition

All changes to your household composition must be reported to your Foster Care Provider, including, but not limited to the following (FFH-Section 89361):

- An addition to the foster parent's family, including when the foster parent becomes a guardian or conservator for any child or other person.
- Any adult moving in or out of the home.
- Except for a foster youth under the jurisdiction of the court placed by the county, any person living in the home who reaches their 18th birthday.

Additionally, all adults (18 years of age and older) must have a recent Tuberculosis test done(within the last 12-months), and be finger printed and cleared by the DOJ, FBI and CACI to reside in the same home as a foster child. This does not apply to children who turn 18 years of age while in foster care.

Foster Parent Responsibilities
(FFH-Sections 89378 and 89387)

Foster Parents are responsible for the care and protection of the foster children placed into their homes, including the following:

- Participation with your Foster Care Provider and other mandatorily involved agencies in planning for the needs of the child.
- Provide assistance in dressing, grooming, bathing and other personal hygiene of foster children as required.
- Maintain house rules for the safety and protection of the child. Protect the child from accidents at home.
- Provide central storage for or distribution of medicine and assistance with taking medicine. Arrange and assist with medical and dental care.
- Provide reasonable transportation to ensure the child gets to necessary treatment, appointments, visitations, training programs, etcetera
- Participation in skill enhancing training.
- Cooperate in completing treatment objectives in the child's Child & Family Plan.

- Assist the child in setting and reaching goals.

- Provide basic services within the home, including clothing, school supplies and the child's personal incidentals.

- Provide or ensure at least three nutritious meals per day, have between-meal snacks available, provide food as necessary, and meet any special dietary needs documented in the written plan identifying the specific needs and services of the child, unless the physician of a child advises otherwise.
    - Foster parents may encourage a child, as age and developmentally appropriate, to learn meal preparation, but should not require a child prepare meals.
    - A child may use kitchen knives and appliances to learn meal preparation, provided that they are properly trained in the safe use of such items and their safety plan does not dictate otherwise.

- Be regularly present in the home when children are present.

- Unless restricted by the child's Child & Family Plan, foster parents must permit and facilitate connections between the child and child's family and non-relative extended family members. However, foster parents are not required to take any action that would impair the health and safety of the child.

- Promote a normal, healthy, balanced and supported childhood experience and treat a foster child as part of the family to the extent possible.

- Maintenance and supervision of the child's cash resources and/or property where appropriate.

- Foster parents must provide supervision when a child is near a swimming pool and other bodies of water, and are encouraged to provide age and developmentally appropriate instruction to a child on water safety skills, including teaching them how to swim.
    - Foster parents shall use the Prudent Parent Standard when deciding whether a child may have access to fish ponds, fountains, creeks and other bodies of water.

Foster Child Activities

Foster children are entitled to participate in age-appropriate extracurricular, enrichment and social activities. Foster parents must use the Reasonable and Prudent Parent Standard as defined in this chapter to determine whether to give permission for a foster child to participate in such activities, taking into consideration the appropriateness of the activity with respect to the child's age, maturity and developmental level. The child's activities must always be kept in accordance with court orders and the Child & Family Plan which identifies the specific needs and services of the child.

Such enrichment and social activities include, but are not limited to:
- Activities that require group interaction
- Physical activities, games, sports and exercise
- Leisure time activities which include other members of the foster family
- Education opportunities through public, private or special school enrollment and assistance with schoolwork
- Learning of basic living skills to include: bathing, dressing, grooming, social skills, shopping, cooking, money management and use of public transportation
- When appropriate, the foster parent should participate in these activities with the child

CONFIDENTIALITY

Foster parents must make confidentiality one of their highest priorities because to knowingly furnish any confidential information regarding a foster child to a person not legally entitled to the information is punishable by state law and may also result in a civil action under provisions of the Welfare and Institutions Code. At a minimum, any intentional breaches of confidentiality may result in immediate decertification as a foster parent.

The Health Insurance Portability and Accountability Act, or HIPAA as it is commonly referred to, sets forth certain requirements related to "protected health information" about your foster child.

As foster parents you are responsible to:
- Safeguard all health information from misuse
- Use and/or disclose health information only as permitted or required by law
- Maintain the security of health information
- Prevent unauthorized use and /or disclosure of health information
- Advise the Agency when any breach of health information has occurred
- Return the child's health information to the Agency or to destroy it, as requested by the Agency as soon as possible.

Most state licensing agencies, including Community Care Licensing, have regulations which specify the following requirements regarding confidentiality (FFH-Sections 89372, 89370, 89468, 89468):

- All private or personal information and records including, any medical condition or treatment; psychiatric diagnosis or treatment; history of abuse; school reports reflecting poor performance or behavior; or information relating to the biological family of the child must be maintained in confidence.

- Foster parents are required to disclose information about the child to the Juvenile Court, the Foster Care Provider's licensing or approval agency, and to the child's biological family, Social Worker, placement worker, probation officer, physician, psychiatrist, CASA, attorney and other authorized representative, unless such disclosure is prohibited by court order.

- As needed to ensure appropriate care, supervision or education of the child, foster parents must disclose information to respite care providers, occasional short-term babysitters, alternative caregivers, school officials, and other persons unless such disclosure is prohibited by court order.

- Foster parents have the right to any known information regarding a child being placed in their home and usually information is provided by the placing agency in the form of a "Health and Education Passport," a needs and services plan, or pre-placement questionnaire. Foster parents are encouraged to ask questions or request further information about a child if they have concerns.

Foster children have the following rights pertaining to confidentiality (FFH-Section 89372 and WIC Section 16001):

- To be free from unreasonable searches of person or personal belongings

- To make and receive confidential phone calls, and send and receive unopened mail and electronic communication, unless prohibited by court order

- To have storage space for private use

- For all juvenile court records to be kept confidential, consistent with existing laws

CARE AND SUPERVISION OF FOSTER CHILDREN
(FFH-Section 89378)

It is your responsibility to provide care and supervision which meets the child's needs. Children in foster care, regardless of age, must have supervision in your home with a few exceptions, including the following:

- **Occasional Short-Term Care:** The Prudent Parent Standard allows foster parents to arrange for occasional, short term care of a foster child in the foster home for periods of **no more than 24 hours** using a reasonable and prudent parent standard.
   - This regulation is intended to make it easier for foster parents to attend various activities such as medical appointments, grocery shopping, social gatherings, an evening out or special event.
   - The law exempts the short-term, occasional babysitter from completing a health screening, CPR certification, training and fingerprinting-background checks.
   - Foster parents are required to use careful and prudent decision making when considering short term care that maintain the child's health, safety and best interests.
   - Occasional short-term babysitters/caregivers may be under the age of 18 but must have the maturity, experience and ability to provide adequate care and supervision to a child.
   - A foster child may act as an occasional short-term babysitter, however the Prudent Parent Standard must be employed when determining whether that is appropriate (or under what circumstances it can become appropriate).
   - Under no circumstances shall a foster child be required to babysit.

The law requires foster parents to provide the caregiver the following information before leaving the child with the caregiver for short-term care:
   - Information about the child's emotional, behavioral, medical or physical conditions necessary to provide care to the child during the time the foster parent is away. **You must always stress confidentiality issues and ensure that the caregiver understands the importance of keeping all information regarding the child in confidence.**
   - Any medication that should be administered to the foster child during the time the foster parent is away.
   - Emergency contact information that is valid during the time the child is in the care of the babysitter. This information should include the foster parent's cell phone number and your Foster Care Provider's on-call Social Worker's number.
   - Make sure the caregiver is aware of the child's right to contact the Foster Care Provider's on-call Social Worker.

Please note that this law only applies to **non-regular periods of no more than 24 hours**. It does NOT apply to:
   - Regular, afterschool care when foster parent(s) are working
   - Regular supervision because a foster parent is enrolled in a college course or other obligations that meet several times a week

- **Alternative Caregiver:** Any adult (even relatives) that you want to provide supervision in your home on a **regular** basis or for a period of **more than 24 hours** at one time, must be approved by your Foster Care Provider, and should provide the following information/documentation:
   - Must be at least 18 years of age
   - Fingerprints with clearance from FBI, DOJ, CACI Child Abuse/Neglect Report Request
   - Out of State Disclosure and Criminal Record Affidavit
   - Current First Aid/CPR Certification
   - Tuberculosis test (completed within 12-months of first placement)
   - Signed Oath of Confidentiality

- Signed Statement to Report Child Abuse
- Current Driver's License, DMV records and Proof of Automobile Registration and Insurance
- Signed HIPAA Compliance Agreement

If an alternative caregiver is going to be used, the child's Foster Care Provider's Social Worker must be notified verbally or in writing prior to the foster parent's absence from the home. Notification must include:
- The dates the foster parent plans to be absent from the home
- The name and contact information of the alternate caregiver
- An emergency number where the foster parent may be reached while they are away
- A list of the child's activities/services/appointments for the time requested

Providing care and supervision through the use of an alternative caregiver is intended to prevent the removal of a foster child from the home, thus maintaining stability and normalization during those infrequent instances where the foster parent will be absent from the home longer than 24 hours.

- **Respite Care:** Respite care is the provision of prearranged child care when a foster parent is absent or incapacitated, and it has been determined that temporary in-home or out-of-home care is in the child's best interest. Respite care is offered to allow temporary respite of parental duties so that the foster parent is able to fulfill other responsibilities necessary to improve or maintain parenting function. Out of home respite care may not exceed 72 hours at a time without approval by your Foster Care Provider and the placing agency (FFH-Section 89378(a)(1)(B)(6). Whenever you require respite care for your foster child, contact the child's Foster Care Provider's Social Worker. Your Foster Care Provider's office needs to coordinate respite care in order to:
  - Comply with licensing regulations and requirements
  - Assure appropriate temporary placement in regards to specific needs of the child and foster family
  - Assure that the temporary care provider receives the child's vital information including medical needs, etcetera
  - Keep records current for proper reimbursement
  - Verify the location of the foster child and who is providing supervision and care

You may apply the Prudent Parent Standard to provide supervision on an occasional basis. However, if you will be out of the home for more than 24 hours, you will need a child care provider who has been fully screened and approved as outlined earlier in this chapter.

Leaving a Child Alone Without Adult Supervision

Most state licensing agencies allow for a foster parent to leave a child at home alone without adult supervision, but only on an **occasional** basis and never overnight.

- Foster Parents must apply the Prudent Parent Standard, use proper risk management and take reasonable steps to determine the appropriateness of leaving a foster child alone without adult supervision, taking into consideration the child's age, maturity, and developmental level (FFH-Section 89377).

- As always, the Child & Family Team should be involved in decisions regarding the child being left unsupervised, and all court orders regarding the child must be followed.

- If a child is left alone, the foster parent must ensure that the child knows where the emergency numbers are posted and that they know proper emergency procedures.

- The child must also know where and how to contact the foster parent while they are away.

- In the case of regular, unsupervised time in the home, such as allowing a child to be in the home after school every day for a couple of hours until the foster parent arrives home from work, an exception from the placing agency must be obtained.

SUPERVISION OF FOSTER CHILDREN OUTSIDE THE FOSTER HOME

Foster children are entitled to (and should be encouraged to) participate in age and developmentally appropriate extracurricular, enrichment and social activities. (FFH-Section 89379). Foster parents may employ the Prudent Parent Standard in determining the appropriateness of allowing children to be unsupervised away from the foster home. However, foster parents must know the whereabouts of their foster child(ren) at all times to insure safety. Foster children should be afforded the opportunity to engage in activities you would customarily allow your own children to do, such as going to the library, movies, park or other event/outing within the parameters of the child's Child & Family Plan.

Here are the guidelines that must be met:

- Remember that you are ultimately responsible for providing supervision and for the safety of your foster child.

- Foster parents must know the whereabouts of their foster child at all times.

- All of the following criteria must be met when allowing your foster child to be away from the home unsupervised.
  - The Child & Family Plan must address this and provide guidelines approved by the placing agency and the Child & Family Team
  - Safety of the child and/or others
  - Court orders or restrictions
  - Age appropriateness, maturity and level of functioning of the child
  - Effects of medications and times to be taken

"You're a great person. It takes a lot of love and compassion to do what you do. I mean, all the time that you invest in making life easier for kids who have had it hard. Things that you taught me will stay with me the rest of my life and for that I am grateful."

-Youth age 16

FAQ: Care & Supervision

What kind of preparations must we make to take our foster child on vacation with us?

Family vacations offer an excellent opportunity to draw close to your foster child and make them feel loved and accepted as part of your family, so do not be intimidated by what may appear to be too much "red-tape" to get approval. Simple preparation can make it both possible and easy to include your foster child in your family's special plans.

If you are going out of county or out of state, you will need to receive written approval (email is acceptable) from the child's placement agency worker and you must obtain a court order. If approved, you must take the court order with you along with a medical consent form and emergency information for the area where you'll be staying. You must notify your placement worker as soon as your plans have solidified. It can take three weeks or longer for an out-of-state travel approval by the court to be issued. Court orders vary with each child, so do not assume permission will be granted. The child's placing agency worker will be able to answer all of your questions regarding the necessary process.

Prepare ahead of time for any possible emergencies that may arise and make sure you have everything you will need for the child to receive emergency medical care. Put together a "packet" to bring with you on your trip which includes:
- The court order
- Medical consent and the child's MediCal or Medicaid Card
- Home File

What options do I have for my foster child during school holidays and summer break?

The Child & Family Team should address this well in advance of school breaks in order to plan for wholesome activities and insure proper supervision is in place for the child. If the foster child is going to be at home, there must be adult supervision by someone who has been approved by the Foster Care Provider or for occasional occurrences under the Prudent Parent Standard. Alternatives could include:
- Childcare in another FFA certified foster parent's home
- Hiring a licensed daycare person
- Make an arrangement with friends or a family member willing to become an approved temporary care provider.

In addition to childcare, there are often community programs available during the summer that can creatively occupy your child, but planning is necessary to meet pre-registration requirements for most of these programs. Some of these programs include:
- YMCA
- Local school programs
- Boys and Girls Club
- Parks & Recreation Department - art and drama
- Summer Jobs

Pre-summer planning is essential and an excellent opportunity to use your "listening" skills to really hear your child's desires and to research different ideas together. Be sure you do this well ahead of time, so they don't miss out on any activity opportunities because of late sign-ups. In home and out-of-home child care and activities are the financial responsibility of the foster parent.

Foster Parents may not sign Release of Liability forms or authorization for photos to be taken. The child's placement agency worker (Probation/CWS) is authorized to do this.

CHAPTER 10

Chapter 10

Is it alright for my foster child to spend the day with his/her friends at the beach, the mall, an amusement park, etcetera, without adult supervision?

Again, the youth's Child & Family Team must address this issue and any plans must be in keeping with the Child & Family Plan. Because of water safety issues, foster parents must ensure that there is proper supervision whenever a foster child is near a swimming pool and other bodies of water (including ponds, creeks, etcetera) and parents are encouraged to provide age appropriate instructions to the child on water safety skills including teaching them how to swim. When applying the Prudent Parent Standard to allowing a foster child to have access to any bodies of water, the foster parent must consider the level of supervision that the child requires.

How old does my foster child need to be before we can leave him/her at home unsupervised?

Most state licensing agencies' regulations do not specify a child's age when addressing s/he being occasionally left unsupervised at home. Foster parents must employ the Prudent Parent Standard in determining the appropriateness of this on a case by case basis.

My foster youth is on probation; does curfew change during the summer?

Please don't assume that it does. Some may think summer would be handled like one long week-end as to curfew requirements, but that is not the case. Check with the child's Probation Officer to find out summer rules.

What do I do when my foster child is sick and I have to go to work?

Pre-planning is the answer. Make arrangements ahead of time with a child-care provider, friend or family member who can watch s/he when they stay home ill. *Note: the Prudent Parent Standard may be exercised at this time.*

 Foster Care Providers do not typically offer infirmary services or babysitting, but may be helpful in securing these services.

Is my foster child allowed to babysit other children?

A foster child may act as an occasional, short-term baby sitter in the foster home; however, the foster parent must apply the Prudent Parent Standard and use proper risk management to determine whether this is appropriate. Under no circumstances should a foster child be required to babysit. Foster children may also babysit outside the home (FFH-Sections 89378 and 89379). In both cases, this activity must be within the scope of the child's Child & Family Plan and Safety Plan.

Children's Records

Foster parents are expected to maintain a separate, complete and current record or file for each foster child in their home (FFH-Section 89370). Whenever a foster child is placed in your home, your Foster Care Provider will supply you with a Home File. The law requires that you keep this file in your home in a safe, locked place. The only people who are privy to the home file are you, your Foster Care Provider's staff and the placing agency's Social Worker. If in doubt, contact your child's Social Worker.

Each Foster Care Provider will have their own policies, procedures, forms, etcetera, and as a foster parent you will need to become familiar with them.

Information Most Often Contained in the Home File

- Acknowledgement of Discipline & Discharge
- Caretaker Log of Parental Contact
- Case Notes prepared by the foster parent, including observations, behaviors, successes, medical information, etcetera
- Centrally Stored Medication & Destruction Record
- Child & Family Plan (Treatment & Service Delivery Plan) within 30 days of placement
- Client Personal Property Form (Inventory)
- Court Documents
- Dangerous Propensities
- Foster Parent Monthly Report completed for every month a child is in your care
- Foster Child Information Report
- Health & Education Passport (within 30 days)
- Health Care Encounter Forms
- Immunization Records
- In-Home Support Informed Consent
- Medical Consent
- MediCal/Health card
- Personal Rights
- Placement Acknowledgement & Consent
- PRN Authorization Form
- Safety Plan
- School Related Documents
- Social Security Card

The following is a more dtailed look at the information your Foster Care Provider may require you keep in your foster child's Home File:

- **Behavior Case Notes:** Any observations, thoughts, concerns, successes, incidents and ideas that you write down to share with your child's Foster Care Provider's Social Worker.

- **Centrally Stored Medication and Destruction Record:** The proper documentation of medications is very important. *Please read the following carefully:*
  - All prescribed medications must be stored so that they are inaccessible to foster children. There are some exceptions allowed in the case of a foster child storing and administering his/her own medications, but only when the child's physician has given written permission to do so.
  - All prescribed medications must be counted and properly logged on the Centrally Stored Medication and Destruction Record as soon as you receive it.
  - Prescription medication not taken with the child upon termination of placement should be counted and destroyed in front of a witness, then documented by the foster parent and the wit-

125

ness, and initialed by a Foster Care Provider representative. Medications that arrive with your child must be accurately inventoried, quantity counted and documented by the foster parent with the help of a Placing Agency worker, Foster Care Provider representative or other authorized individual.
- In the event a medication was prescribed before being placed in your home, enter "prior" into the date started column. This will help everyone understand exactly which medications you are personally responsible for safeguarding and administering to your child.
- If you receive any medication that is not properly labeled or is expired, do not give it to your child! Notify your child's Foster Care Provider's Social Worker immediately. The Foster Care Provider's Social Worker will then contact health care professionals to straighten out the medications.
- Every time you give your child any medication, record it on the Medication Log and initial.
- Medication records must be kept for at least one year.
- Send a copy to your Foster Care Provider, and a copy should be kept in the child's Home File.

It is true that regulations require a lot of documentation, but it is not your Foster Care Provider's intention that foster parents spend a lot of money making copies. Here are a few low cost options:
- **Discuss the option of having copies made for you by your Foster Care Provider.**
- **Mail originals to your Foster Care Provider with an attached request that documentation be returned to you.**
- **Give documents to your Foster Care Provider's Social Worker to deliver (request return service if needed).**
- **For those of you with the capabilities, scanning documents to email or faxing them can be an easy solution.**

Do not email any confidential information, (i.e., client names, medical/medication information) unless you have an authorized encrypted system!

- **Child & Family Plan:** This important document serves as the child/youth's Treatment and Service Delivery Plan required by licensing regulations. It is completed by the assigned Foster Care Provider's Social Worker within the first 30 days of placement through a Child & Family Team Meeting or TDM process which includes the county placement worker, foster parents and the child if possible. The plan is based on information provided by the placing agency, Dangerous Propensities, the Child/Youth Assessment, Educational Assessment, Life Skills Assessment and a personal assessment conducted by the Foster Care Provider's Social Worker. The plan specifically sets forth the child/youth's identified needs and goals, and the objectives and tasks required to meet the identified needs. The Child & Family Plan is updated routinely, often monthly, but must be done at least every six (6) months.

- **Client's Personal Property Record:** Please inventory and record all of your foster child's belongings on the ***first day of placement***. This will help everyone understand what property you are responsible for safeguarding and to know if there is anything dangerous or that requires approval from the placing agency for the child to have in their possession.
  - Don't forget to inventory the clothes the child is wearing!
  - Send a copy to your Foster Care Provider, and a copy should be kept in the child's Home File.
  - Continue to log new items and items that are discarded on the personal property FFH-Section of the Mandatory Foster Parent Monthly Reporting Log as long as the child is in your care.
  - Don't forget to do an exit inventory when the child's placement in your home ends.

- **Consent for Medical Treatment:** An authorization from your child's legal guardian for you or a representative from your Foster Care Provider to obtain medical care prescribed by a duly licensed physician or dentist. Please make sure that you take this form to every appointment! *Without proof of authorization to provide medical care, healthcare providers may refuse treatment to your child.*

- **Court Documents:** Include court reports, notifications of hearings, placement orders and dispositions/judgments.

- **Foster Parent Monthly Report:** An accumulation of information that must be completed and turned in to your Foster Care Provider every month. Be sure to keep a copy for the child's home file. The following information should be contained in the Mandatory Foster Parent Monthly Reporting Log:

  · **No Medication Verification:** If the child has not taken any medication (including over the counter) for the entire month, then sign and date in the space provided.

  · **Medical and Dental Visits:** Please record any medical or dental visits that occurred during the month. At the end of each month, mail copies of completed Health Care Encounter forms along with the Mandatory Foster Parent Monthly Reporting Log to your Foster Care Provider.

  · **Allowance:** Providing a foster child with a regular allowance and a monthly clothing stipend is a Best Practice. As such, your Foster Care Provider has established a policy requiring foster parents to provide both on a monthly basis, with the amounts based on the child/youth's needs and age. Each time you give an allowance, write down the amount and the date, and have the foster child initial the form. For younger children, save receipts, write down the amount and date, and indicate what was done with the funds (e.g., bought a toy, put in savings account, etcetera). Send a copy of receipts to your Foster Care Provider and keep a copy in your child's Home File.

  · **Clothing Allowance:** Each time you buy your child clothing save the receipt, write down the amount and the date, and have the foster child initial the form (for younger children the foster parent will initial the form). A copy should be kept in the child's Home File. Without proper documentation, you could be held liable for unaccounted balances.
  Note: Keep an accurate account of your child's running balance.

  · **Client's Weight and Height:** Within a few days of placement, record your foster child's weight and height, and then record it once a month thereafter. This information is very important, especially sudden weight gains or losses.

  · **Personal Property List:** A list used to keep track of your child's belongings. Over time, your child's property will fluctuate, so record any property that was acquired or discarded during the month. (Please state reasons that items where discarded. For example: "outgrown or torn clothes; broken toy; etcetera.) Without proper documentation, you could be held liable for any items that are reported missing.

Please be aware that certain items that may seem worn out or unusable to you may have great sentimental value to a child (or their biological family). Always check with the child before discarding any of their possessions to make sure they agree with the decision.

- **Foster Parent Records:** Include a record of miscellaneous home checks including disaster drills and expired drugs. Also, there is a space to record training documentation, so indicate the number of training hours and attach documentation (such as certificates, signed general test forms, etcetera).

- **Health Care Encounter Forms (HCE):** Must be taken to every medical/dental visit and completed by the Health Care Provider. A copy of the completed HCE needs to be returned to your Foster Care Provider, and a copy should be kept in the child's home file. *Note: Your Foster Care Provider forwards all HCE to the appropriate county representatives.*

Chapter 10

- **Medical Insurance:** If your foster child arrives at your home with medical insurance, please give your Foster Care Provider a copy for their records. If the child does not arrive with proof of medical insurance, let your Foster Care Provider's administrator know as soon as possible. Temporary Medi-Cal cards can usually be obtained and faxed to health care providers the same day.

> **If you are in need of consent for medical treatment, a healthcare encounter form or proof of medical insurance right away, contact your Foster Care Provider with the medical office's fax number and, as long as the information is on file, it should be faxed to the office as quickly as possible.**

- **Medical Case Notes:** For all health-related information, such as all medications that enter the home; medication changes/errors; all transfers of medications; child-reported ailments and follow-up; and all information from doctor, dental or emergency appointments.

    - The law requires documentation that each foster child has been taken for a **CHDP physical exam and dental exam** within the first 30 days after placement (or an appointment is to be made), and annually thereafter (FFH-Section 89469).

    - **Tuberculosis (TB) Testing** is also required for your foster child within 30 days of placement. Please request a physician's review of TB test status and provide documentation of one of the following:
        - Current TB test with verified results (don't forget to take your child back to get TB test read!)
        - Physician's documentation of reasons not to test

- **Medication Record:** Is located on the reverse side of the Foster Parent Monthly Report. Proper documentation of medications is of the utmost importance, and all foster children's prescription medications must be listed on the Medication Record and initialed every time it is given. Additionally, every time you give your child any over the counter medications (OTC), the following must be recorded on the Medication Record and medical Case Notes (Blue) as directed:
    - Name of medication
    - Dosage
    - Time of day medication was taken
    - Reason for OTC medication
    - Response to OTC medication
    - Initials of person administering the medication (foster parent, Foster Care Provider staff or temporary care provider).

- **PRN Authorization Form:** A physician's authorization to give a foster child medication. Foster children should not be given any medications, including over the counter medication, prior to having the PRN signed (be sure to take a PRN Authorization Form to the first appointment with a physician). A copy of the signed PRN form must be returned to the Foster Care Provider, and a copy must be kept in the child's home file.

- **Safety Plan:** The Safety Plan is one of the most important documents you will receive when a child is placed in your home. It is prepared by the child's Foster Care Provider's Social Worker within 24 to 48 hours, and highlights any dangerous propensities the child may have as well as specific instructions as to how to keep the child safe.

- **School Records:** Include grades, attendance, disciplinary actions (if any), and the child's Individualized Education Plan (IEP) information (if they have one).

Temporary Care Passport

One very important thing to remember is that certain information from the Home File must always be with the foster child. If they go to another home for a few days, send the **Temporary Care Passport**, which is a file containing certain vital information that would be needed by a caregiver, including:

- Information about the child's emotional, behavioral, medical or physical conditions.
- Any medication that should be administered to the foster child.
- Emergency contact information.
- Required forms should they need medical attention.

Important: If you go on a vacation, take the child's Home File with you.

Foster children's Home Files are the property of the Foster Care Provider. When your child is discharged from your care, the Home File is to be returned to your Foster Care Provider for proper storage as dictated by state licensing standards.

Periodic and Annual Inspections

On-Going Inspections

"Inspecting" or "evaluating" your home is an ongoing requirement. By on-going we mean that your Foster Care Provider staff is in your home on a regular basis, and therefore, any problem would be visible and addressed on an on-going basis.

Whenever a child is removed from your home, your Foster Care Provider is required to evaluate the reasons why, and determine if any changes need to be made in selecting children for placement with you.

Formal Inspections

Each year before your Foster Home Certificate of Approval expires, your Foster Care Provider is required to conduct a "formal" evaluation. The purpose of this inspection is to do follow-up training and to ensure compliance with licensing regulations as previously outlined. Other possible inspections may include:

- **State Inspections:** At any time, your Foster Care Provider may be evaluated by their licensing agency to have its license renewed. As part of their evaluation process, the child's files may be reviewed for accuracy and compliance with state regulations. This is why it is so important that foster parents keep accurate, detailed records.

- **Allegation Complaint Investigation:** A state licensing agent will conduct a thorough investigation which may include a detailed inspection of your home and the child's files if they receive a formal complaint against you, (i.e., violation of personal rights, abuse, non-compliance with regulations, etcetera). An interview may be conducted with you and possibly with your foster child.

- **Visits from other agencies (CPS, Probation, Attorneys, etc.):** It is general policy that all placement workers, attorneys, etcetera, coordinate with your Foster Care Provider staff (and you) prior to visiting your home. Unfortunately, this is not always the case. If you do get an unexpected visitor, please be courteous to them and inform your Foster Care Provider.

- **Accreditation Inspections:** The highest quality Foster Care Providers are "accredited" by a nationally recognized accrediting agency. This is a rigorous inspection process conducted every three to four years, and will include visits to certified foster families.

- **Common Deficiencies:** The following are some examples of regulations, which if not complied with, nearly always result in a serious deficiency:
    - Exceeding the limitations on capacity or ambulatory status of children
    - Failure to provide criminal record clearance
    - Violations of children's rights
    - Failure to have working telephone service on the premises of the home at all times
    - Improper storage or dispensing of medications
    - Safety issues related to the home or property
    - Lack of proper toilet facilities or improper hot water temperatures

REIMBURSEMENTS FOR FOSTER CARE

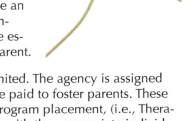

Your Foster Care Provider is committed to supporting foster parents by providing excellent, competitive reimbursement rates for providing care and supervision of foster children. When a child is placed in your home, there will be an "Agency Placement Agreement" to sign. This document sets forth the reimbursement rate for the particular child depending on the level of care, the established reimbursement policy, and what is required of you as a foster parent.

Your Foster Care Provider's ability to set and raise foster parent rates is limited. The agency is assigned a rate for its services by the state, which also sets the minimum rates to be paid to foster parents. These rates are based on the age of the children/youth, services provided and program placement, (i.e., Therapeutic Foster Care, etcetera). Feel free to discuss rates or financial matters with the appropriate individual within your Foster Care Provider.

It is important to note that foster parents are not employees of your Foster Care Provider, nor are they "paid" to provide care. Foster parents are reimbursed for the care and supervision of the foster child. As such, reimbursement is to be used to pay for usual and customary expenses consistent with the quality of care standards related to:

- Food
- Personal hygiene supplies
- School supplies
- Entertainment/recreation
- Transportation
- Housing/utilities
- Clothing
- Allowance
- Child care

From time to time, your Foster Care Provider may cover the expense for special items such as:

- Select medications
- Out of the ordinary school expenses
- Special programs, such as summer recreational or camp programs

Clothing Expenditures

The foster parent is responsible for purchasing foster child/youth clothing as part of their routine "care and maintenance" of foster children. The payments you receive from your Foster Care Provider are for the reimbursement of care and maintenance responsibilities.

Basically, as a foster parent you are expected to take care of the foster child/youth's basic needs just as you would your own child. A failure to do so will result in the decertification of your foster care license.

Don't forget to record the items purchased on the child's personal property record, and always save receipts. This is how you can demonstrate "due diligence" in meeting the basic needs of your foster children/youth.

Reimbursement for Temporary Care (Respite)

Every Foster Care Provider will have their own policy and procedure for reimbursing or covering the cost for temporary care. Please become familiar with these policies before you make temporary care decisions. The "Best Practices" is for foster parents to develop their own support group, including temporary care providers. It is to your advantage to pre-negotiate the fees and arrangements for temporary caregiving services with friends or family members.

The Foster Home and Property

Capacity

Maximum capacity allowed in a foster home is six (6) minors and no more than two (2) infants, contingent on physical space, ambulatory status and other considerations. ***This includes foster children as well as any biological, adoptive and guardianship children residing in your home.*** No more than two (2) children may share a room, including your biological children (FFH-Section 89228).

Please note: Many accrediting agencies will not permit more than three foster children per household unless there is written justification (such as in the case of sibling groups). In Therapeutic Foster Care, the basic standard is one foster child/youth per family.

Fire Clearances

In order to take a non-ambulatory, disabled child/youth, you must have a state Fire Marshall clearance (FFH-Section 89420).

Emergency Procedures

Foster parents must post emergency telephone numbers in a prominent location and must:

- Discuss and practice emergency procedures in the form of a "drill" with the foster child (taking age and developmental appropriateness into consideration) at the time of placement and every six months thereafter and;

- Ensure that occasional short-term babysitters and alternate caregivers know the location of the emergency numbers and are familiar with emergency procedures (FFH-Section 89323).

Confidentiality of your Home Address and Phone Number

Foster Homes are considered confidential. For your protection and that of the foster child, your home address and contact information may be restricted. Meaning only those with the legal "right and need to know" can have access to this information. Your information may be given to others when the Child & Family Team determines it is appropriate to do so.

Telephones

You must have a working telephone on your premises at all times—a landline or cell phone, provided that the cell phone stays on the premises if you are away. You may employ reasonable restrictions regarding phone use by foster children (FFH-Section 89372 (5)). However, calls to the child's Social Worker, authorized representative, attorneys, foster youth advocates and supporters, CASA workers and probation officers may not be restricted (FFH-Section 89372 (5)(D). Additionally, no restrictions may be applied to telephone calls with relatives, including brothers and sisters, unless prohibited by court order (FFH-Section 89372 (5)(C)). Always verify who the foster child is authorized to call as there may be restrictions placed on family members or individuals that they are not allowed contact with.

There are several methods a foster parent can use to monitor, restrict and control use of the phone, including:
- Blocking device on the phone disallowing 900 calls or long distance calls without a specific code
- Set up your phone service to disallow 900 and 976 numbers, international calls, third party calls or collect calls
- Be aware that you cannot block 411 (information) and a child may utilize this feature repeatedly, incurring a charge for every call. Make sure you have a telephone book handy and request that your foster child not use the 411 service
- Prepaid calling cards
- The foster child pre-pays out of their allowance for long distance or toll calls, unless calling his or her authorized representative
- Use of separate lines
- Cell phone that may be handed to the child after the parent dials the number
- Phone log where calls are listed
- Calls made collect

Foster Children's Cell Phones

Unless prohibited by court order or the person or agency responsible for placing the child, a foster child may possess a cell phone. Foster parents may place reasonable limitations on cell phone use as per the Prudent Parent Standard. (FFH-Section 89379 (a)(10)(A, B, C)). At the time of placement in foster care, an assessment will be made for each child individually as to the plan for their use of their personal cell phone. The plan will take into consideration any of the child/youth's dangerous propensities or safety issues. Additionally, Prudent Parent Standards allow for general limitations of cell phone use, such as restricting cell phone use after a certain time at night, or at the dinner table or when the child is attending a meeting. Foster parents are not required to purchase a cell phone for a foster child or pay for the foster child's cell phone service.

Vehicles and Transportation

You must possess a valid driver's license and have current auto insurance. Vehicles must be maintained in safe operating condition and records kept to verify this. You must have working seat belts and use car seats as required by law for infants and children according to age, weight and height requirements.

If anyone other than foster parents or other authorized representatives is going to transport a foster child, the foster parent must ensure their vehicle is in safe operating condition and get the following information from the driver:

- Name
- Address
- Phone number
- Driver's license number (verify they have a license)
- Car registration
- Proof of insurance

If this becomes a regular routine, this person must be fingerprinted and approved.

Foster parents and all individuals who transport a foster child are prohibited from smoking or permitting any person from smoking a pipe, cigar or cigarette containing tobacco or any other substance in a motor vehicle when the foster child is present. This applies when the vehicle is moving, parked or idling.

If a foster parent chooses to leave a foster child in a parked vehicle, consistent with the requirements of Vehicle Code FFH-Section 15620 (see below), the foster parent may apply the Prudent Parent Standard to determine the appropriateness of doing so (FFH-Section 89378 (b)).

Some states, such as California, requires that a parent, legal guardian or other person responsible for a child who is six years of age or younger may not leave that child inside a motor vehicle without being subject to the supervision of a person who is 12 years of age or older under either of the following circumstances (FFH-Section 15620):

- Where there are conditions that present a significant risk to the child's health or safety;
- When the vehicle's engine is running and/or the vehicle's keys are in the ignition.

Physical Environment

Your home must be kept clean, safe, sanitary and in good repair at all times (FFH-Section 89387 (b)). You must take measures to keep your home reasonably free of flies and other insects (FFH-Section 89387 (b)(1)).

- **Pools, Spas and Other Bodies of Water:** Foster parents who accept foster children under the age of 10 years or a child who is developmentally, mentally or physically disabled must ensure that all bodies of water are inaccessible, or that children are supervised at all times if accessible (FFH-Section 89387 (d)). *Swimming pools must be made inaccessible by one or more of the following safety measures:*

    - A fence at least five feet high that does not obscure the pool from view. There must be no more than a two inch gap between the ground and the bottom of the fence, and gaps between fence rails must not allow passage of a sphere of four inches or greater in diameter. Any access gates must be self-closing, self-latching and open out.
    - An approved safety cover that is operated manually or power operated that meets all the performance standards of the American Society for Testing and Materials (ASTM).

- If it is determined by the licensing agency that it is not possible for the foster parent to comply with one of the measures above, the home must be equipped with exit alarms—devices that make audible, continuous alarm sounds when a window or door is opened or left ajar—on all doors and windows that provide direct access to the pool. Additionally, all windows that provide direct access to the pool or body of water must be secured so that they cannot open more than four inches.
- Above ground pools can be made inaccessible by removing or blocking the ladder. If the pool is less than five feet in height, it can be blocked by the use of a barricade which meets the same requirements as mentioned above.
- All pools that cannot be emptied after each use must have an operative pump and filtering system.

An adult who has the ability to swim must provide supervision at all times when a foster child is using a pool or body of water from which rescue requires the rescuer's ability to swim. Foster Parents with foster children 10 years of age or older must use the Prudent Parent Standard when deciding whether a foster child shall have access to bodies of water including swimming pools, spas/hot tubs, lakes, ponds, etcetera, that are not enclosed or safeguarded by the options listed above (FFH-Section 89387 (d)(1)).

- **Outdoor Activity Space:** If you provide outdoor activity space on your property, it must be free from hazards (FFH-Section 89387 (h)).

- **Bedrooms, Furniture, Equipment and Other Supplies:** The minimum requirements for bedrooms, furniture, equipment and supplies for all children in your home (including members of your family, adoptive and/or guardianship children, children of a minor parent and foster children in your care) are as follows (FFH-Section 89387 (a)):

- No more than two children can share a room.
- No child over age five (5) may share a bedroom with any child of the opposite sex. However, foster parents may request a Documented Alternative Plan (LIC 973) permitting a foster child to be in a bedroom based on their gender identity.
- No child can sleep in a room that is used for other purposes such as a hallway, a garage or an unfurnished attic.
- No bedroom shall be a common passageway into other rooms.
- Except for children under the age of two years old, children cannot share a room with an adult. In bedrooms shared by adults and children under the age of two, no more than two children and two adults can share the room.
- Each child in placement must have his/her own bed equipped with clean linen and a comfortable mattress and pillow. Linen must be changed at least once a week or more often to ensure that clean linen is in use at all times.
- Beds should be arranged to allow easy passage between beds and easy access in and out of the room (for safety).
- Bunk beds of more than two tiers shall not be allowed.
- Bunk beds must have railings on both sides of the upper tier to prevent falling.
  - Children under six years old or who are unable to climb into or out of the upper tier of a bunk bed unassisted shall not be permitted to use the upper tier.

- Each bedroom shall have adequate closet and drawer space to accommodate a child's personal belongings.
- Toys, games, books, recreational and educational materials must be provided for children based on their age, and mental and physical development.
- The foster home must be maintained at a safe and comfortable temperature. Most Foster Care Providers recommend between 68 and 85 degrees Fahrenheit.
- Faucets used by a foster child for personal care and grooming must deliver hot water at a safe temperature. Most Foster Care Providers recommend between 105 to 120 degrees Fahrenheit as a safe temperature.
- All rooms must have adequate lighting to ensure comfort and safety in the home.
- All fireplaces/wood stoves must have protective screens.
- Waste must be stored, located and disposed of in a manner that will not permit the transmission of communicable disease or odors, create a nuisance, provide a breeding place or food source for insects or rodents.
- Unless the home is equipped with a sprinkler system, the home must have approved, commercially manufactured and functioning smoke detectors installed in the hallways of each sleeping area in the home. The alarms must be audible in each bedroom.
- A commercially manufactured and functioning carbon monoxide detector must be installed in the home.
- Foster parents are not required to incur a cost to provide computer availability to foster children, however, if the home is equipped with a computer that is made available to other children in the home, it should be made available to foster children of similar age and maturity.

- **Guns and Toxic Material Storage:** All dangerous items and materials must be inaccessible to children. Poisons, firearms and other dangerous weapons must be locked away. Ammunition must be stored and locked separately from firearms (FFH-Section 89387.2 (a)).

- **Storage of Household Kitchen Knives, Cleaning Products and Disinfectants (FFH-Section 89387.2 (b)):** Foster parents must apply the Prudent Parent Standard in determining if it is age and developmentally appropriate for a foster child to have access to and use of items such as household kitchen knives, cleaning products and disinfectants. Household kitchen knives and appliances do not need to be locked or inaccessible to a foster child who is of sufficient age and maturity to use such items. Foster parents must ensure that the foster child has been instructed as to the use and safe handling of such items before they use them. Disinfectants and cleaning solutions must be stored where inaccessible to a foster child; however, foster parents may allow the child access to such items if they ensure that the child knows how to safely handle and use them. Foster parents must consider the child's safety plan and dangerous propensities (if any) before allowing access to equipment or materials that could be used for self-harm or to injure or harm others.

The safety of the child and others in the home must be of paramount importance!

- **Personal Alcohol Use and Storage:** The personal use of alcohol by adults in our culture is common, but carries with it a considerable responsibility. This is especially true when it comes to foster parenting. Given the background of many of the foster children in care, personal use of alcohol within the foster home can be problematic. It is not uncommon for a foster child to come from a home where drugs and alcohol were abused, which possibly led to the abuse suffered by the child. Also, many of these children and youth have personal challenges with substance abuse which could escalate when exposed to alcohol in the foster home. For all of these reasons, many Foster Care Providers have policies established to govern the use of alcohol in foster homes; they include:

- **Alcohol Use:** Most Foster Care Providers discourage the use of alcoholic beverages in the foster home when foster children/youth are present. Foster parents should use great discretion when consuming alcoholic beverages. The rule of thumb is to always consider what is being modeled to the foster child. Their best interest should be your highest priority.

  Excessive drinking or overt drunkenness will not be tolerated and will result in the removal of foster children and your de-certification. Parties where alcohol is freely available must be conducted outside the presence of foster children. Alcohol should not be consumed during regular family activities such as meals, picnics and/or recreation.

- **Storage:** Alcoholic beverages must be stored in a locked, secure location inaccessible to foster children. This includes all alcoholic beverages including beer, cooking wines, liqueurs, etcetera. The consequences of a foster child consuming alcohol obtained from a foster parent or in the foster home, even without the foster parents' consent or knowledge, are extremely serious. These consequences include criminal charges as well as civil litigation.

Intentionally furnishing alcohol to a foster child/youth is absolutely forbidden and will result in a criminal referral and investigation, removal of the foster child(ren) and your de-certification. Some families hold to the belief that it is okay for a teen to have an occasional beer, or drink wine or champagne while in the confines of their own home. THIS IS NOT ALLOWED UNDER ANY CIRCUMSTANCES. Your Foster Care Provider expects all foster parents to strictly adhere to this policy without exceptions.

THE FOSTER CHILD

Many states, including California, have a "Foster Youth Bill of Rights" which provides children in care with a variety of protections for their health, safety and general wellbeing (FFH-Section 89372). It is important that foster parents respect the child's rights and apply the Prudent Parent Standards where appropriate. It is the responsibility of the foster parent to provide each school aged child who is placed in their home with an age appropriate orientation that includes an explanation of the rights of the child and addresses any of the child's questions or concerns.

Each child in foster care has a right to live in a safe, healthy and comfortable home where they will be treated with dignity and respect. They have a right to:

- Adequate, age-appropriate clothing that does not violate school standards when worn during school activities, and are in accordance with the gender identity of the foster child
- Healthy food
- His/her own place to store their things
- Toiletries and personal hygiene products, including enclosed razors used for shaving, as age and developmentally appropriate
- Personal belongings, including items that were gifted to the child/youth
- A home free from corporal or unusual punishment, infliction of pain, humiliation, intimidation, ridicule, coercion, threat, mental abuse or other actions of a punitive nature, including but not limited to interference with the daily living functions of eating, sleeping or toileting, or withholding of shelter, clothing or aids to physical functioning. Foster children must never be locked in any room, building or facility premises

Case Plan/Child & Family Plan

Children 12 years of age or older have the right to be involved in the development of his/her own case plan and plan for permanent placement. They also have the right to review their case plan and to be informed of any changes to the plan. Your Foster Care Provider's policy is for age appropriate foster children to be part of the Child & Family Team and participate in all team decision making.

Visitation and Contact

Children in foster care have the right to visit with parents, grandparents, siblings and other important family members **unless** prohibited by a court order. Additionally, children 10 of age or older who have been in foster care for at least six months or are placed in a group home are **required** to have a case plan that includes identification of individuals important to the child and the actions necessary to maintain contact with said individuals. Foster children also have a right to make and receive confidential phone calls, to send or receive unopened mail unless prohibited by court order. Foster children always have the right to have contact with their Social Worker or probation officer, attorney, or CASA worker.

Telephone/Cell Phone Use

As mentioned previously in this chapter, unless otherwise prohibited, a foster child may possess a cell phone. Foster parents may place reasonable limitations on cell phone use or all telephone use as per the Prudent Parent Standard. Such limitations might include restricting cell phone use after a certain hour at night, at the dinner table or when the child is attending a meeting. Restriction of telephone use by the child may be used as a reasonable discipline measure except that no restrictions shall be applied to telephone calls, mail and electronic communication with relatives unless prohibited by court order.

Court

Foster children/youth have the right to have their own lawyer. They have the right to go to court and talk to the judge about how they feel about their family, lawyer, Social Worker, etcetera, and to tell the judge about what they want to happen with their case. Foster children are also allowed to see and get a copy of their court report and case plan, and to keep their court records private, unless the law states otherwise. Foster children/youth also have the right to contact the Foster Care Ombudsman Office and/or Community Care Licensing at any time to report a complaint.

Discrimination

Foster children have the right to fair and equal access to all available services, placement, care, treatment and benefits, and to not be subjected to discrimination or harassment on the basis of actual or perceived race, ethnic group identification, ancestry, national origin, color, religion, sex, sexual orientation, gender identity, mental or physical disability or HIV status. Foster children/youth have the right to attend religious services and activities of their choice.

Education

A foster child has a right and a responsibility to go to school. They also have a right to the same school resources, services and extracurricular activities as other students in the same school. A foster child has the right to stay in their original school, even if their foster care placement changes, so long as it is in their best interests. Most states' law requires that each county and each school district have a child's educational records and provide assistance with foster child's/youth's enrollment in school.

The child's legal parent or legal guardian retains the right to make decisions about the child's education **unless** the juvenile court specifically appoints another responsible adult to make educational decisions on behalf of the child. The appointed adult will most likely be the child's foster parent, relative caregiver or court appointed special advocate (CASA). It cannot be the child's Social Worker, Probation Officer or anyone who works for the child's school.

Foster youth, age 16 or older have the right to be allowed access to information regarding available vocational and postsecondary educational options including, but not limited to:

- Admission criteria for universities, community colleges, trade or vocational schools and financial aid information for these schools
- Informational brochures on postsecondary or vocational schools/programs
- Campus tours
- Internet research on postsecondary or vocational schools/programs, sources of financial aid, independent living skills program offerings and other local resources to assist youth
- School sponsored events promoting postsecondary or vocational schools/programs
- Financial aid information, including information about federal, state and school-specific aid; state and school-specific scholarships; grants and loans; aid available specifically to current or former foster children; and contact information for the Student Aid Commission
- Requirements for participation in Transitional Age Youth Services and Programs

Health Care

- Children in foster care are entitled to basic health care, which includes medical, dental, vision and mental health services.

- All youth, including foster youth, in California age 12 or older have the right to access "sensitive health care services" without adult's permission. These services include any services having to do with preventing or treating pregnancy (including birth control, abortion or pre-natal/OB care), services related to treatment of STDs, drug or alcohol use, and rape or sexual assault.

- A child may also obtain outpatient treatment of mental conditions without an adult's permission if the doctor finds the child mature enough and if the child presents a danger to themselves or others without the treatment.

- As a foster parent, you are responsible for ensuring that each child receives necessary first aid, medical and dental services. When a child shows signs of a serious illness, they must be immediately taken to a doctor. Whenever a child is taken to a doctor for regular or emergency care resulting from an accident or illness you must notify your Foster Care Provider as soon as is possible (FFH-Sections 89469, 89475).

You must have a first aid kit in your home (FFH-Section 89475 (b)) which should include at a minimum:

- First-aid manual
- Bandages or roller bandages
- Scissors
- Thermometers
- Sterile first-aid dressings
- Adhesive tape
- Tweezers
- Antiseptic solution

Medications

This topic is so important that we have devoted an entire chapter to it as well as in-depth training requirements. *Please refer to chapter 12 for more information*.

- Medications should be stored where inaccessible to a child (FFH-Section 89387.2(b)(2)).

- Unless prohibited by court order, a child may self-administer medication or injections **if the physician of the child gives permission** (FFH-Section 89475.1).
  - Family Nurse Practitioners (FNP), Registered Nurses (RN) or Physician's Assistants (PA) may provide *instruction* to the child as to the proper administration of a medication, but they **may not** give permission for the child to self-administer. Only the child's physician (MD) may do so.

- The foster parent must ensure that the child knows how to:
  - Self-administer their medications and injections
  - Document when they self-administer their medications/injections
  - Properly store their medication so that it is inaccessible to other children

- FFH-Section 89475 regarding Health Related Services states that when a foster child has a health condition that requires medication, foster parents must comply with the following:
  - Assist the child with self-administration as needed and if the physician gives permission in writing, the child may self-administer medication or injections.
  - Ensure that instructions are followed as outlined by the appropriate medical professional.
  - Medication shall be stored in the original container with the original unaltered label.
  - Prescription medication must be administered to the child as directed on the label or as directed in writing by the physician.
  - Non-prescription medication must be administered to a child as directed on the label or as directed by the appropriate medical professional.
  - The administration of prescription PRN medication (taken "as needed") shall require the foster parent to document the date, time and dose of medication administered.
  - If a child cannot determine his or her own need for medication, the foster parent shall determine the need of a child in accordance with medical instructions.
  - Under no circumstances shall a child be required to take psychotropic medication without a court order.

Safeguards for Cash Resources, Personal Property and Valuables

- Foster parents must make an itemized inventory list of the cash resources, personal property, and valuables that a foster child brings into the home and review this list with the child. The list is kept in the child's Home File.

- Foster parents must safeguard the cash resources, personal property and valuables of each child by keeping such items separate and intact, and maintaining accurate records of the cash resources, personal property and valuables of each foster child which are entrusted to the foster parent.

- Foster parents must allow the foster child to have access to and control of his or her cash resources, personal property and valuables in a manner that is age and developmentally appropriate.

- When a foster child's placement in the home ends, the foster parent must surrender the child's cash resources, personal property and valuables to the child if age and developmentally appropriate, or to the placement agency or another authorized representative who is responsible for the care and custody of the child, along with an itemized inventory list of these items.

- The foster parent must request and retain a receipt that is signed and dated by the child (if age and developmentally appropriate) or authorized representative for the child affirming that all personal belongings of the child are being surrendered.

- Foster children have the right to be free from unreasonable searches of their person or belongings, except when conducted by law enforcement for cause, or if reasonable restrictions are imposed by the foster parent if the child/youth's current behavior presents a safety risk (cutting, threats of harm, etcetera). In such a case, a safety plan would be developed to reduce the risk of harm.

CHAPTER 10

DISCIPLINE

The following forms of discipline are prohibited (FFH-Section 89372 (a) (1)):

- Violation of personal rights (see above)
- To be treated disrespectfully
- To be denied safe, clean and comfortable accommodations and furnishings
- Corporal (physical) or unusual punishment
- Infliction of pain, humiliation, intimidation, ridicule, coercion, threat, mental abuse or actions of a punitive nature
- Denial of food, sleep, toileting, clothing, medication or other required aids
- Denial of phone access to social worker, attorney, CASA, approved family members, etcetera, or prohibited from making a verbal or written complaint
- To be locked in any room or building, or to be physically restrained by any locking devise, rope, strap, etcetera.

FOOD

Foster parents are required to provide or ensure at least three nutritious meals per day, have between-meal snacks available, provide food as necessary, and meet any special dietary needs documented in the written plan identifying the specific needs and services of the child, unless the physician of the child advises otherwise (FFH-Section 89376).

- The quantity and quality of food available to household members shall be equally available to a foster child.
    - Providing food to a foster child different from the rest of the family is a serious Personal Rights violation, unless it is prescribed by a physician for dietary reasons; such as a diabetic diet.
- Foster children shall be invited to participate in all household meals.
- An infant who is unable to hold a bottle shall be held during bottle feeding. At no time shall a bottle be propped up for an infant. A bottle given to an infant able to hold his or her own bottle must be unbreakable.
- Foster parents may encourage a foster child, as age and developmentally appropriate, to learn meal preparation, but must not "require" a child to prepare meals.

CHURCH AND RELIGIOUS ISSUES

Many families participate in some type of church or religious activity, and this is in no way discouraged. However, foster children have the right to attend religious services of his or her choice and must never be required to attend church with the foster family (FFH-Section 89372).

- Efforts will be made by the Foster Care Provider to place children in homes with families of compatible belief systems.
- The Best Practice is for foster children/youth to be fully advised of your family's activities before placement and agreeable to them.
- You may feel very passionate about your spiritual beliefs and want to share them with your foster child, but you must adhere to state requirements.
    - It is okay to share beliefs, but it's not okay to force them on a foster child.
    - It is better to "model" your beliefs and not use them to manipulate.
    - Please remember, most foster children/youth have been severely traumatized, including being manipulated, and have very sensitive personal issues to work through.

- The most important thing you can do as a foster parent is to be supportive, nurturing and accepting of your foster child, no matter what/how they believe.

It is rare to have a problem in this area if the foster parent respects the child/youth's distinct culture and values, and works closely with their Foster Care Provider's Social Worker around these issues.

Activities

Foster children are entitled to, and should be encouraged to participate in age and developmentally appropriate extracurricular, enrichment and social activities (FFH-Section 89379), including, but not limited to:

- Sports
- School activities such as band, dances and field trips, 4-H activities
- Leisure time such as bike riding, socializing with friends, shopping and going to the movies
- Sleepovers with friends
- Babysitting
- Having visitors in the home
- Use of computer equipment
    - Computer equipment that is available to other children in the home should also be available to foster children of similar age and maturity, however foster parents are not required to incur a cost to provide computer availability.
- Use of a personal cell phone unless prohibited by court order or the person or agency responsible for placing the child. Foster parents may place reasonable limitations on cell phone use utilizing the Prudent Parent Standard. Foster parents are not required to purchase a cell phone or pay for cell phone service for a foster child.

Overnight Visits

It is natural for children to want to spend a night at a friend's house and foster children have the right to such activities, unless prohibited by court order. Foster parents must employ the Prudent Parent Standard when determining the appropriateness of their foster child occasionally spending the night at a friend's house.

The decision to allow a foster child/youth to spend the night away from their foster home will be based first and foremost on the child's Child & Family Plan, Safety Plan, their age and maturity, and what the foster parents know about the home and family where the overnight visit is to take place. The child's safety is always the most important factor. Your Foster Care Provider must always be notified if a foster child is away from the foster home overnight.

FAQ: Visits And Overnights

What if my foster child asks to call or visit their parent(s) or relative(s)?

Guidelines for visits are spelled out in the child's Case Plan, Court Order, Child & Family Plan and case notes. Don't just assume your child can visit. You should call the child's Foster Care Provider's Social Worker if it isn't clear in the documentation.

What if my foster child asks to visit overnight with their parent(s) or relative(s)?

The same applies. It must be pre-approved.

What if my foster child asks to visit their friend's house?

If you do not know your foster child's friend, first invite the friend to your house a few times so you can see what they are like and what they like to do together. If your foster child is to visit the friend's house you must first connect with the parents of your child's friend. They are taking responsibility for your foster child who is a ward/dependent of the court. They must be informed of the particular rules and regulations for the foster child, especially during the visit. Make sure to talk with your foster child about what information you will be sharing with the friend's parents and why, so that they are prepared. If the child does not want that information to be shared, they may choose not to visit. Follow the Prudent Parent Standard in these circumstances.

What if my foster child wants to stay overnight at a friend's house?

If it is determined by the Child & Family Team that overnight visits with friends are appropriate and in the best interest of the foster child, the foster parent must always consult with the parents of the foster child's friend. Never use the child as a source of information, but rather speak directly with the adults, getting their name, address and phone number. Never be afraid to ask personal information from the parents or the child's friend, because you share the responsibility for your foster child with your Foster Care Provider. The child's Foster Care Provider's Social Worker must be informed of and approve any overnight visits.

Photo by Bobbi Dombrowski

Probation Requirements

Many youths in placement are under the supervision of the Probation Department. As previously mentioned, there are differences between "601's" and "602's" with respect to the law. Due to these differences, probation has specific procedures and expectations for each Welfare & Institutions Code (WIC) Juvenile Court status designation. It is necessary and important for you to understand these differences.

- **WIC 601–"Status Offenders":** Youth who fall into this category do not come under the court's jurisdiction because of breaking the law, but because they have run away, are incorrigible, truant or there is a parent-child conflict. Once 18, they are adults and can do as they please. This is where the term "status" offender originates. There is a problem only by their status as a minor. Probation places 601's in foster care on a voluntary basis. This means the youth has a lot more choice about the foster home and can choose to return to his/her home. There are several considerations with youth in this category:

  · Probation takes on more of a "supportive" role. They do not have the legal "leverage" as with a criminal violator.

  · Family reunification is the primary goal and a lot of energy is expended toward this end.

  · Biological parents may be much more involved with the case, even with the foster family (bearing approval).

  · Probation expects foster parents to keep their staff and your Foster Care Provider informed about the youth's behaviors and maintain age appropriate limits.

- **WIC 602—"Criminal Offenders":** Youth in this category are under the court's jurisdiction for violating the law. There is no distinction as to what type of offense, how many or how severe. They are all considered to come under the jurisdiction of WIC 602. It is not uncommon for 602 wards to be in foster care as many of the dynamics associated with other children in foster care apply to them. There may be problems at home necessitating the youth's out of home placement or their behavior may be too unmanageable for the parents. Please keep in mind, your Foster Care Provider will not refer any 602 youth to a foster home if safety is an issue. Only 602 youths deemed to be capable of living successfully in an open setting will be placed in foster care.

  The Probation Department handles 602's very differently than 601's. There are some important considerations with youth in this category:

  · Terms of Probation: Each 602 ward will have terms of probation ordered by the court. These include specific requirements that must be followed. A violation of a probation term is a violation of law.

  · Accountability: It is expected that the foster parents will hold the child accountable to probation by enforcing terms of probation, thus, it is essential that foster parents know these terms. If the Court orders a 10:00pm curfew, a foster parent cannot make it 11:00pm. Only the Court can change these terms.

  · Enforcing terms can be communicated in a positive and "caring" statement, e.g., "I don't want you to be in any more trouble with the court." You can also emphasize the authority of the court, e.g., "I cannot change an order of the court." Phrases such as this communicate to your foster youth that you did not make the rule, but have to enforce it. Let the Probation Officer be the "heavy" in these situations. It is important to be honest and stress the need for compliance with your foster youth; as it is of no benefit to the youth for you to disregard his/her terms or be lax in enforcing them. In fact, it may result in his or her re-arrest and detainment.

  · Supervision: Most Probation Officers will treat 602's in foster care as a regular field supervision case; meaning that the probation officer will conduct on-going visits to the youth at home, school or at the agency's office roughly every 30 days. The foster parent will need to cooperate with scheduling and transportation for these meetings. Your cooperation will also be needed when the probation officer has to do a routine drug test or personal property search.

Chapter 10

- Even more importantly, the probation officer needs your input. S/he will periodically talk with you in person or by telephone. You, more than anyone else, will know how the youth is doing and are in the position to report on positive or negative changes in youth's behavior or attitude.
- Violations: The foster parent must immediately report to the probation officer or your Foster Care Provider's Social Worker any violation of probation terms. A failure to do so can result in the removal of the youth from your care. Probation can also request that no other children be placed in your home.

We have gone to some length to emphasize the importance of being knowledgeable about probation requirements. Experience has taught us that working with youth who are under the supervision of probation is a plus because the Probation Officer can be a valuable asset to the youth's Child & Family Team.

Probation has the option to arrest the youth for any violation. If this occurs, s/he will be handcuffed and taken away to juvenile hall. This can be very traumatic for you, your family and the youth. The youth may be released back to your home quickly, or in a number of days, therefore it is critical you work together with the youth's Foster Care Provider's Social Worker and the Probation Officer to understand possible outcomes.

In Case of Emergency

Disaster Preparedness and Emergency Communication

CHAPTER 11

Chapter 11

IN CASE OF EMERGENCY
Disaster Preparedness and Emergency Communication

Every family should be prepared for a disaster or emergency. Foster parents are responsible for the safe care and supervision of their foster children in all circumstances. It is prudent to have a thoughtful disaster plan, and most state licensing agencies require that a plan be posted in a public place in your home.

DISASTER PREPAREDNESS

EMERGENCY PLAN

Every Foster Care Provider must provide an **"Emergency Plan for Foster Family Homes."** This form lists emergency phone numbers and other information that may be needed in an emergency situation.

Important points your plan should consider:
- Every foster home should have an agreed upon location where the family will meet outside of the home in case of an emergency. This location should be far enough away from the structure that it will be safe in case of fire or earthquake damage.
- A second meeting place outside the neighborhood and a contact plan in case of a mandatory evacuation.
- Don't forget your pets when planning emergency preparedness!

EMERGENCY KIT

The American Red Cross recommends that families assemble an emergency kit that contains at least a three-day supply of items that every member of your family requires to live. Be sure to include medication and extra eye glasses as needed. The American Red Cross provides free instructions for building a customized kit that will meet your family's needs.

STAY INFORMED

Be aware of the various types of disasters or emergencies that might occur in your area. This includes those unique to your family members such as health emergencies or other possibly dangerous situations. Every child placed in foster care will have a **Safety Plan**, which is initiated by the child's Social Worker and given to the foster parent. This document outlines any specific risk factors the child may have and describes a safety plan to be implemented.

EMERGENCY COMMUNICATION

There must always be at least one person capable of and responsible for communicating with emergency personnel when there is a foster child present.
Your Foster Care Provider is responsible for providing you with effective afterhours emergency communication options. The following is a framework for emergency communications which will give you an idea of what to expect or what to request from you Foster Care Provider.

IMPORTANT NOTE: In the event of a life threatening emergency, you are to always contact 911 before calling your Foster Care Provider.

All Foster Care Providers must provide foster parents with a list of 24/7 emergency contact phone numbers, including coverage for weekdays, evenings, weekends and holidays.

Emergency on-call staff will vary from agency to agency, but generally the following staff should be available:
- A Social Worker – this is required of all Foster Care Providers
- An In-home Support or Behavioral Counselor – this is especially important for Therapeutic Foster Care families
- A Family/Parent Partner or similar foster parent peer mentor
- Supervisory/management staff
- Personnel from placement agencies

When to Make an Emergency Call

If there is a life threatening emergency, the foster parent must first call 911 and then, as soon as possible, contact their Foster Care Provider.

The foster parent must contact the Foster Care Provider when:
- There is an emergency requiring immediate outside-agency assistance
- A child needs or has received emergency medical attention
- Any suicidal ideations, gestures or behaviors are exhibited by the foster child
- For all medication-related issues, such as adverse reactions, missed dose or a child's refusal to take medication
- When needing advice for de-escalating a situation or providing a specific behavioral intervention
- The foster child is exhibiting or threatening dangerous or violent behaviors to themselves or others
- A foster child/youth runs away
- A foster parent needs support or assistance with care and supervision, scheduling problems or asks critical questions that need to be addressed outside of normal business hours. NOTE: These types of calls should be rare and infrequent!

When Not to Make an Emergency Call

- For routine matters which can be resolved during normal business hours
- Situations where the agency has provided specific written instructions and/or policy for foster parents to follow
- Routine parenting issues which fall within the scope of Prudent Parenting
- You are feeling frustrated and/or angry, but there is not an immediate emergency

When in doubt, call! It is better to be safe than sorry concerning the wellbeing of a foster child/youth.

Information Needing to be Reported

When making an emergency contact, be prepared to provide the following:
- Your name and phone number
- The foster child/youth's name
- A clear, precise description of the emergency
- The immediate/current status of the foster child/youth
- The time and place of the incident being reported
- The names of others involved, if any
- What interventions have been initiated

Non-Emergency Information or Questions

- Foster Parents should never hesitate to request information, counseling, guidance or ask questions. The role of a foster parent and the wellbeing of foster children are too important not to seek help when needed.

- Always start by calling your foster child/youth's Foster Care Provider's Social Worker. However, many times the office support staff can be of assistance, or your Social Worker's Supervisor.

- Some foster care agencies have staff dedicated to foster parent certification and support who are able to answer many questions. Learn who is available for you to call at your Foster Care Provider when you have questions.

- Competent Foster Care Providers maintain voicemail systems allowing you to leave a fairly detailed message for your foster child's Social Worker. Some of these systems will forward messages to cell phones as well.

- Some agencies will provide foster parents with staff's cell phones to make them more readily available to provide assistance.

- Please be patient! It is important to remember that Social Workers have a very demanding work load. They are often out of the office visiting other foster children/youth, families, schools, attending court or participating in team meetings.

Basic Communications Policy

Your Foster Care Provider should encourage open and honest communication at all times. Effective foster parenting is a team process which requires free and unrestrained communication. Foster parent "voice" and feedback is essential to the healing and success of each foster child/youth, and for ensuring that case plans are effectively executed and updated. Whenever a foster parent feels there is a breakdown in communication, or that their input is not valued, they must immediately contact the appropriate person within their Foster Care Provider to seek an immediate solution. Remember the basic premise: effective communication produces successful foster children/youth.

CHAPTER 12

Prepare, Prevent & Protect

Risk Management and Responding to Allegations

Chapter 12

Prepare, Prevent & Protect
Risk Management and Responding to Allegations

This chapter is designed to help you as a foster parent prepare and protect yourself in regards to allegations. It is an unfortunate fact that many foster parents who have been providing care for any length of time, may, at some point, have an allegation made against them. When this happens, it may be very unsettling and upsetting to the whole family. It is important that you are educated in what you can expect if an allegation is made against you, and how you can effectively manage your risk as a foster parent.

Allegations

Allegations against foster parents fall under two categories. The first involves the child's **personal rights** and the second has to do with **health and safety** issues.

Personal Rights Violations

It is essential that foster parents become very familiar with the personal rights of foster children/youth established by law and every foster home must display a poster highlighting these rights.

You must always make sure your parenting methods and discipline approach does not violate your foster child's personal rights.

Refer to the chapter entitled, "Child Development and Behavior," for more information on effective and acceptable parenting methods.

Some examples of personal rights violations are:

- **Physical**
    · Corporal punishment (Hitting, spanking, slapping, etcetera)
    · Inappropriate punishment
    · Rough handling or force

- **Emotional**
    · Threats
    · Depravation
    · Spiritual manipulation
    · Defamation of biological family
    · Inappropriate criticism
    · Sarcastic comments and put-downs
    · Discrimination based on sex, race, color, religion, sexual orientation, ethnic group, ancestry, national origin, gender identity, mental or physical disability, or HIV status

- **Sexual**
    · Inappropriate boundaries
    · Inappropriate touching
    · Inappropriate affection
    · Overt sexualized behavior
    · Exploitation and sexual acts

- **Neglect**
    - Food
    - Clothing
    - Personal hygiene issues
    - Social depravation
    - Allowance: money
    - Telephone
    - Lack of attention
    - Supervision
    - Medical attention

- **Privacy**
    - Violating the child's confidentiality by disclosing their history, diagnosis, behavior issues, etcetera, to those not authorized to have that information
    - Searching or going through the child's belongings, their bedroom, closet and drawer space.

HEALTH AND SAFETY ISSUES
(Be sure to review your state's licensing regulations for clarification.)

- **Cleanliness**
    - House
    - Clothes
    - General sanitation
    - Condition of the exterior areas of the house/yard – safety hazards
    - Animals or byproduct of animals

- **Inappropriately Stored Items**
    - Medications
    - Household cleaners
    - Tools
    - Guns

- **Inadequate Space and Equipment**
    - Beds and bedding
    - Privacy and personal space
    - Room size and configuration
    - Dresser
    - Children sharing bedrooms

- **Vehicle Safety**
    - Insurance
    - Tickets and accidents
    - Maintenance and repair
    - Riding in the vehicle with proper seatbelts
    - DMV compliance

- **Water and Activity Safety**
    - Pool/Spas- covers/fences where required
    - Riding bikes/skateboards with helmets and other protective gear

Allegations

Allegations against foster parents can originate from a number of different sources. Besides the child and his/her birth parents, anyone who is involved in the life of the child or the family is a person who can potentially make an allegation.

Please understand, by and large, most foster children have been subjected to child abuse and neglect and/or have experienced traumatic events, therefore there is a greater level of sensitivity surrounding them and much is done to protect their wellbeing. These are children in **protective** custody and we are here to protect them. All persons who work in the foster care system are, by law, mandated reporters, and are required to report suspected child abuse. The law presumes that these employees will always protect the foster child and if there is ever a question, the rule is to put the safety of the foster child first.

Allegations may be made by:

- **The foster child**
- **A foster child's biological family**
- **Agency Workers:** This could include a Social Worker, Probation Officer, Court Appointed Special Advocate (CASA) Worker, Mental Health therapist, etcetera.
- **School Personnel**
- **Foster Parents:** As a professional Foster Parent, you are expected to take ownership of your mistakes, and be honest and cooperative, and have integrity. Self-reporting a breach of licensing regulations or the child's personal rights is looked on with much more credibility and tolerance by the investigating community; usually producing a less punitive response.
- **Others:** Including peers, neighbors and family friends; basically any individual who has a personal relationship with the foster child/youth.

The Role of Abuse in Allegations

Foster children are first and foremost, survivors; having already overcome multiple obstacles with their resiliency and perseverance. These qualities help them to become healthy, well-adjusted and successful adults. However, it is important to remember that children who have been victims of abuse have experienced the ultimate manipulation and coercion of their mind, body and soul, and, at times this can manifest itself in unhealthy coping strategies which, on occasion, can include story-telling, a false understanding of events and confusion. All of these factors may lead to a child making an allegation that may or may not have occurred.

Risk Prevention

It cannot be stated too often or too strongly enough—it is Best Practice to proactively minimize risk in order to prevent problems and allegations.

Remember and live by this definition of **RISK: It is a probability or threat of damage, injury, liability, loss or other negative occurrence that is caused by external or internal conditions, events or vulnerabilities, and that may be neutralized through preemptive action.**

It is your job as a foster parent to be continually *"neutralizing risk through preemptive action!"*

Because allegations can be made even in the most pro-active foster home, it is imperative that you take steps to **PREPARE, PREVENT AND PROTECT!**

Prepare

Before a child is placed in your home, you should:

- **Learn and follow all state and agency licensing regulations.** It is essential for you to be knowledgeable of your Foster Care Provider's governing regulations. Avoid the "I didn't know that" situation; it will not lessen your chances of being cited.

- **Make sure you are well trained.** Always take advantage of training and skill building opportunities. Not only do you learn skills and techniques which can help prevent allegations, it also demonstrates your "due diligence."

- **"Risk-Proof" your home.** Work closely with your Foster Care Provider in making sure your home is health and safety compliant. It's all about making sure that foster children/youth have no opportunity to access anything dangerous or potentially harmful, and that you are fully complying with all regulations governing physical facility requirements.

- **Have a well-defined "Supervision Plan."** One of the most cited areas of foster parent deficiency is lack of proper supervision. Learn exactly what is required of you by your Foster Care Provider. Make sure you always have qualified temporary care providers; have them lined up before you start accepting children. Discuss with your Foster Care Provider what is expected for different ages, needs and behaviors, and plan accordingly.

- **Become fully informed and knowledgeable of each foster child before they are placed.** Is important that you know your foster child's specific needs, dangerous propensities, treatment plans, behaviors, placement history, family history, placement goals, etcetera. The more you know, the better you are able to be proactive in developing "risk-neutralizing" strategies.

- **Join and become an active member in your local, state or national foster care provider association.** There is strength in numbers and connections. Foster parent associations and/or support groups provide a wonderful opportunity to learn risk prevention techniques and strategies.

- **If a child has Dangerous Propensities and/or a history of making allegations,** make sure there is a very clear "Safety Plan" provided to you <u>before you accept the child for placement</u>. The Safety Plan should address every potential issue, how to prevent re-occurrences and what to do if something does happen. It is also a very effective strategy to work very closely with your Foster Care Provider's Social Worker who can work with the Placing agency and your state's licensing agency in order to make them aware of this child's history.

It is important to assess all possibilities, expect the unexpected, be proactive and minimize potential risk. Make the extra effort and take the extra steps. Do not assume that you are prepared. Reduce Risk by thinking of potential problems before they occur and implement prevention strategies.

Prevent

Once a child is placed in your home, you should follow these guidelines to prevent the possibility of allegations:

- **Make safety and supervision a top priority.**

- **Know your child** and what triggers s/he to recall past traumatic experiences and/or act out inappropriately. Have a plan for reducing the stressors that might activate anger, defiance or other inappropriate behaviors.

- **Check your home and yard daily** for any unsafe conditions and make sure all hazardous materials are inaccessible to children.

- **Make a point to be visible and accountable** in everything you do as a foster parent. Don't ever leave room for "suspicion" or be seen as "secretive" or "elusive."

- **Communicate, communicate and communicate!** One of the most important preventive strategies is to maintain excellent communication with your Foster Care Provider's staff and other key stakeholders in the foster child/youth's life. Ask questions, ask for help and advice, present concerns, and give ongoing updates on how your foster child is doing.

- **Always be courteous and professional** when working with the agencies involved with your foster child.

  · **Work with the Child & Family Team** and make sure that you bring up the child's successes as well as challenges.

  · **Communicate and cooperate with the child's professional support team**—therapist, counselor, teachers and medical professionals.

  · **Remember, you are a "Professional Foster Parent"** and must act accordingly. Maintaining an excellent relationship with all other stakeholders involved with your foster child greatly enhances your credibility if the allegations are made.

- **No one is perfect.** If you make a mistake or lose your temper with your foster child/youth, or react in anger with harsh words, acknowledge your mistake and apologize. This can be one of the most empowering and bonding experiences for child/youth. Also, don't forget to "self-report" to your Foster Care Provider. It is much better that they hear it from you first, and not your foster child/youth!

- **Never spank or hit a child or threaten to do so.** Any form of corporal punishment with a foster child is illegal, and carries with it severe consequences for the foster parent. You must always model appropriate behavior and teach your foster child how to solve problems in a non-violent way.

- **Deploy safety and preventative strategies with sexually active, reactive and provocative children.**

  · **Always work with your Foster Care Provider** in developing and implementing safety and prevention strategies and plans, preferably before the foster child/youth is placed, and if you see any sexualized behavior after they are placed.

  · **Be cautious if you are alone with a child** who acts out sexually or has provocative behavior. Use safe boundaries and teach those boundaries to your foster child. Never allow yourself to be seen by the foster child/youth as provoking or welcoming a sexual gesture.

  · **Always take any allegations the child makes seriously.** As a mandated reporter of child abuse, you must bring any suspected child abuse to the attention of the child's Social Worker and be prepared to file a Suspected Child Abuse Report.

Protect

It is important that you always protect you and your family, including your foster child. Here are some important things you can do to protect yourself, your family and your foster child:

- **Document, document and document.** Keeping accurate notes, records and observation cannot be stressed enough. It takes time, but it is well worth it should you ever be in the position of having to defend yourself. Your documentation and notes should include the following:

  · **Always document any injuries or accidents** that the child has, especially if they come home from an activity with an injury or tell you about an accident they had while out of your home.

- **Keep a record of any serious conflicts** the child may have with parents, other children, social workers, teachers, etcetera, and make sure to bring this up at the Child & Family Team meeting.
- **Keep notes of observed behaviors and conduct.** This is information that is very valuable in the treatment process, especially for updating treatment plans. Include both positive and negative behaviors.
- **Provide your Foster Care Provider with copies of your notes and written observations**, not opinion or judgments. This is another way that you can demonstrate your due diligence.

- Make sure you know who your child is with. Always have a name, address and/or a contact number. Always ask to see the credentials of anyone who you do not personally know who wants to be with your foster child/youth.

- Immediately ask for help if behaviors or issues arise beyond your ability to safely handle or if you have any concerns.

- Always report suspected child abuse to local child protection authorities or your child's Foster Care Provider's Social Worker assigned to the case.

The Investigation Process

Whenever an allegation is made against a foster parent, a rather complicated process begins. As a result of the legal requirement to protect children, the investigative agencies are required to investigate complaints/allegations. Often you may not even know there is an ongoing investigation. Once you become aware of an investigation, one may feel pre-judged, but it's important to remember that the spirit of the law is to protect children and this is a normal part of the investigation process. At the conclusion of any investigation, if you feel that you were treated unfairly, you have the right to file a complaint with the investigating agency and have your voice heard. The initial investigation process may go as such:

- Depending on the nature of the allegation, the response can be immediate or in a matter of days.

- If the risk is perceived to be imminent, meaning that the child is in immediate danger of further harm, in most cases, the child will be removed from the home. However, if the risk is perceived as moderate, the child may remain in your home during the investigation process.

- Allegations can be investigated by multiple agencies, including:
  - **State Licensing Agency.** Your state licensing agency has the primary responsibility to investigate all allegations against foster parents. Your state licensing agency can receive allegations from anyone. Their role is to determine the truth of allegations and initiate the appropriate corrective or legal action. Depending on the nature of the allegation, your state licensing agency may send several investigators.
  - **Child Protective Services (CPS).** CPS also has a legal responsibility to investigate any allegation of child abuse or neglect. In most cases, CPS will defer or subrogate their investigation to your state's licensing agency or to law enforcement when there is a potential for a criminal charge(s).
  - **Law Enforcement.** Law enforcement will usually be involved in complaint investigations if it involves physical abuse to the extent that criminal charges could be made and in all cases of sexual abuse.

- These agencies will most likely work together, but that is not always the case.

- ***It is important that you cooperate with all investigating agencies openly and honestly.*** They have the legal right and obligation to investigate all allegations. They have the legal right to enter your home, interview foster children and other residents of the home, and inspect your records.

- The speed of the response to an allegation will depend on the nature of the allegation. There are two classifications of complaints, which have legally mandated response times.
    - **Physical and Sexual Abuse:** Depending on the urgency, must be initiated within **24 hours**, otherwise within **10 days.**
    - **All other allegations** must be initiated within **10 days**.
- The length of the investigation can vary depending on the severity of the allegation, depth of investigation, availability of staff and the coordination required between agencies. It has been our experience that investigations are generally completed **within 30 to 90 days**.
- Typically the investigation includes:
    - Initial contact with the Foster Care Provider, but sometimes investigators will go directly to your home.
    - If not already done, investigators will contact the family at the home.
    - Investigators will contact all parties involved.

Investigators can interview foster children alone but cannot interview your biological children alone.

- Investigators will review all of the records and files at the Foster Care Provider's office and at your home.

Investigators have the right to copy any records in your home file.

- It is against the law for your Foster Care Provider to inform you of or discuss with you an allegation which has been reported until they are notified that the investigation is complete. This is to ensure that nothing interferes with an ongoing investigation.
- Once the investigation is complete, the investigative agency will compile their report, make a finding and review it with your Foster Care Provider. Your state licensing agency has the authority to order the implementation of consequences, if necessary. Your state licensing agency has three "finding" options to choose from for concluding their investigation:
    - **Substantiated:** meaning that the allegation is valid because the preponderance of the evidence has met the standard.
    - **Inconclusive:** meaning that there is not a preponderance of the evidence to prove or disprove that the alleged violation occurred.
    - **Unfounded:** meaning that the allegation is false, could not have happened, and/or is without a reasonable basis.
- During the investigation process, foster parents should:
    - Make every effort to remain calm.
    - Work closely with your Foster Care Provider. Understand that while your Foster Care Provider cannot share information with you until the investigation is completed, your Provider will give you as much support and guidance as is possible and appropriate.
    - Be cooperative.
    - Be honest and forthright.
    - Own your mistakes.

- Do not get defensive or hostile.
- Do not talk about the details or share information with others outside of your Foster Care Provider and investigator; this includes, media, newspaper reporters, social media sites such as Facebook, Twitter, etcetera.
- Ask questions.
- Be patient.
- Seek wise counsel and emotional support. Use your support system such as another Foster Parent or Family Partner, Foster Parent Association and your personal support system, (i.e., family and friends, but do not talk about the details).
- Seek legal counsel if necessary. The more serious the allegation, the more important to seek legal counsel.

What Happens to Foster Children After an Allegation is Made?

One of the first concerns of most foster parents when they learn of an impending investigation is what will happen to their foster children. Any action taken with regard to your foster child(ren) will depend on the nature and severity of the allegations. Here are some possible scenarios:

- An allegation is made by a foster child that they are being routinely locked in their bedroom.
  - The investigation will be initiated within ten (10) days and foster children/youth will most likely not be removed unless the placement worker deems it is necessary for his/her safety and protection.

- An allegation is made of inappropriate corporal punishment to the child.
  - Whether a foster child/youth will be removed from the home will be determined by the placement worker depending on his or her assessment of any injuries and the imminent danger to the child.

- An allegation is made that the home is untidy, unkempt and below acceptable standards of cleanliness.
  - Most likely children would not be removed.

- An allegation is made that a teenage foster youth is being sexually abused by the foster father.
  - The foster youth will be immediately removed and provided a SART exam (sexual abuse resource team). CPS, law enforcement and the state's licensing agency will immediately engage in an investigation. Usually CPS will defer to law-enforcement on these matters.

In most instances of allegations, foster children are not removed. But it is important to note that if a repeat allegation is made, the chances of children being removed from the home can increase.

Your Foster Care Provider's primary role during an investigation is to protect the interest of the foster child by cooperating with investigators, working towards finding solutions and initiating plans of corrections that the state might require.

An investigation is a very upsetting experience for foster parents and your Foster Care Provider should offer you support, and help guide you through the process to the extent that is legally allowed. This may include advocating for your family (when appropriate) and serving as a liaison between you, the parent, and outside investigating agencies.

Consequences & Penalties

If an allegation (or allegations) is substantiated, found to be true, there are a variety of consequences depending on the nature of the investigation. Minimally, your state licensing agency will issue a citation to the Foster Care Provider and require a Plan of Correction. This does not generally mean removal of children. A Plan of Correction is a specific step or action(s) designed to prevent a recurrence of the allegation. This could include specific training, counseling, physical environment improvement, etcetera.

The required removal of a child from a foster home by a state licensing agency is rare and usually involves physical or sexual abuse, or gross misconduct on the part of the foster family. In extreme cases, the state may order the decertification of the family. Once a foster family has been decertified by the state, they are unable to work in any state licensed capacity with children again. Including:

- Foster care (both County and private)
- Daycare
- Group home
- Elder care

How the Foster Care Provider is Affected

When you are found out of compliance, so is your Foster Care Provider., and your agency can be subjected to "civil penalties." Check with your Foster Care Provider for specific penalty amounts. A serious allegation against a foster parent of a Foster Care Provider can have an adverse effect on the agency, including the termination of its state license.

There are several things that a foster parent can do in these situations:

- They can request or obtain legal counsel through the process. There are legal service programs that are specific to foster parents.

- Foster parents can purchase "liability" insurance (quality, competent Foster Care Providers offer foster parents the opportunity to enroll in foster parent liability insurance, or purchase it for their certified families).

- Foster parents have the right to appeal any decision by the state to decertify their home and if they are dissatisfied with the outcome, they have the right to have the matter heard in superior court.

Foster Parent Risk

It is unreasonable to assume that allegations can be prevented 100% of the time; however, much can be done to substantially reduce the risk of allegations being made. Prevention is the key to effective risk management.

Risk management is a planned series of steps/activities which are designed to minimize potential risk and liability. We want to emphasize that risk management is about thinking, planning and initiating steps for preventing allegations from occurring. It's about thinking of all the possibilities (i.e., worse case scenarios) that could occur.

Understanding the Law

The first step of good foster parent risk prevention is understanding the basic legal framework which applies to foster parenting. And remember, at any time, you have the right to seek legal counsel. The following is a summary of legal terminology you should become familiar with:

- **Liability:** A business or Independent Contractor can be sued not only for something it does, but for things it does not do.

- **Direct Liability:** Refers to Liability on the part of an individual, business or Independent Contractor that has been established on the basis of *negligence* or other factors *resulting in harm or damage to another individual or their property*.
    - People can be held liable for bodily injury, in which someone is physically harmed, as well as financial damages, psychological damages, and damages to property. In all cases, *direct liability implies that the person potentially obligated to pay damages is directly responsible for the injury*.

- **Negligence:** The key element of Direct Liability. There are two types:
    - **General Negligence**
        - The failure to use reasonable care.
        - The doing of something which a reasonably mindful person would not do, or the failure to do something which a reasonable person would do under like circumstances.
        - A departure from what an ordinary reasonable member of the community would do in the same community.
        - Negligence is a 'legal cause' of damage if it directly and in natural and continuous sequence produces or contributes substantially to producing such damage, so it can reasonably be said that if not for the negligence, the loss, injury or damage would not have occurred.
    - **Negligence Per Se**
        - Negligence resulting from a failure to follow a law, statute, regulation, contract or company policy and procedure, specifically related to the safety or protection of another.

- **Due Diligence:** The conduct that a reasonable man or woman will exercise in a particular situation, in looking out for the safety of others. If one uses due diligence then an injured party cannot prove negligence. Due Diligence is one of the key standards by which negligence is tested.

It is this important that you know this because:

- As a foster parent, **you are an Independent Contractor!**

- As an Independent Contractor, you are subject to specific liabilities and responsibilities; separate and independent of your Foster Care Provider's responsibilities and liabilities.

- It is very important that you remember to always view yourself as an Independent Contractor, and carry out your duties and responsibilities as a foster parent with this first and foremost in your mind.

"Due Diligence" is the key for successful Independent Contractor risk protection.

- Remember, Due Diligence is the conduct that a reasonable man or woman will exercise in a particular situation, in looking out for the safety of others.

- Due Diligence is being able to *"prove"* you are doing the very best you can to preserve the safety and wellbeing of your foster children.

- Due Diligence means you are organized, follow the rules and keep good documentation so you are able to *prove* what you do. With no "proof" you put yourself at a greater risk.

Chapter 12

The following Risk Management Tips are to help you perform Due Diligence. So, pursue them diligently.

- Remember, you are a "Professional Foster Parent," so make every effort to protect your reputation and integrity.

- Be Risk Minded; always on the lookout for "neutralizing risk."

- Be Proactive; think of potential problems before they occur. Prevention is the best policy.

- Perform "Due Diligence" every step of the way, especially:

    - Maintaining excellent financial records so that you can demonstrate how you spent your foster care reimbursements. It is very important that you can show how you have provided for basic "care and maintenance" (e.g., clothing, toiletries, basic necessities of life, allowances, extracurricular activities, etcetera).

    - Maintaining excellent communication with your Foster Care Provider staff as well as other stakeholders. Keep a log of your conversations, including the date and items/issues discussed. Another option is to track all of your conversations via email and save your emails to a specified folder.

    - Maintaining excellent, age-appropriate communications with your foster children/youth. If your lives and schedules are very busy, schedule specific times to talk and interact. Put things in writing in a clear visible place, such as: house rules, expectations, chores, emergency phone numbers, emergency exit route, etcetera.

    - Continually document your foster child/youth's behaviors, both positive and negative, and include how you responded (i.e., with rewards or consequences). When you share this information with the client's Social Worker or the Child & Family Team, make sure someone signs off as having received the information.

    - Keep well maintained and properly secured files on your foster children/youth and on your foster care certification/license. Maintain a checklist of what must be included in these files and be persistent to make sure you are provided everything you need. When documents are required to be signed, make sure that they are.

    - It is essential that you learn, know and follow licensing regulations and your Foster Care Provider's policies and procedures. Maintain documentation of all regulations/policy-related training.

    - In addition to your initial and mandatory training requirements, continually seek to improve your skills as a Therapeutic Foster Parent and maintain documentation to support your training. There are many online or community-based resources for foster parent training and education. Check with your Foster Care Provider to see what they recommend to supplement your skill building efforts. Whenever you seek guidance or instruction about foster parenting from your Social Worker, therapist or other professional, document the date, content of the discussion and the amount of time that was spent. In most cases, this is acceptable to use for your ongoing training requirements.

    - Immediately report any unusual incidents; unusual behaviors; injuries or medical emergencies; personal threats; violent or destructive behavior; suicidal ideations or gestures; or any suspicions that the child/youth may have been abused and/or neglected. It is common for foster children/youth to report physical and/or sexual abuse which occurred previously in their life. This too must be immediately reported, just as if it were brand-new information.

Photo by Andreas Krappweis

- Conduct routine safety inspections of your home and grounds; as well as routine fire/emergency drills. Be sure both of these activities are documented, including the date. This should include testing smoke and carbon monoxide sensors and making sure your first aid supplies are fresh and up-to-date.
- Have emergency disaster supplies on hand (e.g., water, food, flashlights, radio, first aid supplies, etcetera). There are plenty of emergency "check lists" online, and many stores sell pre-made emergency kits. Make sure you receive an emergency plan policy from your Foster Care Provider.

■ Know as much as you can about each foster child/youth that comes into your home. This must include dangerous propensities and/or special needs; medical history: family history, culture and background: dietary needs and allergies; and plan accordingly. Be assertive and insist on getting the information you need.

■ Child-proof your house, especially if you will be or are parenting children 0-5.

■ Have clear expectations and routines, and explain them to your foster children/youth at the time of their initial placement and as often as is needed to ensure they are fully understood.

■ Know your own boundaries and limitations, and keep yourself "healthy" physically and mentally. You cannot effectively foster parent if you are overstressed, unhealthy or are attempting something you are not skilled at doing. Always remember to "Stop, Drop, & Roll!"

■ Seek wise counsel and support. If your Foster Care Provider uses Family or Parent partners, seek their support. Make every effort to participate with other foster parents through some type of foster parent support group. Your foster care provider is responsible to support, guide and assist you, so make them do their job.

■ Remember, the Child & Family Team is there to serve you as well as the foster child/youth. Be honest and assertive in sharing your needs, frustrations and ideas. You do have "voice, choice and preference."

■ Maintain solid healthy family relationships with your spouse, partner, children in the home and your extended family. One of the most important roles of a professional foster parent is modeling "healthy family behavior."

■ Do not personalize behavior or set up conflicts with foster children. Foster parents are very often "safe targets" for foster children/youth to vent or project their anger and/or frustrations. Learn the skills necessary to deflect and diffuse. Once again, be sure to "Stop, Drop & Roll."

■ Make sure you know who your foster child/youth is with:
- **Always** use well vetted and screened foster child/youth care workers when you are absent from the home.
- **Always** know your foster child/youth's peers and have their names, addresses and contact numbers.
- **Always** ask to see the credentials of anyone who you do not personally know who wants to be with your foster child/youth.

■ Take care of yourself. Avoid being stretched or taking on more than you can effectively do. Know and respect your limits.

Remember: Expect the unexpected. Be well prepared. Err on the side of caution—it's better to be safe than sorry!

Healthy Kids

Managing Medical Issues and Medications

CHAPTER 13

CHAPTER 13

HEALTHY KIDS
Managing Medical Issues and Medications

Children in foster care have high rates of physical, developmental and mental health needs, and oftentimes many of these needs have gone unmet. It is therefore very important for foster parents to make sure that the children receive regular medical attention and that they follow all doctor recommendations to ensure that the child receives the best care possible. In some instances, foster children may already be taking medications before they are placed in your home and may arrive with their medication, however, quite often, children coming into foster care may have undiagnosed physical or mental health issues. In either case, **you are an important source of observation, information and feedback for medical professionals.**

As foster parents, you should be careful not to "practice medicine" by attempting to diagnose or suggest treatment for any medical issues your foster child may be experiencing. This chapter lays out the specific regulations and protocols most Foster Care Providers have in regards to managing a foster child's medical issues.

Your Foster Care Provider must provide extensive training and support to foster parents in the area of medical issues and medications. Not only is following correct policies and procedures an extremely important part of the foster parenting job, but it is a regulatory requirement.

Foster parents must also follow the proper procedures in documenting and handling medications and medical issues in order to adhere to your Foster Care Provider's state licensing requirements. If you are unclear about any of the required policies and procedures, contact your foster child's Social Worker who can arrange for additional training and support.

Foster parent documentation is extremely important, particularly with regard to medical and medication issues. As is indicated elsewhere in this Handbook, the Best Practice for foster parents is to maintain personal case notes as a way of demonstrating "due diligence" in the care, maintenance and supervision of foster children.

The following are the basic requirements for maintaining a foster child's medical care:

- Most states require that every child placed into foster care be accompanied by a **Health & Education Passport** within 30 days of placement. This passport must include a summary of the foster child's health and education information or records, mental health information or records, and include:
    - The names and addresses of the child's health, dental and educational providers
    - The child's grade level performance, the child's school record, assurances that the child's placement in foster care takes into account proximity to the school in which the child is enrolled at the time of placement
    - A record of the child's immunizations and allergies
    - The child's known medical problems
    - The child's current medications, past health problems and hospitalizations
    - A record of the child's relevant mental health history, the child's known mental health condition and medications
    - Any other relevant mental health, dental, health or education information

- The law requires that each foster child be taken for a **Child Health and Disability Prevention (CHDP) physical exam and dental exam** within the first 30 days after placement and annually thereafter. Foster parents must schedule appointments, even if they fall past the 30-day mark to ensure that the foster child is seen.

- If appointments are past the 30-day mark, be sure to contact the child's Foster Care Provider's Social Worker so this instance can be properly documented. Your Foster Care Provider's licensing agency will most likely accept medical examinations beyond the 30 days, so long as the appointment was made within the statutory 30-day timeframe. For more information on this point, please consult with your Foster Care Provider.

■ For every medical, dental and emergency appointment, some type of authorized **Health Care Encounter/Screening Form** must to be filled out by the attending physician/dentist. Some agencies use a state issued LIC 602; while others will use similar forms they have developed. A copy of the completed form will remain in the child's home file, and the original form must be given to your Foster Care Provider for their records.
  - The form must be signed by the attending physician/dentist or a licensed nurse practitioner.
  - These records are also given to the placing agency so they can be compiled in the child's **Health & Education Passport**.
  - Be sure to log the outcomes and follow-up needs from appointments in your personal case notes.

■ **Completing Patient Intake Information Forms:** Every healthcare provider's office will have some type of intake, patient information form. The following information is a basic guide to properly completing the health encounter/screening forms:

  - **Patient Information**
    - Give the foster child's full name, gender, date of birth and social security number.
    - If you are asked to provide other information about the child, such as previous medical history, allergies, etcetera, you should provide as much information as you can. ***NOTE: you should have received this information in the Health & Education Passport.***
    - For "Address" it is generally recommended to use the address for your Foster Care Provider, but check first to determine your provider's specific policy.
    - Also, use the Foster Care Provider's phone number for the primary contact phone. However, it is also appropriate for you to list your personal home/cell phone number as a secondary or message phone.
    - Leave other fields blank that don't apply, (i.e., "Employer")

  - **Responsible Party Information**
    - This is an area which causes significant confusion and produces many problems, especially with billing. Please make sure your Foster Care Provider thoroughly instructs you in their policies, procedures and practices.
    - The basic rule of thumb – the placement agency, (i.e., DHSS, DSS, CPS, Probation, etcetera), is the **Responsible Party.**
    - You can identify yourself by name as the "foster parent" and provide a contact phone number. **NEVER** provide the following personal information:
      1. Date of birth
      2. Social Security number
      3. Address
      4. Employer information
      5. Credit Card information

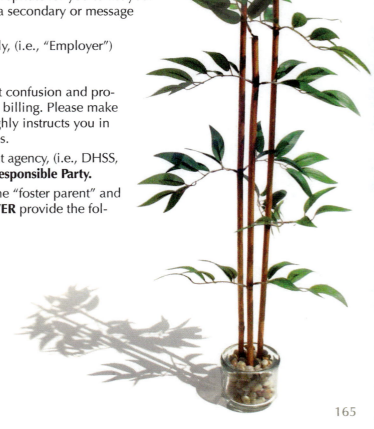

165

- **Insurance:** In most cases your foster child will be insured by a state or federal insurance (i.e., Medicaid or MediCal for those residing in California). Make sure you have the foster child's insurance information/card with you. In rare instances, a foster child may have private health insurance, and you will need this card/information as well.
    1. In many communities there is a distinct shortage of physicians and dentist who accept Medicaid or MediCal for those residing in California.
    2. Competent Foster Care Providers will provide a comprehensive list of available healthcare providers who accept your foster child's insurance. It is their legal obligation to ensure that the medical needs of each client are fully met.

- **IMPORTANT:** Most patient information forms have a section that requires the "Responsible Party" to sign a statement that authorizes the provider to provide care, release medical information about the child and accept financial responsibility for any charges incurred in the treatment of the child.
    1. ***Under no circumstances should a foster parent sign in this section.***
    2. Instead, write the words, "Department of Social Services" or "Probation Client" on the signature line.
    3. Foster parents do not have the authority to authorize medical procedures, and they are definitely not responsible for the foster child's medical bills.
    4. ***Foster parents who provide personal information and accept financial responsibility have found that their credit can be compromised because a child's medical bills weren't paid by the state's insurance in a timely way.***
    5. If you experience any difficulties in this regard, contact your Foster Care Provider's Social Worker or County placement worker for assistance.

· **Other Information**
  - Always leave questions which do not apply to a foster child blank, such as: marital status, income, employer, etcetera.
  - For Emergency Contacts, the list in order:
    1. Your name and telephone number
    2. The Foster Care Provider's Social Worker and telephone number
    3. The child's Placement Worker's name and phone number
  - You may be asked to sign a child in or out of a doctor's office or hospital. This is something you **are** authorized to do.
  - You are also authorized to sign a HIPPA form (this is a form that states the privacy rights of the patient.) By signing this form you are simply stating that you received the confidentiality form.

■ **Tuberculosis (TB) testing** is also required for your foster child within 30 days of placement. TB test information should be included with the immunization records in the foster child's Health & Education Passport. If not, please request the physician to conduct a new TB test, with verified written results; or provide a written statement containing the reasons not to conduct a new TB test.

- **First Aid Requirements**
    - Every foster parent must have a current First Aid/CPR certificate, preferably with Water Safety certification.
    - You must always have a fully stocked First Aid Kit in your home that includes at least the following:
        1. Current edition of a First Aid Manual approved by the American Red Cross, the American Medical Association or a state or federal health agency
        2. Sterile first aid dressings
        3. Bandages and roller bandages
        4. Adhesive tape
        5. Scissors
        6. Tweezers
        7. Thermometers
        8. Antiseptic solution
    - There must always be at least one person in the home capable of and responsible for communicating with emergency personnel when there is a foster child present.
- **Posting Requirements:** All foster homes must have an **"Emergency Plan for Foster Family Homes"** form posted in a conspicuous place, near a telephone. This mandatory form lists emergency phone numbers and other information that is necessary in emergency situations such as the location of utility shut off, location of fire extinguishers, first aid kit, etcetera.

Foster Parent's Role in a Foster Child's Health Care

Foster parents play a crucial role in making sure that their foster child receives appropriate care for any health-related issues. As their primary caretaker, you are closest to the child, and the person most likely to know how the child is feeling and responding to prescribed care.

Helpful Tips:

- Talk to your foster child about how they feel about their medications; use of available resources such as "Possible Side Effects of Stimulants" and "Possible Effects of Antidepressants" and "Understanding Psychotropic Medications" to help the foster child assess his or her reaction to a particular medication.

- Chart your foster child's reactions and comments about medications to discuss with his/her physician. You should also pass this information on to his/her Foster Care Provider's Social Worker.

- Document everything! Keeping thorough personal case notes assures quality medical care and protects the child, the foster parents and the agency. This is another way for you to demonstrate "due diligence."

- If possible, attend all of your foster child's doctor visits including medication evaluations. When you cannot attend, make sure you provide your input and observations about the child's behavior to the prescribing physician.

- Ask questions if you are unsure about anything related to your foster child's medical needs.

- Be sure to immediately communicate all medical interventions, medications prescribed, etcetera, to the child's Foster Care Provider's Social Worker.

Routine or Emergency Surgery

- Children in foster care may not undergo surgical procedures without court approval.

- Anytime anesthesia is administered (even in the case of dental work) the child's placement worker must obtain a court order allowing the procedure.

- In the event a child requires emergency surgery, you must contact the Foster Care Provider's on-call Social Worker, who will contact the placing agency who must then contact an on-call Judge to issue the court order.

- Obviously, in a life threatening emergency, the treating physician will take every measure to preserve life. But, foster parents must initiate the court approval process as soon as possible.

Under no circumstances should a foster parent sign for or authorize any surgery for his/er foster child. However, please know that a physician will proceed without approval if s/he deems the situation is life threatening.

Medications

Your Foster Care Provider should have developed a comprehensive protocol for the handling and administering of prescription and over-the-counter medications that satisfies all state and county regulations. By following these steps, foster parents will ensure the best possible care for their foster child, as well as protect themselves from possible liability.

It is important to note that a court order is required before any foster child may take a psychotropic medication (a medication that acts upon the central nervous system causing changes in a person's perception, mood, consciousness, cognition and behavior). Your child's physician may not be aware of this requirement. So, it is very important that you do not allow an attending physician to prescribe a psychotropic medication without the proper court order.

If a Child Arrives at Your Home with Medications

- Contact the foster child's physician(s) to ensure that they are aware of all medications currently being taken by the child.

- Verify medications that are currently taken by the child and dispensing instructions.

- Inspect containers to ensure the labeling is accurate.

- Log all medications accurately on the **Centrally Stored Medication and Destruction Record** (LIC 622), and log all medications received using your agencies assigned form.

- Discuss medications with your Foster Care Provider's Social Worker and the foster child (if appropriate).

- Store medications in a locked compartment; this includes all over the counter medications/ointments/etcetera. This also includes medications which need to be refrigerated.

- Do not hesitate to ask questions if you are not sure what to do.

When Prescriptions Are Filled

- Coordinate with the foster child's Foster Care Provider's Social Worker to determine who is responsible for ordering medications, paying for medications, etcetera.

- Before filling prescriptions, make two copies of the prescription form, one for the child's home file and one for the Foster Care Provider's office file.

- Never let medications run out unless directed by the physician.

- Make sure refills are ordered promptly. Ordering one week in advance ensures the medication(s) will be refilled promptly, and will allow time in case there are insurance and/or financial issues.

- NEVER allow a medication to run out! This could jeopardize the health and wellbeing of the foster child, and it is a licensing violation.

- Inspect containers to ensure all information on the label is correct.

- Ask for a duplicate container with the exact information to be used when the child may be taking medications outside of your homes (at school, home visits, etcetera)

- If the medication is in the form of a pill, count them to make sure you have received the correct amount.

- Note any changes in instructions and/or medication in the child's medication log (for example, change in dosage, change in brand, etcetera). Log any changes in your personal case notes as well.

- Log newly received medications on the form given to you by your Foster Care Provider and in your personal case notes.

- Discuss any changes in medications with the child and his or her social worker.

A Note about Sample Medications: Sample medications may be used if given by the prescribing physician. They must have all the information required on a regular prescription label except for the pharmacy name and prescription number. **They must, however, contain the name of the child and the dosage information.** Sample medications are to be logged in the case notes and the Centrally Stored Medication and Destruction Record.

Prescription Changes

Many times when a child is prescribed medication, the physician will make changes to the dosage based on the child's response to the medication. If this happens:

- Obtain **written** documentation of the change from the physician, and document the date, time and the person you talked to in your Case notes.

- Remember, if the medication is psychotropic, a court order is required even in the case of dosage adjustments.

- Prescription labels may not be altered by the foster parent. Take the new prescription from the doctor and the old medication bottle to the pharmacy to get an accurate label put on the bottle to reflect the change in directions.

- Note the change in the Medication Log.

- Discuss the change with the child, and be sure to inform the child's Social Worker.

If Medications are Temporarily Discontinued and/or Placed on Hold

- You may keep medications temporarily discontinued by the physician with all stored and locked medications.

- Discuss the change with the child and his or her Social Worker.

- Obtain a written order from the physician to HOLD the medication, and document the date, time and the name of the person you talked to regarding the HOLD in your personal Case notes.

- Use the Medication Log to note the HOLD and potential re-start date.
    - To avoid altering the original prescription label, a post-it note can be taped on the bottle (with the ability to still see the original prescription label below) which notes the HOLD and the potential restart date.
- Be sure to contact the physician after the discontinuation/hold order expires to receive new instructions regarding the use of the medication and document the instructions in your personal case notes.

When Medication Is Permanently Discontinued

- Obtain written documentation of the discontinuation from the physician and document the date, time and the person you talked to in child's case notes.
- Discuss the discontinuation with the foster child and the Foster Care Provider's Social Worker.
- Use the Medication Log to alert your Foster Care Provider of the discontinuation (black out remaining dates).
- Destroy the medications (see below).

Expired Medication

- It is very important that foster parents check containers regularly for expiration dates and that you communicate with your foster child's physician and pharmacy promptly if a medication expires.
- Do not use expired medications. Obtain a refill as soon as possible if needed.
- Over-the-counter medications and ointments also have expiration dates which need to be adhered to.
- Be sure to destroy all expired medications and document the reason for the destruction in your personal case notes.

The Destruction of Medications

There are several circumstances discussed in this chapter that note when a medication(s) must be destroyed. The following is the required procedure for doing so:

- Two people are required to destroy medications, and can be foster parents, Social Workers or other staff from your Foster Care Provider (any adult).
- Both people destroying the medication need to sign the required documentation form from the Foster Care Provider's state licensing agency.
- The FDA released a report in October of 2009 outlining the government approved method for destroying medications.
    - It is recommended that medications NOT be flushed down a drain or toilet unless specifically directed to do so on the drug label or information that accompanies the medication.
    - The recommended method of destruction (unless otherwise directed) is to take the unused medication out of its original container and mix it with an undesirable substance such as used coffee grounds or kitty litter. This method will make the medication less appealing to children and pets, and unrecognizable to people who may intentionally go through your trash.
    - Place this mixture in a sealable bag, empty can or other container to prevent the medication from leaking or breaking out of a garbage bag and put it in the trash.
    - The FDA has a hotline that you may call if you have any questions about the proper method of destruction for a specific medication. The number is 1-888-INFO FDA (1-888-463-6332).

- Medications that need to be destroyed may sometimes be taken to the pharmacy from which they originated. Be sure to check with your pharmacy ahead of time to make sure they will accept medications for destruction. The person who takes the medication to the pharmacy and staff from the pharmacy can be the two adults required to sign the required documentation form from the licensing agency.

IF A CHILD REFUSES MEDICATION OR MISSES A DOSE

It is important to remember that no foster child can be forced to take any medication. Sometimes, refusal of medications may indicate changes in the child that require a reassessment of his/her needs. Please keep the following in mind:

- Medications should always be given according to the prescribed frequency, but in the event a dose is missed, foster parents must contact the child's physician to see if a medication can be taken at a later time to avoid being "missed." If this occurs, you must document the situation and persons contacted in your personal case notes.

- Some medications can be taken at alternate times, while others must be taken at specific times and could cause health/behavioral reactions or adverse reactions with other drugs the child is taking if directions are not followed accurately.
    · Some foster parents find it helpful to use timers to help remember when medications are needed.

- Missed/refused medications must be documented in your personal case notes and the Medication Log, and the prescribing physician needs to be contacted immediately.

- Immediately notify the child's Social Worker or your Foster Care Provider's on-call Social Worker of any missed/refused medications.

- An incident report must be filed for all missed medications regardless of the reason.

PSYCHOTROPIC MEDICATIONS

Many of the children and youth in foster care are prescribed psychotropic medications at some point during their care. These medications may be indicated to treat various mental and emotional issues.

Again, it is essential for foster parents to understand that **a court order is required before any foster child may take a psychotropic medication.** The judge will sign a form which is given to the physician authorizing the prescription.

Please note the following regarding psychotropic medications:

- It is not uncommon for a child/youth to be resistant to taking these medications and sometimes they may have good cause to not want to take what they've been prescribed. It is their right to refuse.

- Many drugs (especially psychotropic medicines) come with a wide range of side effects which can be uncomfortable and problematic for patients, including weight gain, increased anxiety or agitation, and listlessness to name just a few. Some medications have been known to cause suicidal thoughts and life-threatening side effects.
    · In an age-appropriate manner, you can help your foster child understand why they've been prescribed the drug and what they may experience regarding side effects and for how long they should last. Your personal knowledge of the diagnosis and the drug will increase their confidence in your encouragement.

- It is beneficial if the child knows how the drug is supposed to help them and when to expect a positive change. Some psychotropic drugs have a delayed reaction, so it takes a while for it to build within a patient's system before they notice improvement.

Parenting Tips in Regards to Medications

- Active Listen in regard to the child's concerns or complaints; and in a therapeutic voice, encourage them to compare the outcome to the symptoms and/or consequences to the behaviors they are displaying.

- Let them know that once they start the drug, it is extremely important they take it consistently to avoid adverse affects.

- Immediately call the child's Social Work or the on-call Social Worker who will assist you in contacting a medical professional when a dose is missed or rejected so that you can ask for directions about dosing.

- Be sensitive of how the child feels about him/herself by using only supportive and strength-based language.

- Learn how to talk with the child to help them change their motivations for adherence to the whole treatment plan and to take medications as directed.

- There may be other medications or forms of medications (liquid, patch, etcetera) that might be more agreeable to the child, so be sure to discuss alternatives with the child's doctor.

- If the child is considering to refuse to take the medication, encourage him/her to wait until they have a chance to talk to their doctor about what they're feeling and to ask lots of questions so they feel comfortable with the plan.

Advocating Effectively for a Foster Child to a Health Care Provider

Your Foster Care Provider's licensing agency requires that you continually observe your foster child's progress and discuss with the child's physician any changes from satisfactory conditions. To be an effective advocate for the child in your care, you need to know what's going on with them physically, socially, emotionally and educationally. Please note the following points for advocating on your foster child's behalf effectively:

- Share accurate information with health care providers and advocate to your team all that you observe. You will need to share your genuine concern about your foster child as well as any unusual signs and behaviors that you observe.

- Tell the doctor what you know about the child's allergies, sensitivities, and about existing drugs or vitamins s/he is currently taking. Describe their sleeping and eating habits, and unusual tendencies or complaints.

- To assure accuracy, a description of side effects (and degree of affect) that you notice and your child tells you s/he is experiencing should be documented, preferably as it occurs.

- Utilize the medication related forms that your Foster Care Provider gives you (including a medicaiton log or side effects worksheet) along with your personal case notes to accurately document and share what others need to know, especially if you can't be present during the medical evaluation. Be prepared and professional to ensure the highest quality of care for the child.

- Whenever a foster child is prescribed a new medication, talk to the doctor and use the following "Five R's" method to protect the foster child's wellbeing.

The Five R's Method

Right Person

- Make sure the doctor knows the child's age, weight, allergies, eating and sleeping habits, and common physical complaints.
- Are there activities the child should avoid while taking this medication?
- What are the general reasons for non-compliance of this drug?
- How can you change the child's motivations regarding terms of adherence?
- Is this medication addictive? Can it be abused? This is an important consideration if the child/youth had or has drug/alcohol issues.
- How will this medication be monitored?
- When dispersing, is this medication for the right child?

Right Medication

- Share the child's sensitivities, (i.e.. stomach issues, headaches, difficulty sleeping, etcetera)
- Share other medications or vitamins being taken
- What are the long term effects of the drug?
- If multiple medications are prescribed, how will they affect one another?
- Are there any other medications or foods that should be avoided?
- When dispersing, is the right medication being given?

Right Time

- Share the child's daily schedule (i.e., school, meals and sleep time).
- What is the window of time the medication can be given?
- How late is "too late" to administer the drug?
- When should the medication be stopped?
- What do you do if the medication is missed?
- What is the expiration date of the drug?
- When the prescription indicates every two hours does that mean after bedtime too?
- When dispersing, is this the right time to administer this medication?

Right Dose

- What are the possible side effects and are they recognized?
- What is the expected outcome of the drug?
- When will the medication begin to work?
- What is the recommended dosage?
- How does the drug work, (i.e., time release, fast acting, delayed effect, etcetera)?
- When should you be concerned about the side effects and call the doctor?
- When dispersing, is this the right dose?

Right Method

- Share child's ability to swallows pills, liquids or receive shots.
- Discuss options (i.e., creams, patches, nasal sprays, drops, suppositories, etcetera).
- When dispersing, is this drug being administered using the right method?

Side Effects with New Prescriptions

Know what to look for in regards to side effects with every new prescription, and how to respond.

- It is imperative that you educate yourself. Having knowledge of the diagnosis and the prescribed drug is essential to know what to look for and what to report to the health care provider. Know the possible side effects of the medication. This can aid in the doctor's determination of modifying dosage or changing medication to better meet the child's needs and certainly help them better tolerate the medication they've been prescribed.

- Communicate the child's needs quickly and professionally to the health care provider and your Foster Care Provider's team. Some drugs present considerable risk to the child's health and safety, and require regular monitoring of blood work and liver function. Your Foster Care Provider should have developed a form to be used to record side effects experienced by a child who has been prescribed stimulants or antidepressants. The forms should be filled out, then accompany the child at his or her next visit to the doctor or med evaluation.

- Follow the doctor's instructions with accuracy, and report errors and concerns immediately. If you don't understand directions, call for clarification.

When Medications Need to be Crushed or Altered

Medications may be crushed or altered to enhance swallowing or taste, **but never to disguise or "slip" them to a child without his/her knowledge**. The following written documentation must be in the child's file if the medication is to be crushed or altered:

- A physician's order specifying the name and dosage of the medication to be crushed.

- Verification of consultation with a pharmacist or physician that the medication can be safely crushed, identification of foods and liquids that can be mixed with the medications, and instructions for crushing or mixing medications.

- If age-appropriate, a form consenting to crushing the medication signed by the foster child. If the child has a Guardian ad litem or conservator with authority over his/her medical decisions, the consent form must be signed by that individual.

Over The Counter (PRN) Medications

- **"PRN"** Medication (pro re nata) means any non-prescription or prescription medication that is to be taken **as needed**.

- At placement, each foster child undergoes a Well Exam. At this appointment, foster parents should have a PRN form completed and signed by the physician.

- The PRN Form notes which over-the-counter medications can be used for ailments, and the physician will note if the child is able to communicate symptoms clearly and communicate the need for medications.

- Procedures you must follow:
  - Log all PRN medications purchased on the form given to you by your Foster Care Provider (may be called the Centrally Stored Medication and Destruction Record) as well as in your personal case notes.
  - The child's name should be on the over-the-counter medication container.
  - Use the medication log form given to you to note when PRN medications are given. Log the day and time the medication was given, in addition to the reason given and response (there is a key at the bottom of the log to help determine the "reason" and "response").
  - Log in your personal case notes as well when PRN's are needed. Continued and consistent complaints of ailments from a child may be cause for a re-assessment of their needs.

Injectable Medications

- Injections may be administered by a foster child as long as the child's physician has given approval and properly trained the child to do so, or may be administered by the foster parent or other caregiver provided that the foster parent/caregiver has been properly trained to administer injections by a licensed health care professional.

- Only Psychiatric Technicians (P.T.) can administer subcutaneous and intramuscular injections to children with developmental or mental disabilities, and in accordance with a physician's order.

- The physician's medical assessment must contain documentation of the need for injected medication.

- If the child does administer his/her own injections, physician verification of the child's ability to do so must be in the file.

- Sufficient amounts of medications, test equipment, syringes, needles and other supplies must be maintained in the home and stored properly.

- Syringes and needles should be disposed of in a "container for sharps," and the container must be kept inaccessible to all children (locked).

- Only the child or the licensed medical professional can mix medications to be injected or fill the syringe with the prescribed dose.

- Insulin and other injectable medications must be kept in the original containers until the prescribed single dose is measured into a syringe for immediate injection.

- Insulin or other injectable medications may be packaged in pre-measured doses in individual syringes prepared by a pharmacist or the manufacturer.

- Injectable medications that require refrigeration must be kept locked.

Dispensing Medication

Remember, no child can be given any medications without a physician's order. Medications must be stored in their original containers and not transferred between containers. Unless prohibited by court order, a foster child may self-administer medication or injections *if the child's physician gives permission*. The foster parent must ensure that the child knows how to:

· Self-administer their medications/injections
· Document when they self-administer their medications/injections
· Properly store the medication so that it is not accessible to other children

Foster parents may help with administering eye drops, injections, enemas, suppositories, etcetera, if a foster child needs assistance with such. However, the child's physician must authorize this and provide instruction to the foster parent as to the proper method of administration.

The following are some important tips on handling medications:

- Have clean, sanitary conditions (i.e., containers, counting trays, pill cutters, pill crushers and storage/setup areas).

- Cups or envelopes containing medications should not be left unattended. Wait to give medications until the child is present and able to take medications without interference. The name of the child should be on each cup/utensil used in the distribution of medications.

- Pour medications from the bottle into the individual child's cup/utensil to avoid touching or contaminating medication. Use gloves and pour medications over a paper towel for extra caution.

- Medications that have been spilled or contaminated must be destroyed.

- Anyone assisting a child with self-administration of medication needs to ensure that the child actually swallows the medication (no "cheeking" the medication).

- At the time a medication is given to a child, foster parents must sign the appropriate medication log on the appropriate date and time.

Foster parents are responsible for informing their Foster Care Provider's staff if a medication is to be administered in their absence.

Foster parents are also responsible for communicating the directions for giving medications to a child, logging these directions and where the locked medications are located.

Medication Log

- As already incidated several times throughout this chapter, your Foster Care Provider's State licensing agency requires that every foster child will have a medication log in their Home File for each month.

- This medication log notes what medications a child takes, and the times and directions.

- After a medication has been given and confirmed that it has been swallowed, the foster parent must initial the date and time given.

- If a child is not present during a dosing period (i.e., s/he is at school or on respite), a medication is on HOLD or a child REFUSES it, this would need to be documented on the form.
  · **Reminder:** for a HOLD on medications or if a child REFUSES to take a medication, the child's Social Worker and physician need to be notified, and the reasons why and a follow-up plan need to be documented in your personal case notes.

- Each time a child reports an ailment, make note of it in your personal case notes (even if no medication was administered). Continued and consistent complaints of ailments from a child may be cause for a re-assessment of the child's needs.

Transferring Medications for Home Visits, Outings, Etcetera

Each time there is a transfer of medications to and from your home, the entire prescription bottle must be given to the responsible person, or a second identical prescription bottle obtained from the pharmacy may be used and the exact amount of the medication needed for the time your child is away from your home may be placed in the bottle. You must also adhere to the following:

- For all transfers of any medications, complete information must be logged in your personal case notes (including medication name, strength, quantity, RX number, the date/time the medication left the home, and the date/time the medications are returned to the home), and have the responsible person accepting the medication sign for such.

- If there is a count discrepancy after the transfer of medications, your Foster Care Provider's Social Worker must be notified immediately.
  - Additionally, errors made while on home visits or respite could mean that responsible persons need to be trained on the handling of medications.
  - An incident report must be filed for medication errors, and the child's Social Worker will determine the plan of action from that point forward.

Emergency Medication(s) (i.e., Nitroglycerin, Inhaler, Etcetera)

Foster children who have a medical condition requiring the immediate availability of emergency medication may maintain the medication in their possession if all of the following conditions are met:

- The physician has ordered the medication, and has determined and documented in writing that the foster child is capable of determining his/her need for a dosage of the medication and that possession of the medication by the child is safe.
- The physician's determination is maintained in the foster child's file and available for inspection.
- The physician's determination clearly indicates the dosage and quantity of medication that should be maintained by the child.
- It has been determined that the medications do not need to be centrally stored due to risks to others or other specified reasons.

If the physician has determined it is necessary for a foster child to have medication immediately available in an emergency but has also determined that possession of the medication by the child is dangerous, then the Child & Family Team will need to create alternative solutions.

Important foster parent requirements:

- Be sure to communicate with the child's Social Workers and physicians if two orders of emergency medications are needed (i.e., one for the home and one for school).
- Log all emergency medications purchased on the Centrally Stored Medication and Destruction Record, or whatever form your Foster Care Provider gives to you, and in your personal case notes.
- The child's name should be on the emergency medication container.
- Use the Medication Log to note when emergency medications are taken. Log the day and time the medication was given, in addition to the reason it was given and the response.
- Log when emergency medications are taken in your personal case notes as well.

Proper Storage of Medications

- All medications, including over-the-counter, ***must be locked at all times***.
- All medications must be stored in accordance with label instructions (refrigerate, room temperature, out of direct sunlight, etcetera).
- Medications requiring refrigeration need to be locked in a receptacle, drawer or container separate from food items.
- If one foster child is allowed to keep his/her own medications, the medications need to be kept in a lockable container to prevent access by other children or youth in the home. Also, the prescribing doctor must provide documentation that the child is able to keep the medications, and the same must be noted in your personal case notes.

Birth Control for Foster Youth

Birth control, because of how it may be obtained and by its nature, is not considered medication for the purposes of most Foster Care Provider's regulations, and is outside the boundaries of said regulations. Birth control, both oral and intravenous, are not subject to our requirements for medication storage and supervision.

Federal statutes provide minors with the legal right to obtain confidential reproductive health services, which could include a prescription for birth control. Under these statutes, minors are allowed to obtain these services without the consent of their parent or guardian. The federal law reference to "guardian" would extend the confidentiality requirement to foster parents.

Foster parents are encouraged to initiate a conversation with their foster youth about some of the things they should be aware of regarding birth control, such as what protections are afforded by different methods (and what protections are **not**). For instance, your foster youth needs to know that oral birth control pills do not prevent the transmission of sexually transmitted diseases (STDs) and birth control medications may also become ineffective when taken with other certain medications. If your foster youth is not comfortable talking about this topic with you, encourage him/her to talk with their doctor, Social Worker or to visit a health clinic where they may obtain this important information.

Even though you are not required to store birth control medication with the youth's other medications, if you know for sure that your foster daughter is taking birth control pills, make sure she knows to keep the medication in a safe place away from the reach of other children in the home.

When a Child Leaves Your Home

All medications, including his/her specific over-the-counter medications, should go with the child when possible. If it is not possible to transfer the medications to the child's new location, they must be destroyed according to the proper procedure listed above.

- Document when medication is transferred with the child in your personal case notes and have the responsible person/authorized representative accepting the medication sign as well. Be sure to accurately count each medication and log all prescription information (name/dosage/count/RX#).

- When a child transfers out of a home, make a list of their current medication orders, and a list of upcoming medical/dental/mental health appointments for the home the child is transferring to.

CHAPTER 14

OFF TO SCHOOL
Supporting Your Foster Child's Education

Photo by Andreas Krappweis

Off to School
Supporting Your Foster Child's Education

Like many other areas of a foster child's life, school can be challenging, bringing to the surface a variety of feelings and behaviors. In a recent research report, it was found that three quarters of foster children perform below their grade level and over half are held back in school at least one year, and 30% to 52% of all foster youth receive Special Education services.

The "Best Practice" as a foster parent is to provide **mentorship** and **guidance** in regards to school, focusing on your child's strengths. Some foster children are not used to being affirmed of their strengths. When asked, these children may not even know what to say about their hobbies, interests, strengths or goals. As a foster parent, you can really help a child develop a sense of hope for their future and discover who they have the potential to be, what they have the potential to do, and how they could get there. By encouraging them in their strengths and goals, you create a trusting relationship which enables you to share any concerns that you may have about their educational direction and goals.

Redefining Success

As we have mentioned in other chapters of this Handbook, success for a foster child can look a lot different than success for your own children or even yourself. For a child who has been absent from school frequently due to traumatic experiences, just showing up every day to class is a huge accomplishment. Or a child who prior to care was consistently getting referrals to the office or being called out for his/her behaviors, to reduce the number of these negative outcomes shows great success. Every success, no matter how small, is a great accomplishment for a child dealing with the aftermath of trauma.

Education Services Provided by your Foster Care Provider

Because education is so important, it is necessary to devote a lot of manpower and resources to assist foster children and foster parents to achieve the best results. Your Foster Care Provider may have an Education Coordinator or dedicated staff assigned to provide direct support and consultation to foster children and foster parents, including the following services:

- Educational Assessment
- Tutoring
- Attendance at Individualized Education Plan (IEP) or Student Study Team (SST) meetings
- Advocacy
- Vocational Aptitude Testing and Assessment
- Graduation/Emancipation/College Planning
- Application Assistance (FAFSA, job applications, college applications, etcetera)
- Educational Planning/Placement
- Consultation for enrollment, Special Education rights and responsibilities, literacy, extending foster care eligibility, collaboration with schools and school-related structure in the home (i.e., homework time, reading hour, etcetera)

Your Foster Care Provider's Social Worker provides case management (including the Child & Family Plan) that addresses:

- Educational advancement
- Advocacy for appropriate school placements
- Therapeutic interventions to help work through challenging school issues
- Collaboration with the educational staff, schools and other agencies

Educational Rights

Most foster parents would assume that as the child's caretaker, they would have the right to make decisions regarding their foster child's education; however, *this is not the case unless the court has granted such rights*. Educational rights are usually the last rights that a biological parent can lose. If those rights have been terminated, the court appoints someone to assume educational rights. Guardians ad litem or Court Appointed Special Advocates (CASAs) are usually given this responsibility, but sometimes the court appoints a close relative or a foster parent.

The school district may appoint a **Surrogate Parent** as well. Surrogate parents are determined when a child's parent(s) cannot be located or if they are imprisoned. A surrogate parent does not necessarily hold educational rights; they may simply represent the child like a guardian would.

It is very important for foster parents to know who has educational rights because that person is responsible to sign any school-related legal documentation. For example, if your foster child receives Special Education services and an Individualized Education Plan (IEP) meeting is scheduled to change the current IEP, then the person who holds educational rights will need to be present in order to sign the new IEP into effect.

School Enrollment

Most children should be enrolled in school immediately upon coming to your home. However, some children may have needs that cannot be met in a regular school setting. In cases such as this, your foster child's Social Worker should let you know if there is a better alternative such as Independent Study, Community School, Continuation School, Adult School, a vocational program, Home School, home/hospital services or another alternative program in your area.

Every school has a slightly different process for enrolling students. High school and Junior High students will meet with their assigned counselor. Elementary school students will enroll through the school office. In general, you will want to follow these steps:

- Contact the school to make an appointment, if necessary.

- Be sure to bring the foster child's **Health & Educational Passport**. This should contain all mandatory immunization records and other pertinent school-related records.

- Ask your foster child's Foster Care Provider's Social Worker if the child has an IEP. If your child does, you will need to bring a copy of the IEP at enrollment. Consult the **Special Education Needs** in this chapter for further information on this subject.

- If you or the Social Worker is unaware of an IEP for your foster child, then ask the school to contact the child's previous school to find out if the child received Special Education services and if a copy of the IEP can be faxed to the current school.

- The school will need a copy of the IEP to create an appropriate school schedule with accommodations that fit the child's specific academic/emotional needs. IEP accommodations include settings, techniques and materials that do not change the basic curriculum but assist the child in reaching meeting educational standards.

- You do not need special paperwork to enroll your foster child in school, but be sure to let the school know who has educational rights over the child (if you do not) and that you serve as the child's foster parent.

- Make sure your name **and** the Foster Care Provider's Social Worker's name is entered on the emergency notification card.

- Do not reveal confidential information about your foster child's family history and background. If the school has specific questions, direct them to your child's Foster Care Provider's Social Worker.

- You may be asked to provide the child's immunization record. This should be in the Health & Education Passport, but may also be obtained from the child's previous school or from the placing agency.

- You may also be asked to give permission for your foster child to be photographed, however ***you are not authorized to do this*** because of confidentiality laws and privacy protection.

SCHOOL ATTENDANCE

Remember, all foster children must receive some form of education. Each foster child's school history is different, but many foster children have had very inconsistent school attendance and some may have never attended school. Children in foster care, due to trauma and instability, have also ended up changing schools as a result of frequent moves. It is therefore very important that foster parents enroll their foster children in school as soon as possible. Research supports a direct correlation between regular attendance and school achievement.

Under current law, every effort must be made to maintain a foster child in their current school in order to maintain continuity, essential linkages and to prevent educational disruptions. It is not uncommon for foster children to be behind in their skills and need consistent attendance to make adequate progress. Dental, medical and other appointments should be scheduled after school hours whenever possible.

Every state/county has a Department which is required to monitor foster child enrollment and attendance. This department may regularly mail out a School Verification Form, or other similar form, to your Foster Care Provider several times per academic year. A foster child who is **not enrolled** in school will not qualify for Federal foster care funding which is used to pay for foster care services.

If your foster child refuses to go to school on a regular basis, get assistance from your Foster Care Provider's Social Worker immediately, and initiate a conversation with the child's teacher or educational counselor.

It's important to note that:

- There may be a motivation behind your foster child's refusal to go to school besides defiance, such as an issue with bullying (foster children often become the victims of bullies), or it may be that the child experienced trauma or abuse at home because of school issues.

- With children who are victims of violence and abuse, there is always something under the surface, something deeper than what you see or understand that the child is experiencing which motivates him/her to react to certain situations.

- Think creatively when your foster child refuses to go to school. There may be a better alternative than the current educational program. It is important to seek help from your Foster Care Provider's Social Worker and the child's Child & Family Team. It is also important to keep a log of events, and comments or conversations you have with your foster child about school.

SCHOOL RECORDS AND PRIVACY

There is strict Federal and state legislation controlling the confidentiality of foster children's school records. These records are private, with the exception of parents, placement workers and qualified school personnel. Additionally, because of specific laws surrounding Special Education students, even greater care is taken in these cases to insure appropriate confidentiality.

It is very important for foster parents to view and be aware of the documents in their foster child's school file. Knowing your foster child's educational background is a key to understanding them. The school files, called cumulative files, contain:

· Immunization records
· Report cards from previous schools
· Disciplinary reports or referrals
· IEPs (if applicable)
· Other documents, including an updated list of every school the child has attended.

Often, foster children do not remember all the schools they may have attended. Having that information can be very helpful in understanding and interacting with your foster child about school.

Whether or not the school will allow you to view the child's file seems to depend on the school. Ask the school personnel if there is a specific process for obtaining permission to view confidential school records. Often, schools will ask you to acquire a release of information document from the placing agency. However, some records may still be closed unless a release of information is obtained from the person who holds educational rights for the client.

The following education-related records should be kept in the foster child's Home File:

- Immunization records
- Proof of residency
- Documentation on who has educational rights
- Grade reports (including progress reports)
- Attendance reports
- Standardized testing scores
- High school exit exam results
- Credit assessment/transcripts (should have one each semester)
- Awards/Certificates
- Disciplinary reports
- IEP—current and previous (if applicable)
- Independent Living Program materials and job information
- Letters from teachers and/or administrators
- Personal notes

All school-related information must be shared with your foster child's Placement Worker (Social Worker/Probation Officer). They need this information on a quarterly basis to complete court progress reports. It is also very useful in order to track a child's progress. However, be sure to keep a copy for your child's Home File.

Special Education Needs

Often, foster parents will be involved with special education services for their foster child, for which nearly 50% of foster children qualify. Children with identified special education needs have a legal document called an Individualized Education Plan (IEP) which is a specially designed plan that addresses the unique needs of a child who has been diagnosed with learning disabilities and/or a condition which impedes his/her ability to learn or perform in school. The IEP calls for certain accommodations/adaptations that allow the child to have access to the general curriculum in a way that enables him/her to meet educational standards.

There are many qualifications for Special Education. Learning disabled children are given an assessment by a School Psychologist. Qualification is based on the results of the test. If the child qualifies, the school team meets to develop a plan that will provide appropriate services for the child. This plan contains yearly objectives and quarterly benchmarks to meet those objectives. The IEP is reviewed yearly and reassessed every three years.

It is important to understand that children who have been designated as Special Education students may have learned to dislike school. The feeling of being different and always behind can affect self-esteem and a child's general attitude toward school. Focusing on areas of strengths and interests, especially creative ones, can help counter these feelings. Make sure to talk with your foster child about expectations that are reasonable and realistic for him/her. Help him/her set goals and let them know that you are a resource to help them when they need it. Even if the foster parent does not hold educational rights for the child, s/he play a crucial role in not only working with the child to encourage his/her educational growth, but also as the person who has the most knowledge of how the child is responding and whether the services are meeting the child's needs.

Special Education services provide accommodations for a variety of needs and disabilities, including:
- Sensory—hearing, visual, speech/language
- Orthopedic Impairment
- Developmental
- Autism
- Traumatic Brain Injury
- Emotional Disturbance (mental and emotional problems manifesting in behavior)
- Specific Learning Disability—a learning disability that can manifest itself with a deficit in one or more of these areas: attention, reasoning, processing, memory, communication, reading, writing, spelling, calculation, coordination, social competence and emotional maturity.

If your foster child has a pre-existing IEP, the school must continue the previous IEP accommodations when they are enrolled. IEP accommodations must not be interrupted.

Like all children, not every foster child will need to have Special Education services. However, once your child has been in your home for a while (two to three months at least), you may begin to recognize patterns in the way your child is particularly challenged by school and homework, such as a significant discrepancy between a child's abilities and his/her performance. If you observe school-related challenges, you should:

- Contact the foster child's teacher(s) to see if they are observing similar behaviors.
- Contact the child's Foster Care Provider's Social Worker so they are fully informed and can participate in creating solutions.
- Also, bring your concerns to the Child & Family Team. If the child has a learning disability that has not yet been discovered, you may do him/her a great service by detecting it, so that appropriate supports might be set into place.

"I am getting to start a new life as being able to do kids' stuff like I am supposed to do."

—Youth age 12

Typical Characteristics of Learning Disabled Students

Reading
- Confusion of similar words; difficulty using phonics; problems reading multi-syllable words
- Slow reading rate and/or difficulty adjusting speed to the nature of the reading task
- Difficulty with comprehension and retention of material that is read but not with material presented orally

Writing
- Difficulty with sentence structure; poor grammar; omitted words
- Frequent spelling errors; inconsistent spelling; letter reversals
- Difficulty copying from board or overhead
- Poorly formed letters; difficulty with spacing, capitals and punctuation

Oral Language
- Difficulty attending to spoken language; inconsistent concentration
- Difficulty expressing ideas orally
- Problems describing events or stories in proper sequence
- Residual problems with grammar; difficulty with inflectional or derivational endings

Math
- Difficulty memorizing basic facts
- Confusion or reversal of numbers, number sequence or operational symbols
- Difficulty copying problems and aligning columns
- Difficulty reading or comprehending word problems
- Problems with reasoning and abstract concepts

Study Skills
- Poor organization and time management
- Difficulty following directions
- Poor organization of notes and other written materials
- Needs more time to complete assignments

Social Skills
- Difficulty "reading" facial expressions and body language
- Problems interpreting subtle messages, such as sarcasm
- Confusion in spatial orientation; getting lost easily; difficulty following directions
- Disorientation in time; difficulty in telling time.

Please note that many of these learning disability characteristics may be seen in non-disabled students as well. Just because a child displays some of them does not mean that s/he have a learning disability and require Special Education services. Some foster children may experience delays in learning because of factors such as frequently changing schools, cultural and language differences, running away from home or a history of poverty and/or neglect, among others.

Again, it is important to be calm and sensitive toward your foster child in school-related areas. If you think s/he may have a learning disability, contact the child's teacher with observations and questions, and always bring the issue to the Child & Family Team.

Chapter 14

Emotional Disturbance Disability

A common disability that qualifies a child for special education services is called **Emotionally Disturbed (ED)**, and can also be referred to as **Seriously Emotionally Disturbed (SED)** in the mental health context. A student is considered emotionally disturbed if, because of a serious emotional disturbance, s/he *exhibits one or more* of the following characteristics over a long period of time and to a marked degree, which adversely affects educational performance:

- An inability to learn which cannot be explained by intellectual, sensory or health factors
- An inability to build or maintain satisfactory interpersonal relationships with peers and teachers
- Inappropriate types of behavior or feelings under normal circumstances exhibited in several situations
- A general pervasive mood of unhappiness or depression
- A tendency to develop physical symptoms or fears associated with personal or school problems.

The disability category "emotionally disturbed" is not a recognized psychiatric diagnostic category. Thus, it does not require a particular psychiatric diagnosis—such as schizophrenia, depression, etcetera. A student does not need to have a psychiatric label to be eligible for special education services.

Requesting Special Education Services

If your foster child does not currently receive special education services, but you feel they may benefit from this type of assistance, the child must be evaluated by the school district.

- The process begins by submitting a simple, one page letter to the school Principal or school psychologist stating concerns and requesting an assessment. This letter may be submitted by the foster parent, CASA worker, Social Worker or the person with educational rights. Social work staff from your Foster Care Provider will assist you with this.

- The school will usually request a SST (Student Success/Study Team) meeting and then the assessments will occur after that.

- If it is determined that the child has one or more of the learning disabilities mentioned above, the school will prepare an Individualized Education Plan (IEP) and the child will receive the help s/he needs to achieve school success.

While the foster parent may request services for the child, only the person with the educational rights over the child may sign the IEP making it official.

The following are some important terms and definitions related to Special Education:

- **Assessment:** Testing and observation in order to identify a child's strengths and needs for the appropriate development of an educational program. Assessments also serve to monitor the child's progress in an education program.
- **Individualized Education Plan (IEP):** the plan developed for every Special Education student setting forth annual educational goals and determining classroom placement.
- **Student Study or Success Team (SST):** a team of people consisting of the child's parents/guardian, teacher(s), administrator and/or counselor. An SST meeting convenes when school life becomes interrupted by poor attendance, poor grades and behavior issues, or if an IEP is being considered.
- **Least Restrictive Environment (LRE):** Children with disabilities must be educated with children who are not disabled in mainstream classes to the maximum extent appropriate.
- **Modifications:** Changes in the delivery, content or instructional level of a subject or test. Learning disabled children with modifications in a specific class or classes, operate according to different standards with different expectations than non-disabled students without modifications.
- **Resource Class:** A Special Education classroom for children who are in a regular classroom for more than half of the school day.
- **Special Day Class (SDC):** A classroom adapted to meet the needs of children who require specialized services for over half of the school day.
- **Day Treatment Facility:** A specialized program run by the local school district that provides education and occupational assistance.
- **School Psychologist:** A specialist trained to evaluate a child's ability to learn by administering IEPs, conducting tests, arranging programs and placements (not to be confused with clinical psychologist or therapist).

Transitional Age Youth

For transition age foster youth (ages 16 to 19 years old), other educational elements become increasingly important, such as finding a job, learning independent living skills, (e.g., grocery shopping, budgeting, managing their own apartment, etcetera); becoming aware of available community resources (e.g., public transportation systems, financial aid resources, Independent Living Program, etcetera); and thinking through future goals and life after emancipation.

There are many school-related differences that should be taken into account when parenting a transitional age foster youth in your home, including:

- California legislation (AB 12) allows foster youth to remain in government funded foster care until age 21. So, just because a youth turns 18, it no longer means that s/he will have to leave your foster home. However, there are some specific educational and/or training requirements which the youth must follow in order to remain eligible for care. These youth must be:
  - Completing high school or an equivalent program (GED); OR
  - Enrolled in college, community college or a vocational education program; OR
  - Participating in a program designed to remove barriers to employment; OR
  - Employed at least 80 hours a month; OR
  - Unable to do one of the above requirements because of a medical condition, including mental/behavioral health

A significant focus in supporting a foster youth is helping them prepare for their emancipation. Therefore, foster parents should encourage foster youth to get a part-time job by the age of 16. A job will provide money that the foster youth can save for later as well as an opportunity to gain marketable work skills.

Most states/counties have a program called the Independent Living Program (ILP) which offers free independent living skills classes to current or former foster youth from age 16 to 21; as well as assistance locating work, housing and developing an emancipation plan. Participation in ILP is often times required by law, but regardless, it is an important resource for foster youth.

ALTERNATIVES TO TRADITIONAL HIGH SCHOOL

Unlike elementary schools, junior, middle and high schools have public alternatives to regular school. Alternative programs include:

- **Community School:** A school program operated by your state/county's Office of Education which provides services to meet the needs of junior high and high school students who are referred by the School Attendance Review Board (SARB) or are expelled from their school district. The SARB deals with all chronic-truancy and school behavior problems. SARB meetings will include a representative from the school, probation, law enforcement, mental health, etcetera, who convene to determine how to intervene in order to curb truancy problems. A community school's primary purpose is to help students transition back to their school districts; however, youth may also receive a graduation diploma from a community school.

- **Continuation School:** An alternative high school program for students over age 16 who are referred by SARB. Unlike Community Schools, Continuation Schools are operated by the school districts and are designed to assist students who want to graduate but are unable to succeed in a traditional high school.

- **Adult Education:** Students can attend high school classes that are held in the evenings to accommodate people who work during regular school hours. Students who are attending full-time high school during the day can make-up failed classes by attending adult "night" school classes as well.

- **Independent Study:** A program offered at most schools where the student works on his/her own for most of the time and meets once weekly with a teacher to turn in work and receive assignments. The youth's placement worker must approve of this schooling option.

- **Home School:** Depending on the needs of the child/youth and the approval of the Child & Family team, education may be provided in the home by the foster parents.

- **Home Hospital:** If a student experiences an injury or illness that requires them to miss weeks or months of school, arrangements can be made with the school to provide class work and tutoring in your home. In some instances, Home Hospital can be used for children experiencing acute emotional and/or mental health issues. This arrangement must be approved by the child's Social Worker.

Each of these school options is different and uniquely appropriate for various needs. There are also private schools as well as vocational programs available to Transition Age Youth where they can learn trade skills. Older youth can take community college courses and earn college and high school credits. There are also parenting classes available for pregnant youth. Reading and learning centers in your community can be very helpful as a compliment to traditional education. Contact your youth's Foster Care Provider's Social Worker or the local school district for further information about alternative education opportunities.

GED and High School Proficiency Diplomas

Students have the option of gaining the equivalent of a high school diploma before the traditional age of graduation. After age 16, the student may take your state's High School Proficiency Exam (if it has one) or at age 17 and 10 months they may test for the General Education Diploma (GED). While the GED is recognized nationally, it may not be accepted by some colleges and universities.

Your Role in Your Foster Child's Academic Development

Before gearing up to "help motivate" your foster youth to do better in school, take a moment and consider why they may be "unmotivated." There could be many things happening that a foster parent might not see, such as unrealistic expectations of the foster family or teachers; fear of failing; lack of understanding of curriculum; self-defeat because of a lack of success; or the foster youth may be having difficulty with teachers, peers or administrators. Consider the tensions and difficulties of your foster youth's life before assuming that they are being lazy. Remember that no one wants to fail, though s/he may give up.

It is important to talk with your foster youth about their past experiences in school and short/long term goals. Be observant of his/her strengths and interests, noticing patterns and creating strategies to set realistic goals. Help them understand that achieving a goal comes down to small, daily decisions made toward that goal—in this way, mistakes can be made and lessons learned can work to further motivate them to make better decisions. Again, look for your foster youth's strengths, and consider how you can give him/her more opportunities to use his/her strengths in school, your home and within the community. Build on the instances of motivation that you discover within each individual youth. Some foster children may not have been nurtured in these ways, and they will gain motivation just by your interest and concern.

Another way you can assist your foster youth in the area of education, is to help him/her start an **Academic Portfolio**. Many foster youth experience difficulty continuing their education after transitioning out of care because they don't have complete and accurate school records. Encourage your youth to create a binder or folder that includes:

- Their Social Security card (or copy)
- Certified copy of their birth certificate
- Official Record of their Immunizations
- Official transcripts from each middle school and high school the student has attended. Transcripts should include a list of courses taken, credits earned, grades and GPA
- Report cards—as a back-up to any missing transcripts
- Diplomas of graduation or GED
- Copies of all IEPs and other testing for students with disabilities
- Records of extracurricular activities in which the youth participated
- Records of any internships, volunteer work and part-time or summer jobs. Help them take this information and create a resume. Be sure to include a description, dates and their supervisor's name and contact information.

Behavior at School

It is not unusual for foster children to have difficulties in school. Problematic behavior at school is often the way a child responds to traumatic experiences in their lives. Unfortunately, few foster children have "normal" school experiences, but rather they deal with conflict with peers and teachers, and can struggle to feel accepted or to be successful in an academic setting. It is important that you understand these challenges that your foster child may face, as it will help you to focus and remain calm when dealing with your foster child's possible behavioral issues at school.

Remember, with a child dealing with the effects of trauma, there is always something happening beneath the surface. The challenge is in discovering what may be causing behavior problems and how the child can be supported and his/her behavior modified without isolating or casting judgment.

School is a very difficult place for some foster children. Be patient and affirming when working through difficult behaviors with your foster child. Also, be sure that you have the support and insight of your foster child's Social Worker, therapist, the school counselor, teachers, etcetera. It is important to note that schools serving students in grades 8 through 12 are required to establish programs that promote school safety and emphasize violence prevention among children in public schools. Contact your child's school to learn more about these programs and communicate with the school if you feel that your foster child may be at risk.

Along with the Child & Family Team, you may decide to try some of the following ideas to help your foster child succeed in school:

- Establish a behavior contact
- Tutoring (to provide positive attention to the child)
- Assessment—there may be a Special Education service that can provide support for the child
- In-Home Support Counseling support for during school hours

Some schools are very aware of the emotions, experiences and needs of foster youth. But many are not. Therefore, it is important that foster parents are patient and professional in working with the schools and use such opportunities to educate school personnel in how to work with a foster child.

Resources

- **Foster Parent Support Groups:** these meetings are a great opportunity for foster parents to connect and openly share feelings, ideas and techniques.

- **Tutoring:** talk with your Foster Care Provider and/or the School District about the availability of free tutoring either through their agency or within the community. Often, local colleges and/or universities will provide free tutoring services through their education department.

- **Agency or Public Library:** a small video and reading library may be available through your Foster Care Provider to foster parents and children, and the public libraries have access to a broad range of related resources. Look for materials covering themes such as: parenting skills, therapeutic issues for children and academic skill building. There are also some very helpful and enlightening DVDs and books on topics such as ADD/ADHD and other learning challenges.

- **Special Education Information:** for more in-depth information about the rights and responsibilities under Special Education, contact the Community Alliance for Special Education (CASE) for a copy of their excellent handbook at (415)-431-2285.

- **TASK – Team of Advocates for Special Kids:** TASK is a non-profit organization offering support to families of children with disabilities. They provide assistance in seeking and obtaining education, early intervention, medical and therapeutic support services. (866) 485-1717 (toll free in California) www.taskca.org

- **Websites:** the following is a list of websites with good articles and links to other resources that may help you understand your foster child and guide him/her in education.

    www.casey.org
    www.ldonline.org
    www.chadd.org
    www.childrenwithdisabilities.ncjrs.org
    www.ericed.org
    www.fape.org
    www.pbs.org/wgbh/misunderstoodminds/
    www.schwablearning.org

CHAPTER 15

Adolescence to Independence

Challenges and Opportunities

Chapter 15

Adolescence to Independence
Challenges and Opportunities

It is important to remember that adolescence is a key transitional period. This critical time in your foster youth's development is so important, that we have devoted an entire chapter in this Handbook to the subject. However, many of the concepts in this chapter are also discussed in Chapters 6 and 9, so be sure to use those as a reference as well.

> **Points to Remember**
>
> - Successfully parenting foster adolescents and youth is a matter of helping them make a successful transition from childhood to adulthood. This is a healthy, yet challenging process of youth empowerment.
>
> - For the transition of power to be successful, the foster parent must be willing to hand over responsibility on a gradual basis, empowering the youth to make decisions and be in control whenever possible.
>
> - This "transfer of power" includes allowing them the opportunity to experience the consequences of their choices, which means they might "fail."
>
> - However, with a caring foster parent's support, these short term "failures" will lead to confident, healthy young adults.
>
> - Most people think working with teenagers is a chaotic and irrational experience, but it doesn't have to be. It can actually be a life changing experience when a foster parent is willing to work from a strength-based perspective with understanding and compassion.

It's not Rocket Science—It's Biology!

It is absolutely essential for parents of adolescents and youth to remember that much of what they are seeing and experiencing is directly related to the biological changes that the youth is going through.

- Hormonal changes not only affect the body but the brain as well.

- As a youth's body chemistry changes, remember that you, as the foster parent, can remain a permanent, consistent support by not overreacting to changes in behavior.

- Remember to exercise patience on a daily basis, respecting the youth's self-esteem, continually reassuring him/her that you are always available to talk.

> Make every effort to be observant and sensitive to a youth's natural biological changes. This approach will help you to be more tolerant and able to support your youth through this important transition to adulthood.

Other important considerations:

- Boys and girls mature at different rates and in different ways, so expect to see them progress toward adulthood in different ways and at a different pace.

- Our society's emphasis on the perfect body adds to adolescent adjustment problems. Because self-worth is equated with personal appearance, young people live with a constant fear of fitting in or not being "cool."

- We may say that appearance doesn't make a difference, but to an adolescent, it does! Be sure to never make a negative statement, tease or joke about their appearance.

Common Problems and Behaviors

Communication

- **Open the Door to Communication:** The ability to talk openly about problems is one of the most important gifts a foster parent can give to a foster youth. Developing a relationship of open communication takes time and patience, particularly for youth who have never had this type of relationship with an adult. Sometimes the best opportunities to communicate happen in unexpected ways, such as while driving somewhere, doing a simple chore like grocery shopping together or cooking a meal together. Casual, non-threatening times can be just what a foster youth needs to allow them to open up and talk about what is on his/her mind.

- **Listen More, Talk Less:** Active listening is the secret to effective communication. Think of yourself as a sponge, able to absorb a youth's feelings, emotions, etcetera, without reacting. Admittedly, staying neutral while we listen is much easier said than done, so practice, practice, practice.

- **Affirmation:** All kids need to know that they are okay, especially foster children. Even when your child communicates otherwise, s/he needs to have our affirmation to know that s/he are loved and accepted unconditionally. This stimulates positive change and motivates your foster child to set and achieve new goals.

Important communication points:

- All adolescents and youth will test limits and break rules. The parent's responses need to be consistent and fit the behavior. When young adults question your value system they are often trying to establish their own values. They need and want consistent boundaries, even when their outside behavior suggests otherwise.

- Ask yourself if you're responding to a youth's behavior the way your parents did when you were young. How did you feel when your parents yelled at you or punished you for typical teenage behavior?

- If you feel triggered by the youth and there is a chance that you might yell, use profanity or verbally put the youth down in any way, **STOP, DROP and ROLL**. This means, *stop* talking or interacting, *drop* into deep calming breathing and then when you are able to respond rather than react, *roll* back into the communication.

- Avoid the use of the word "never" in giving consequences or making threats, for example "You'll never see that friend again!" or "You'll never use the phone again!" or "You can never be trusted again!" These types of statements can make a young person feel powerless and hopeless, and you cannot realistically follow through with these types of threats.

- Never physically threaten, gesture or place your hand on them when you are angry or emotionally upset.

Behaviors

Important tips when addressing a behavior:

- Describe what happened using "I" messages. "I need to get to work on time, so I expect everyone up, dressed and ready for school by 7:30am. "When you don't get ready in time, I am late for work."
- Describe what you want done beforehand. Clearly let the youth know your expectations. For example, "I count on you getting up and ready for school on time." "I have to leave by 7:30. Is there anything you need to do tonight to enable you to be ready by that time?" Give the youth an opportunity to think, plan and prepare for success.

When praising a behavior:

- Show your approval, such as, "You really did a nice job with…" and "Thanks for…"
- Describe what was done well, "Sweeping and mopping the floor" "Studying hard all week and getting a B on your quiz."

Setting Limits

Believe it or not, even young adults want boundaries, rules and consistency. Youth who have come from chaotic backgrounds with little discipline and routine thrive when they can count on parents who respond predictably; parents who show them respect, acceptance and an unwavering desire for their success. One of the surest ways to facilitate a successful transition to adulthood is by setting limits and then holding the youth accountable to live within those limits.

Here are some helpful ways to set appropriate limits:

- Clearly communicate the rules and expectations for each youth in a way s/he can understand.
- Take time to listen to the youth's ideas and needs, and validate their concerns. Involve them in the rule setting. S/he will be more agreeable to following the rules if they have had a part in the decision making.
- Explain the reasons why you have set a rule or limit with a youth. Whenever possible, tie your rules to *your* needs, not what you deem as "good for them." For example, setting a curfew time because you need to get to bed at a decent time. Or, having telephone or computer use rules that allow you to use those items when you need to. Avoid the statement, "Because I said so."
- There should be different limits based on the maturity and understanding of every youth. In most instances, a youth can earn more freedoms by demonstrating personal responsibility and building healthy relationships based on mutual trust.
- Always consult with the Child & Family Team to discuss what appropriate limits look like for the week, and then re-evaluate how those limits are working at the next team meeting.
- Always be consistent, fair and impartial.
- Foster parents within the home must agree on setting and enforcing rules and limits. When there are differences between parents, each must respect the other in front of the youth. Obvious parental disagreements and arguing creates confusion and offers the potential for the youth to "split" the parents and become manipulative. An example might be, "the TV volume doesn't bother me, but your Dad has a headache and we need to respect his need for quiet."
- Enforce limits through "thinking" words not "fighting" words, for example:

  Thinking: "Are you planning on doing your homework before or after dinner?" ("Isn't your favorite program on tonight?")

Fighting: "Do your homework NOW!"

- Evaluate your own beliefs and opinions about what is acceptable. Try to be flexible and accepting of your foster child's cultural and family background, behavior and appearance, unless it is potentially dangerous to themselves or others.

- Learn more about "problem ownership." Don't make their problem your problem. Remember, their reactions are more about them than you, so don't personalize it!

Power Struggles—Pick Your Battles

Power struggling is part of a normal transition from childhood to adulthood. By using the following tools and strategies, you should see a significant decrease in power struggles.

- **Start with active listening** when you know your youth is upset about something. Keep things **"Slow and Low"**— speak in a quiet tone of voice, physically get down to their level, reduce loud noises and bright lighting. Make eye contact and be attentive.

- **Use reflective statements and listen.** This will be much harder than you think, especially when s/he may be reacting very emotionally. It's important that your statements are genuine invitations that show your concern for the youth and his/her feelings. Examples of reflective statements include:
  - "You seem very upset, would you like to talk now or wait until you feel calmer?"
  - "Tell me what happened; I want to hear what you think."
  - "I can see you're very upset."
  - "It's okay, let's talk about it."

- **Avoid the temptation to immediately problem solve.** In most cases, young people just want to vent their feelings and thoughts without hearing anything from the parent. When they are ready, help them brainstorm solutions allowing them to take the lead. Your role is to teach them to problem solve, not to do it for them.

- **Give instructions in a positive way; ask—don't order.** Be clear and detailed, and check to make sure the youth understands you. Give choices and set time limits. Give warnings in a supportive way such as, "Did you lose track of time? If you want to go to the basketball game tonight, you only have five minutes to clean your room."

- **Allow them the right to fail.** All of us have made mistakes and have hopefully learned by them. It is your job to use the process of "choices and consequences" as a teachable moment. The process of making a successful transition to adulthood must include some stumbling and failure along the way. Better they make mistakes while at home with parents, than later with little or no support.

- **Don't be so protective or controlling** that you prevent the youth from experiencing natural consequences. We all want to protect our children from hurt, pain, failure, etcetera. Unfortunately, this desire is not always possible or healthy. In fact, if you allow natural consequences to do the teaching, you won't be perceived as the "bad guy" as often.

- **Be willing to swallow some pride and bite your tongue.** We all have some tendency to want to win, no matter what the cost. With adolescents, taking this posture is a relationship killer, and can subvert forward progress. Do your best to be solution-focused, creating a "win-win" opportunity whenever possible.

- **Apologize.** It is very important to acknowledge your short comings and mistakes as well. A parent's ability to admit a wrong and apologize can be key to successful parenting and can be a powerful model for the youth. Youth and adolescents especially, demand honesty, fairness and justice.

- **Pick your battles.** Don't throw away your relationship over behavior that has no great significance or which is based on fear or other personal feelings. This is what we mean by picking your battles. For example, if your youth insists on wearing provocative clothing, you have the opportunity to share your values in a teaching mode where there may be more room for negotiation. However, if the youth is using drugs or alcohol, this becomes a safety issue and needs to be addressed as such. Restated, focus on major issues which have significant moral, social or health consequence; treat everything else as insignificant annoyances.

- **Maintain a sense of humor.** Adolescents and youth can be very serious and every problem/situation can seem like the "end of the world." Developmentally, they live in the "here and now," so help them see the lighter side of life, the big picture. Step back and laugh with them from time to time.

GIVING CONSEQUENCES

- The process of "consequences" is at work all the time. We experience them every day, at work, at home and with friends. Consequences affect us all, positively and negatively. Giving appropriate consequences to foster youth is essential because it helps them learn that their actions lead to results, both positive and negative. They learn that life is full of choices and the choices they make have an impact on what happens to them and those they care about.

- Simply giving a youth consequences does not mean you are automatically going to change their behavior. Negative behavior is an indication of deeper feelings. When you address the feelings, the behavior usually resolves as a result.

- It is essential for the youth to understand how their behavior affects their relationships and their life experiences. Helping the youth reflect on such things can only happen when the youth is in a calm, regulated state of mind. Only then can they understand how their behaviors bring about consequences.

- There are two basic kinds of consequences: *positive* and *negative*.
  - Positive consequences are things people like and are willing to work for. Behavior that results in positive consequences is likely to be repeated. A reward is a positive consequence.
  - Negative consequences are things people don't like and want to avoid. In most cases, negative consequences encourage people to change their actions so they don't receive more negative consequences. Removing a privilege is an example of a negative consequence.

- Providing consequences for negative behaviors, when administered effectively, is an important tool for teaching children and youth. The process or the way you do this develops and strengthens relationships.

- You can be a much more effective parent through a genuine, nurturing relationship with the youth than through external rules and punishments.

- All mistakes have consequences which are opportunities to learn.

- We suggest being as pleasant as possible, calmly making statements such as:
  - "The choice to _____ (behavior) has created _____ (tangible effect) and _____ (possible feelings)."
  - "How can you make this better?"
  - "What will help you remember not to make this choice again?"

- Research has shown that even when a negative consequence is given, young people are more likely to respond positively and learn more from adults who are calm and reasonable, and when the youth is involved in the disciplinary action.

It is important that members of the youth's team (including the youth) talk about both real consequences in the future and ways to avoid them and to develop consequences together.

Tips on applying effective consequences:

- **It is important to stress *learning*** rather than punishment after the fact. Plan positive and negative consequences ahead of time. Make sure the youth knows what the expectations are for each situation, and what s/he needs to do to prevent actions that would result in negative consequences.

- **The consequence has to mean something to the youth.** Taking away or giving something the youth isn't interested in will probably have little effect on behavior.

- **Use active listening** and give the youth the opportunity to tell you what happened. Explore with them how they are feeling in general. Find out if something happened which upset them.

- **Get both sides of the story.** Know the facts before giving consequences. Get as much accurate information as you can. Don't assume that the youth is guilty just because of past behavior.

- **Don't accuse** or ask your youth to admit to something they've done wrong in a way that's going to make them upset or defensive. Especially if you know s/he did it. Don't feel that they need to admit to wrong doing in order for them to learn a lesson.

- **All foster parents in the home must be involved** in making decisions about appropriate consequences. Don't give out consequences unilaterally. This sets up the possibility for the youth to "split" or manipulate one parent against the other.

- **Don't feel pressured to administer an immediate consequence.** If a consequence is given, it must fit the behavior. For example, if curfew is violated, a logical consequence might be to shorten the curfew time by an hour the next time. If they succeed in coming home on time, they gain the hour back. If they don't succeed, the curfew is set earlier until they do succeed. This motivates the youth to make a change in their behavior, rewards their performance and empowers them to be in control of their future.

- **Sometimes it's okay not to impose any consequences**, especially if the youth is receiving consequences elsewhere, like school. Remember, it's about creating teachable moments—not punishment. Some behaviors involve value differences and these take consistent modeling and time to positively change.

- **Make consequences short-term and specific.** Focus on teaching for positive change rather than being punitive and requiring "payment" for doing something wrong. Make consequences as natural as possible so that they become tools to help the youth develop self-control and mature thinking.

- **Be creative, but consistent**. Do what you say you are going to do, stay with the plan, but always assess the plan to determine if it is effective.

Examples of consequences for adolescents and youth:

- Restricting phone use to five minutes from ten minutes (be mindful of the youth's right to make allowed calls).

- Restricting participation in a certain event, (i.e. school dance, movie or party), but don't be unreasonable—restrict for one event, giving them an opportunity to earn back the privilege for the next event.

- Ask for a personal apology, verbal or in writing. Be sure you model this behavior when you wrong them.

- Restitution—the youth is responsible for replacing or fixing something that they have damaged. Don't withhold allowance as payment for damages.

- Part of any family routine is participation in household chores. It's reasonable to expect your foster youth to do chores, but assigning extra chores or manual labor as a punitive measure may not be okay. Logical consequences that involve chores are usually appropriate, such as:
    - Assigning a youth to pick up trash around the yard if they contribute to littering on the property
    - Washing the car if they had a hand in getting it dirty
    - Assigning the youth extra days of unloading the dishwasher if they continually have to be reminded to do so

  These are types of acceptable consequences that correspond to their behavior. However, assigning strenuous chores or physical exercise is never appropriate and can be construed as corporal punishment, a violation of the youth's personal rights.

- Restrict TV/computer time (an evening, a single show, or a weekend is usually all that is needed).

- Restrict visiting with friends, but not for more than one or two days, unless the youth was involved in criminal activity with their friend.

- Require the youth to come home right after school.

Music, Drugs and Alcohol

So often music, drugs and alcohol are a part of the whole peer group structure which present difficult issues for parents and youth. Nonetheless, the foster parent has a responsibility to their foster youth to help them make proper decisions in this regard.

Chances are, you may not like the music they like. This is not the kind of issue worth fighting over. It is an area where both foster parents and youth need to compromise. In the event that you feel the youth is listening to music that is offensive, vulgar, drug-related or advocates negative behaviors, you should:

- Initiate a non-threatening discussion explaining your concerns without being condemning or critical, and using active listening to hear the youth's point of view.

- Tell them how their music makes you feel. The key is to get them to think about the effect their music is having and what message they are giving to others by their music choices.

- Make an assessment of how strongly the youth is connected with this musical orientation.

- You might ask the youth not to share this kind of music with the family, and suggest they listen to music with headphones.

Many adolescents and youth experiment with drugs and alcohol, so you should be prepared to work with them through these types of behaviors and not reject them for it. The key is to educate your foster youth. There are many resources for this, including the youth's school, the internet, community resources, etcetera.

If you suspect your foster youth is using drugs and/or alcohol, before you do anything, talk to the Foster Care Provider's Social Worker assigned to your foster youth. Ask yourself what your suspicions are based on. Make notes, observations, get your facts!

- Don't be afraid to ask the youth directly if they are using alcohol or drugs, especially if they seem under the influence. This lets them know that you care about them and that you are paying attention.

- Avoid power struggling and confrontations, remember they're not going to stop just because you want them to. Threats and demands will not make them stop.

- Let your youth know that their safety is your #1 concern, and while you expect them to use good judgment when they are with their friends, they can always call you to avoid a situation that is not in their best interest. When they do call for your help, acknowledge their good judgment by helping them out, and then when things calm down, let them know that you expect them as minors to abide by the law at all times.

In dealing with drug or alcohol use, it is essential for you to be an appropriate role model. Foster parents are discouraged from consuming alcohol in front of foster children/youth. Also, all alcohol in the home must be locked up and out of sight. Never drink alcohol and drive! Be aware of your foster child's history and whether alcohol was an issue in their past.

In working with youth that have an addiction to drugs or alcohol, learn as much as you can about causes and treatment (also see Chapter 9). Look into support groups such as Alcoholics Anonymous, Narcotics Anonymous and Alateen in your community. The Child & Family Team will be involved in coming up with strategies and solutions for helping you and your foster youth.

School Problems, Homework and Cutting Class

Difficulty in school is not uncommon with foster youth, for many valid reasons. They may have missed a fair amount of school due to moving from placement to placement, they may be deficient in credits or possibly have learning disabilities/Special Education needs.

Tips for addressing school-based issues:

- Don't make school issues a battleground between you and the youth. Remember that the school is responsible for providing an education to your foster youth and for working through problems that happen there.

- Your involvement with the school in identifying solutions and areas of responsibility is essential; however, it is not necessarily your job to assign consequences for school-related difficulties. Most of the time, allowing the youth to experience school imposed consequences is enough.

- Be involved in the youth's school experience. Establish clear communication with teachers and school personnel. Show the youth you're interested in their school activities. Attend Back-to-School night and parent-teacher conferences.

- Sometimes it is necessary for parents to support the school imposed consequence for a school-related problem. Your cooperation and positive attitude about the school's decision prevents a "split" between you and school staff, and provides a consistent message to the youth. Help the youth stay focused on the "learning" aspects of the consequence and help them develop a strategy for changing problem behaviors.

- Be supportive of your youth and the school. Use active listening when a youth comes home from school with a problem and don't problem solve unless they ask for your help. Avoid asking lots of questions and giving advice.

- Establish a routine for homework. Make sure they have a quiet, well-lit place to work and be available to help them with assignments at a set time each day.

- Positive feedback and rewards are great incentives for youths to attend class and achieve good grades.

- Allow for natural consequences when homework assignments aren't completed (they will receive a lower grade or may fail the class). Use email to stay in touch with teachers. Most schools now have grade and homework information available online and full email access to teachers and administrators.

> If the youth has any learning disability, homework assignments can be very frustrating and anxiety producing. Communicate with your Foster Care Provider's Social Worker if you see that the youth's sincere efforts at school do not keep them on par with their peers.

Dishonesty

A common mistake parents make when they know a youth has been dishonest is to confront them, requiring them to tell the truth. Statements such as "I know you did it; don't lie to me" or "If you tell me the truth you won't get in trouble" are never helpful. Please keep the following in mind:

- Don't set the youth up to lie.

- Avoid statements that may cause the youth to feel shame.

- It's very important to remain calm, address the issue, focus on the behavior and not the person, and then move on.

- Create a learning experience for the youth by helping them look at how they might have done things differently.

- Give praise for positive behavior, especially if the youth comes forward and admits to dishonesty. Always use logical, age appropriate consequences.

Below are two scenarios and possible responses:

- You drop the youth off at school in the morning. Later, you receive a call from the school informing you that s/he missed the first two periods. From prior experience, you know s/he has a problem with telling the truth, especially regarding school.
    - Don't try to trap him in a lie: "Well, how was first and second period today?" Which is immediately followed by, "I know you weren't there today."
    - Instead, share your information with the youth, "The school called and said you weren't in first and second period today." Then start active listening, avoiding arguments and power struggles.
    - Remember, this may be a tool the youth uses to get his or her needs met, by avoiding embarrassment or fear. If you listen long enough you may get to the real problem and help them work through their issue in a more acceptable manner.
    - As previously mentioned, the youth will receive school imposed consequences for his absence.

- Your foster youth tells you s/he is going to a football game. Later, you get a call from another parent (unbeknownst to your youth) telling you that s/he was actually at a party at their house.
    - Again, avoid setting the youth up to lie: "How was the football game? ...you went to a party.... why did you lie to me?" This will set up an immediate power struggle because you are accusing him/her of lying, especially if you know s/he is going to deny what occurred.
    - Instead, present the statement that Mrs. Jones called and said she saw him/her at the party. Then start active listening. Remember, there is a lot of information you need to find out before making a judgment.

- Avoid making generalized statements like, "I can't trust you anymore." "I don't know how you could do this to us," etcetera. Statements such as these will not help change the behavior and may suggest that the youth will never regain your trust, thus s/he will give up trying.

STEALING

As with dishonesty, if you know a foster youth has a problem with stealing; don't set him/her up for confrontation. Stealing can sometimes be the result of feeling powerless or angry, inadequate socialization and/or deprivation.

As a general rule:

- Keep valuables or items that are easily taken (money, wallet, car keys, etcetera), in a secure place out of sight. Protect your personal information such as bank statements, PIN numbers and social security/driver's license numbers. This is a good idea even if you are not aware of any past stealing behavior.

- Closely supervise your foster youth when visiting stores or other homes.

- Don't accuse the youth of stealing unless you are absolutely sure of all the facts.

- Don't rely on other youth to tell on each other (they could be setting each other up).

Just as was suggested with lying, don't set your youth up to deny s/he has stolen. It is not necessary to insist on an admission of guilt when you know they have stolen something.

- Admitting guilt is a separate issue from stealing.

- When you know that they have stolen something, proceed with active listening, allow natural consequences and, if imposing a consequence, make sure to relate it to improving that specific behavior.

- It is important to take the approach of teaching them rather than punishing. Often the natural consequences of stealing, such as getting caught and confronted by store management or law enforcement, will do more than any punishment you could come up with.

FIGHTING

Angry and/or depressed youth often engage in frequent verbal and/or physical altercations. Sometimes youth learn these behaviors by observing others engage in violent behavior, or because they may have been victims themselves. It is not unusual for adolescents to experience moments of anger and/or exhibit some form of verbal or physical aggression from time to time. This is part of normal development in adolescence. It's important to distinguish between normal behavior and what could be a pattern of aggressive behavior.

Youth need to be taught how to manage their anger and how to express their feelings in socially acceptable ways, such as:

- Teach them new ways to work through their anger when in conflict with peers.

- Model for them ways to resolve conflict with others.

- Work with them to help them empathize with others.

- Allow for natural consequences when this behavior occurs at school or in the community (i.e., suspension, arrest, etcetera).

- Remember to reward appropriate handling of anger with praise and positive statements.

Self-Destructive and Abusive Behaviors

Self-destructive and abusive behaviors can include issues such as poor personal hygiene; frequent accidents; scratching; carving or cuts on arms/limbs; self-inflicted cigarette burns; excessive ear or nose piercing; self-induced vomiting; self-administered tattoos; punching walls and injuring knuckles; placing themselves in situations of high risks; abusing drugs and/or alcohol; fighting; and threats of suicide, suicidal ideations (fantasies or thoughts of suicide) or actual suicide attempts.

Dealing with these dangerous behaviors requires a great deal of skill, active listening, patience, support and professional intervention. Again, it is important not to panic, personalize or become overly emotional; but to respond professionally. Contact the youth's Foster Care Provider's assigned or on-call Social Worker right away, and do not respond by punishing or disciplining the youth.

Don't attempt to change or solve these behaviors by yourself. Immediately document your observations and seek the assistance of the youth's Foster Care Provider's Social Worker.

Suicide

Suicide is the second highest cause of death for adolescents and youth next to alcohol-related auto accidents. Foster youth are the highest risk group because they may have experienced trauma or abuse in their past, and may have feelings of depression, helplessness or hopelessness. Also, recent research has shown that some prescription medications, which many foster youth are prescribed, may have the side effect of suicidal thoughts and feelings in those taking them. Foster youth also have the added pressure and fear that comes with not knowing what the future might hold for them following their emancipation from the system, especially if they have no family and no plan. It's important to note that most of the time, people who kill themselves have given definite signals or talked about suicide.

Any suicidal remark, gesture or attempt that you learn of, or observe, must be taken very seriously and be reported to the youth's Foster Care Provider's Social Worker or on-call Social Worker immediately.

What to look for:
- Sleep disturbance (lack of sleep or always tired)
- Lack of appetite
- Isolation from friends
- Giving away personal belongings
- Preoccupation with death
- Obsession with music or writings of death
- Depressed mood
- Withdrawal or extremely quiet
- Marked personality changes; mood swings—very low to very high
- Express feelings of hopelessness and helplessness (i.e., "Life means nothing", "What's it worth?", "Nobody cares about me", "I'd be better off dead", "I won't be a burden to you anymore", etcetera
- Mood changes that occur after certain events such as family visits, court appearances, receiving upsetting news, etcetera
- Unwillingness to share feelings
- Increased problems with drugs or alcohol
- Unusual neglect of personal appearance
- Not tolerating praise or rewards

These warning signs are especially noteworthy in light of a recent death or suicide of a friend or family member, a recent breakup with a boyfriend or girlfriend, conflict with parents or others such as being the target of bullying, or news reports of other suicides by young people in the same school or community.

If you notice any of the above mentioned signs, contact the youth's Foster Care Provider's Social Worker or on-call Social Worker immediately!

Please remember:

- Don't discount or minimize your concerns

- Don't be afraid to ask the youth if s/he is having suicidal thoughts or desires (i.e., "Have you had any thoughts of hurting yourself?") Asking a youth or adolescent whether s/he is depressed or thinking about suicide can be very helpful.

- Rather than "putting thoughts in the youth's head," such questions let the youth know that someone cares and gives him/her a chance to talk about his/her concerns or feelings.

- USE ACTIVE LISTENING without offering advice.

Supervise and watch closely and immediately contact the youth's Foster Care Provider's Social Worker or on-call Social Worker. In an acute emergency, always call 911 first!

Most suicidal people do not want to die, they want to be rescued. They are looking for someone to take control of their life for them because they are so confused. Most suicidal people are very vulnerable and will respond to someone in authority.

Threats—When are they Serious?

Foster parents must take *every* threat a foster child or youth makes seriously and bring the issue to the Child & Family Team immediately! Sometimes these threats are a reaction to a perceived hurt, rejection or attack. However, there are instances when a youth has injured or killed themselves or others after making threats. When these instances occur, everyone asks, "How could this happen?" and "Why didn't we take the threat seriously?" For this reason, Foster Parents must be very proactive in their response to youth who make threats.

Examples of potentially dangerous or emergency situations with an adolescent or youth include:
- Threats or warnings about hurting or killing someone
- Threats or warnings about hurting or killing themselves
- Threats or warnings about hurting or killing an animal
- Threats to run away from home
- Threats to damage or destroy property

Most people would agree that it is impossible to predict a youth's future behavior with complete accuracy. However, a person's past behavior is one of the best predictors of future behavior. A youth with a history of violent or assaultive behavior is more likely to carry out his/her threats. In most cases this information would be in the child/youth case file and would be one of the areas of focus for the Child & Family Team.

The presence of one or more of the following increases the risk of violent or dangerous behavior in youth:

- Past violent or aggressive behavior, including uncontrollable angry outbursts
- Bringing a weapon to school
- Past suicide attempts or threats
- Family history of violent behavior or suicide attempts
- Blaming others and/or unwilling to accept responsibility for one's actions
- Recent experience of humiliation, shame, loss or rejection
- Bullying or intimidating peers or young children, or being the victim of bullying
- Being a victim of abuse or neglect, or witnessing abuse or violence in the home
- Repeated themes of death or depression in conversation, writing, reading selections, artwork
- Past destruction of property or vandalism
- Cruelty to animals
- Poor peer relationships and/or social isolation

When a youth makes a serious threat it should not be dismissed as just idle talk. Foster parents should immediately talk with the youth. If it is determined that the youth is at risk to harm themselves or others, and they refuse to talk, become argumentative, respond defensively or continue to express violent or dangerous thoughts or plans, you should immediately contact the youth's Foster Care Provider's Social Worker or the on-call Social Worker to arrange for an evaluation by a mental health professional.

In an emergency situation, it may be necessary to contact local police or to take the youth to the nearest emergency room for evaluation. A youth who has made serious threats must be carefully supervised while awaiting professional intervention.

Runaways

One common action that adolescents and youth use to cope with their emotions and feelings is to run away. This behavior usually has nothing to do with the foster parents and should not be construed as a personal reflection on you or your parenting. Some common reasons youth run away include:

- They are getting too close to foster parents and the foster family; and therefore they might run away to protect themselves from experiencing potential hurt and loss.

- They may be doing poorly in their foster home and run away anticipating that they will be removed from the home due to their behaviors. It is their way of taking control and making it their decision to leave rather than be rejected.

- Youth may be easily persuaded by peers and make impulsive choices to run away.

- Youth who fear punishment, consequences or are embarrassed about their behavior may run rather than face his/her foster parents or other authority figures.

In the event a foster youth runs away:

- After reporting the situation (see Emergency Section), be aware of and recognize your own feelings of rejection, anger, loss, guilt or frustration. As a foster parent, it is natural to feel as though you have caused the youth to run away even though this is just not the case.

- Try not to personalize this experience, but try to understand the youth and the reasons behind his/her choice to run away. Contact your Foster Care Provider's Social Worker as soon as possible to share these feelings and your own personal responses.

- The "Best Practice" for working with any foster child/youth who runs away is to accept them back into your home; be supportive, help them process their feelings through active listening, and to not respond in anger or be harsh.

- A child/youth who continually chooses to run away may be returned to your home on numerous occasions.

- An effective way of establishing strong relationships in order to change a youth's habitual response/behavior of running away is to support the child/youth's placement in your home.
    · In these circumstances, the goal is to teach the foster youth that running away will not solve his/her problems. It also reinforces the fact that they are wanted and cared for.

- When a youth is returned back to your home, it's important that you don't pass judgment on them for the choice s/he made, but welcome him/her back, and let the youth know you are happy s/he is home safe and sound.

Supporting LGBT Youth

Many adolescents and youth who identify as Lesbian, Gay, Bisexual or Transgender (LGBT) experience a great deal of trauma and stress.

Some of the stressors of LGBT youth might experience include:
· Stigmatization
· Social isolation
· Bullying
· Harassment and violence
· Lack of family support
· Discrimination in housing and employment
· Rejection by religious institutions

The risks associated with these stressors include:
· School-related issues such as excessive absences, fighting, poor academic performance and dropping out of school
· Sexually transmitted diseases including HIV
· Prostitution
· Risky and dangerous sexual encounters
· Alienation from family, expulsion from home
· Increased drug and alcohol use
· Low self-esteem, self-hatred
· Feelings of hopelessness and helplessness
· Attempted or completed suicide

It is essential for foster parents to provide a safe environment for LGBT youth, and the best way to do that is to become educated. Foster parents need to learn more about the unique differences and challenges that these youth face and the supports available to them in your community.

It is important to note the following:
· Don't assume that all youth are heterosexual; accept the youth for who they are.
· Be understanding, empathetic and unbiased.
· Use appropriate and gender neutral language, and never tolerate jokes or derogatory remarks about LGBT people or community.
· Above all, show your foster youth genuine acceptance, support and affirmation.

Parenting Young Parents

It is not uncommon for a Foster Care Provider to place a pregnant youth or young mother and child in a foster home. These foster families are carefully selected and the foster parents participating in the program receive specific training to assist a young parent in developing the skills necessary to provide a safe, stable and permanent home for her child.

Of course, everything previously covered in this chapter also applies to foster youth who also happen to be parents, but young mothers require special understanding, medical care and education, particularly about nutrition, infections, substance abuse and complications of pregnancy and what constitutes an emergency. It is important for pregnant teens to learn how tobacco, alcohol and other drugs can harm their unborn child, and to be connected with community resources that can assist her and her child in numerous ways. Other important issues that need to be understood include:

- Young moms are, well, young! In essence, you have "children parenting children." Don't expect that maturity and responsibility automatically comes with having a baby.

- Don't expect adolescent parents to have any parenting skills or intuition—anticipate that you will need to teach them.

- Respect that these teens are doing the best that they know how to do and never assume they have been shown how to appropriately provide for an infant's needs.

- The young mom may view the baby differently than you would expect. The child might be seen as a cute "toy" or like a friend, someone to love and need them or to meet her needs. You may even detect an ambivalent attitude toward the infant, even some hostility because that baby is now intruding on her life.

- She may have plans to marry the father of the child and "live happily ever after." Sometimes she might be preoccupied with her boyfriend to the point of seeming to ignore the baby, or at least not showing much interest in parenting/care giving.

- She may expect you to be the child's babysitter or to even parent her child—but remember that this is not your role!

Your Role in Parenting a Young Parent

- You and the young parent will work with the Child & Family Team to create a Shared Responsibility Plan which will outline the duties, rights and responsibilities of the youth and the foster parent caregiver with regard to the youth's child.

· The plan will identify supportive services to be offered to the youth by the foster parent and the Foster Care Provider.

· The plan is designed to strengthen the youth's family unit and to facilitate a supportive home environment for the youth and her child that ultimately enables the youth to independently provide a safe, stable and permanent home for the child.

· The plan may not limit in any way the youth's legal right to make decisions regarding the care, custody and control of her child.

· Some of the responsibilities outlined in the plan include:
   - Feeding
   - Transportation
   - Child care
   - Discipline
   - Sleeping arrangements

- Your Foster Care Provider should have developed a form that serves as a "contract" between the youth, you as the foster parent and Foster Care Provider.

- You will need to be a good instructor, providing hands-on guidance on the proper care and nurturance of the child. Begin by asking the youth what they know about parenting and what they would like to learn. They may know quite a lot, but never assume that the youth knows how to be a parent.

- Do not become the primary parent figure to the baby. It may become easy to assume that role, especially if you see the young mother's hesitance or limited amount of skills. Remember, your role is to teach her to be a good parent, not to be the parent yourself.

- It is important to note that as the foster parent of the young parent, you are ultimately responsible for the care and supervision of not only the youth but his or her child as well. However, this does not mean that you are the child's babysitter. Although there may be times when it is okay to help as a babysitter, the message you need to communicate is, "This is your baby and you are responsible for taking care of him/her."

- Especially in the beginning, be very observant of the mother's behavior toward the child and watch for any signs of inappropriate behavior. Again, consider yourself an instructor. Don't condemn or be critical, but give careful instruction regarding your concerns. Report right away to your Foster Care Provider any questionable behavior or abusive tendencies.

- Teach the young mother the importance of her role as a parent in the healthy development of her child.

- Encourage relationship building! There is no greater gift you can give this young family than to help them develop a solid, bonded relationship.

- Work very closely with the Child & Family Team. These cases always present greater logistical issues and require excellent coordination and planning.

Financial Considerations

Babies of foster youth are not normally considered a foster placement, nor are they usually under any type of court jurisdiction. Thus, they are not funded as a foster child. However, due to the fact that the mother is in foster care, the baby is automatically eligible for AFDC (Aid to Families with Dependent Children) on a monthly grant. This also qualifies the baby for Medicaid and a host of other services, such as:

- WIC—a program that supplies formula, and other food products such as milk, juice and cheese.
- Well Baby Care—ongoing check-ups and health care.
- Subsidized Child Care—this service may be limited to availability or teen might be subject to a waiting list.

The AFDC will issue separate checks to your Foster Care Provider payable to you and the foster youth. This money is only to be used to meet the baby's needs (formula, diapers, clothing, car seat, stroller, toys, etcetera). The following is important in regards to AFDC funding:

- Youth should be encouraged to establish a monthly budget
- Part of this money can be budgeted to repay you for extra cost for utilities, laundry, food or even housing if this is agreed upon by the entire Child & Family Team.
- These funds provide a great opportunity for teaching accountability and how to create a realistic budget to meet the needs of the infant.

School Issues

Ideally, the young mother and her baby can become enrolled in TAPP (Teen Age Parenting Program), or some similar state educational program. TAPP offers on-grounds child care, specialized instruction about caring for a child and the academic courses needed to complete a high school diploma. Unfortunately, TAPP schools are not available in every community. In the alternative, some regular and continuation schools have programs for young mothers. Home study programs, adult school, limited attendance programs are other options for teens wanting to continue/complete their education.

Please discuss school issues with the youth's Foster Care Provider's Social Worker, and/or agency staff designated to provide educational supports and services.

Help Them to a Good Start

Imagine what it's like to be a teen mother. Raising children is tough enough for mature adults, let alone a youth. Please be sensitive to this challenge and make it your goal to get mother and child off to a good start. Keep these guidelines in mind when foster parenting a teen parent:

- Have reasonable expectations.
- Be very patient and tolerant.
- Be positive and rewarding—reinforce even the smallest things they do well.
- Constantly tell them they are a special family, reinforce their value and worth.
- Be involved with the youth in their Independent Living Skills development.
- Remember, you're teaching them to be a good parent by being a good role model.
- Be there for them!

PREPARING YOUTH FOR TRANSITION TO ADULTHOOD

A TOUGH CHALLENGE

Young people transitioning out of the foster care system are significantly affected by the instability that accompanies long periods of out-of-home placement during childhood and adolescence. Without the support of foster parents, the typical outcome for these youth includes a higher risk for unemployment, poor educational outcomes, health issues, early parenthood, long-term dependency on public assistance, increased rates of incarceration and homelessness. Approximately 20,000-25,000 young people age out of the foster care system in the United States each year; with many doing so without support of any kind to help them succeed.

Foster youth do not usually have the option of turning to their families for support. Alone, these young people are confronting the harsh reality of the gap between the wages they earn and the cost of living on their own. As a result, youth are aging out of the foster care system and becoming homeless at disconcerting rates. Nationally, nearly 50% of young people transitioning out of foster care experience some degree of homelessness.

POSITIVE CHANGES

- In 2008, the Federal Government passed legislation entitled Fostering Youth Connections and Increasing Adoptions Act. This legislation made federal foster care funding available to foster youth up to age 21.

- In 2010, California became a model state by passing Assembly Bill 12 which allowed California foster youth to remain "in the system" until age 21; plus, it created a new program: Transitional Housing Program Plus – Foster Care (THP+FC) which is very similar to the state's Transitional Housing programs. Foster youth can participate in AB 12 services as long as they are:
    - Completing high school or equivalent program (e.g. GED); OR
    - Enrolling in college, community college or a vocational education program; OR
    - Employed at least 80 hours a month; OR
    - Participating in a program designed to promote or remove barriers to employment; OR
    - Unable to do one of the above requirements because of a medical condition.

Basic Services for Foster Youth Transitioning to Independent Living

The Federal "Foster Care Independent Act," referred to as the "Chaffee Act," requires that all Foster youth ages 18-21 can voluntarily remain in the foster care system as "Non-Minor Dependents" (NMDs). As such, they are treated as adults with a different set of rules and they can leave placement any time with no questions asked.

Additionally, foster youth ages 16-21 participating in any of the above stated Transitional Age Youth programs or placed in your foster home, are eligible to receive comprehensive lifeskill development instruction and guidance in the following life domains:
- Planning and Organization
- Educational Advancement
- Employment and Career
- Community Supports
- Personal Living
- Finances and Savings
- Health and Safety

All foster youth over 16 years of age are required to participate in a State or County operated Independent Living Program (ILP) and develop of a Transition to Independent Living Plan (TILP). These support service help to achieve the following:

- Foster and/or former foster youth receiving lifeskill training/education and/or supportive transitional housing, benefit substantially. Major, multi-state research of transitional age foster youth recently conducted by Mark Courtney, PhD, at the University of Chicago, clearly demonstrated that for every $1 spent on foster youth ages 18-21 returns $2.40 to the economy through increased employability and productivity, and decreased consumption of public services.

"Thanks for showing me that I am worth being loved...I am worth getting mad at...I am worth being concerned about. Thank you for showing me I am worth something."

−Youth age 18

Chapter 15

A Snapshot of Success in a Transitional Housing Placement Program (THPP)

Learning to Take the Reins

Courtney was a very timid and awkward 16 year old girl. As a foster child for most of her life, Courtney lacked strong social skills and was reluctant to speak up for herself. With the hope that by learning more independent living skills Courtney's self-esteem would improve, Courtney's Social Worker referred her to her state's THPP program.

While excited about the idea of living independently, Courtney's initial apprehension about the program was evident. Because THPP is a voluntary program, Courtney underwent an interviewing process which demonstrated to staff just how introverted she was. However, it was also evident to staff that underneath her timid exterior, Courtney was a survivor who had the potential to blossom into a confident young woman. Once accepted into the program, Courtney was placed in a THPP apartment where she and her Youth Development Specialist (YDS) addressed her short- and long-term goals. Being encouraged to voice her own ambitions was Courtney's first taste of self-empowerment, and it worked to set an encouraging tone for her THPP journey.

Many of Courtney's goals involved learning necessary life skills, such as cooking, grocery shopping and budgeting. Courtney's team worked patiently with her on each skill, addressing not only the skill itself, but how each skill would increase her independence. Courtney's team also addressed her social skills by connecting her with community social events and Independent Living Program activities. With each learned skill and each new experience, Courtney began to emerge as a more self-assured person.

> *"Amazed by her assertiveness, Courtney's team applauded her newfound ability to take the initiative in her life."*

Six months into THPP, a more confident Courtney started to take the reins at her THPP team meetings, voicing not only her needs but also ways she thought each need could be met. For example, one of Courtney's goals was to prepare herself for college. At one team meeting, Courtney voiced her intent to enroll in a community college course in order to strengthen her college applications and get acquainted with college life. Amazed by her assertiveness, Courtney's THPP team applauded her newfound ability to take the initiative in her life.

Courtney spent two years in THPP, learning vital life skills while growing into a more confident and capable young adult. While Courtney may always be shy, her time in THPP did help her find her voice and become more assertive; enabling her to tap into her inner strength in ways that will certainly help her reach all of her life's goals.

The Foster Parent's Role—Enhancing Your Foster Youth's Success

- Encourage your foster youth to actively participate in the Independent Living Program (ILP) services available to them. ILP truly serves as a wonderful gateway to many resources and Lifeskill training.

- Remember, foster youth learn living skills better by observing and practicing in a home setting than in any classroom; basically, your home is the best classroom.

- It is never too soon to engage your foster child in activities that will build his/her independent living skills. As part of your family, it is natural that your foster child be involved in household chores and activities. Look for these natural opportunities to build upon your foster youth's strengths and abilities, empowering them to become self-sufficient young adults.

Here are some tips for helping your foster youth develop Lifeskills in critical life domains:

Employment

Foster youth from age 16 on should be encouraged to get a part time job unless there is a reason they shouldn't. The obvious benefit is that they will be earning money and can begin saving towards emancipation. But they will also learn how to keep a schedule, follow directions, establish work ethics, etcetera. Some of the ways in which you can help your foster youth get a jumpstart on their employment journey is to:

- Help them create a resume and cover letter (show them your resume as an example)

- Fill out a practice job application that your foster youth can keep with them when they go to fill out other applications so they have all of their information ready

- Review common interview questions and practice answering them together

- Help them pick out appropriate clothing to wear to job interviews

- Talk to them about the importance of following up with employers once an application is turned in and sending a thank you note after the interview

Money Management

Money is a crucial area of learning for every young person. Here are some excellent points to remember:

- Receiving their first paycheck is one of the most exciting, rewarding and tempting things they will experience. They will most likely have thought about what they want to do with that money before they even receive it, so it's very important to plan with your youth ahead of time how they will handle their income.

- Talk to them about the importance of understanding the difference between "needs" and "wants."

- Help them to set up a savings account, possibly even a checking/debit account.

- It is recommended that you create a budget together, which includes a significant portion for savings. You should also budget for special purchases that are important to the youth, they need to be able to spend some of their paycheck as a motivation to keep earning paychecks.

- When tax time comes around, help your youth prepare their first tax return as this is another important aspect of money management.

Chapter 15

Education

It is not unusual for a youth who has experienced a lot of disruption in their lives to be behind in school credits. You can do a lot to help them overcome this deficit.

- While they are still in your care, ask your Foster Care Provider if they offer tutoring or a reading-assistance program. If not, ask them to locate a service to support your foster youth.

- Youth in foster care who are age 16 or older have the right to access information regarding available vocational and college education opportunities. There are many grants and scholarships available to children who have been in foster care, so it's important to talk with your youth about his/her academic goals and interests.

- Exposing foster youth to higher education opportunities such as college and vocational schools can help broaden their horizons. You might even visit some college campuses with them.

- Encourage them to start thinking about their future education plans well ahead of emancipation and to apply for financial aid early. Their Foster Care Provider may have staff to assist your youth in this process or they can direct them to someone who can.

Health Management

This is an often overlooked area of training for a foster youth. Many foster children/youth have had inadequate health care until they entered the foster care system. They may not know even the basics of proper health care management. You can help strengthen this life area by doing the following:

- Teach foster youth how to keep their bodies healthy by eating right and getting enough exercise.

- Help them to understand what to do when they become ill; what is an emergency requiring a visit to the Emergency Room and when a regular doctor appointment will be sufficient.

- Learning basic first aid training is very important and is available through your local Red Cross or through your Foster Care Provider.

- Make sure they know how to use their Medicaid/MediCal insurance (finding doctors and dentists who accept their insurance) and how to make sure they receive continuing Medicaid/MediCal coverage after they leave foster care.

- Teach them about the actual costs of health care and how important it is to have some form of health insurance even after their Medicaid/MediCal benefits expire.

Basic Home Maintenance and Repair

- It cannot be stressed enough how important it is to instruct a young person in the basics of house cleaning, laundry, yard work and minor home repairs.

- You can help youth avoid a lot of disasters by explaining and demonstrating how to use cleaning products.

- Teach them how to do household chores and let them work alongside you, giving praise for jobs done well.

- Show them some of the basics of simple home repair and how to use the proper tools for the job.

Grocery Shopping and Cooking

This is another very important skill building area that requires a lot of instruction.

- Young people need to learn how to select food items like produce and meat as well as how to understand pricing and value.

- It is important for youth to learn about food costs and how to get the most value for his/her money, including looking for sales and using coupons.

- Planning meals and shopping for the ingredients can be a fun and bonding time if done with patience and forethought.

- When it comes to cooking, patience and encouragement is required. Most young people are pretty nervous about cooking for the first time, especially if it's for the whole family.

- Working side-by-side with your youth to create a meal can be one of the most rewarding things the two of you can do together. Find out what foods your foster youth enjoys and what s/he would like to learn how to cook.

- Teach different cooking methods like sautéing, baking, barbequing and how to use a slow-cooker such as a crockpot. Include how to use different types of utensils.

- Be sure to teach the youth about food safety, such as proper refrigeration, adequate cooking temperatures and food storage. Don't forget the importance of keeping a kitchen workspace clean and sanitary, especially when cooking meat.

- Don't assume your child knows even the basics about cooking; show him/her each step in the process.

Housing Realities

A great learning experience for your foster youth is to help him/her perform a mock house/apartment hunting exercise.

- Explore how to find housing (classifieds, property management agencies, internet, etcetera), and how to determine the associated expenses, such as utility set-up, internet, cable, telephone services, furniture needs, security deposit, and on-going living essentials (cleaning supplies, food, laundry money, toilet paper, trash bags, etcetera).

- You might provide some samples of actual utility bills to help the youth understand how to read and interpret the information.

- In addition to finding housing, it is important for the youth to learn his/her rights and responsibilities when renting a place and to understand the importance of following rental property rules, maintaining a good relationship with his/her landlord and paying rent on time.

Transportation

Youth in foster care have the opportunity to obtain a driver's license and even own a vehicle; however, this is not the norm and many will not obtain a vehicle until they are out on their own.

- It is important to help your youth learn how to use alternate methods of transportation, such as busses, shuttles, etcetera.

- Even if your foster youth doesn't have his/her own car, teaching him/her the basics of purchasing insurance, doing basic auto maintenance and repair will help his/her long after s/he has left your care.

Chapter 15

GETTING A DRIVER'S LICENSE

Driving is probably one of the most important goals for every teenager. It is a "right-of-passage" issue in our culture that helps usher the youth into adulthood.

- In past years, there was considerable confusion and contradiction around the issue of youth in foster care obtaining a driver's license and driving a car. Finally, due in large part to the lobbying of foster youth themselves, the legislature passed a law that resolves this problem. Foster youth may drive, but under the following specific guidelines:

  · When a youth applies for a learner's permit (the initial license application) it must be signed by either the youth's natural parent, a grandparent, a sibling over the age of 18, or an aunt or uncle. In the absence of a relative, the youth's Foster Care Provider's Social Worker, Probation Officer or Guardian ad litem acting as an officer of the court on behalf of the youth may also sign.

> **Foster Parents should never sign for a foster youth driver's license! If you were to sign, you would become jointly liable with the youth for all financial claims or damages as a result of an accident. Under current law, if a Probation Officer or Placement Worker signs, they are immune from any such liability, thus, the youth would have sole liability.**

  · The youth must show proof of auto insurance prior to obtaining a license, with the minimum coverage required by the youth's state of residence. For youth in California, the minimum is $15,000 for bodily injury to or death of each person as a result of any one accident and, at least $30,000 for bodily injury to or death of all persons as a result of any once accident, and at least $5,000 for damage to property of others as a result of any one accident.

  · The decision for a foster youth to drive should be made by the Child & Family Team and should be a collaborative process with all of the key stakeholders.

  · The youth must also complete the required driver's education and Behind the Wheel Training as does every underage driver. A big decision to be made is what car will be used by the youth for his/her DMV driving exam. The youth can use a foster parent's car or a vehicle from his/her Foster Care Provider, as long as the insurance carrier approves it.

- Driving is an important skill to learn in our culture, but it is a privilege, not a right.

- The tremendous responsibility associated with driving must be understood and communicated to the foster youth.

- A foster youth should not be denied this opportunity to learn to drive when it is appropriate. On the other hand, all the details need to be worked out pursuant to your Foster Care Provider's policy and your state's law. If you have any questions, please ask the youth's Foster Care Provider's Social Worker.

SOCIAL SKILLS AND RELATIONSHIPS

One area that is too often overlooked, is helping a youth learn how to appropriately interact with others, especially those outside of his/her age group.

- Foster youth will want to go on dates, attend dances and other school events, and do things that youth their age do. By encouraging them to participate in positive social activities, you will allow them the opportunity to gain social skills that will serve them later in life.

- Take your foster youth out to dinner to a nice restaurant so s/he can learn proper protocol. Also, take him/her to a play or music event, or have the youth attend the events of other children/youth in the home, such as sporting events, concerts, etcetera. Expose youth to social opportunities they might otherwise never have.

- Let your foster youth make his/her own appointments (in person and over the phone), empower youth to talk to his/her doctor about his/her needs and concerns rather than doing it for him/her.

- Encourage the youth to advocate for themselves. In this high-tech era, with cell phones, the internet and less face-to-face communication, help your foster youth understand the difference of communicating in person versus over email or text messaging, and how non-verbal communication can be interpreted differently. All of these experiences will help build confidence and will broaden their understanding of life.

- Instruct your foster youth about appropriate conduct at work, how to properly interact with employers, adults, senior citizens, people with disabilities, etcetera. Don't expect the youth to know, but rather make this another learning experience.

GIVING BACK

- Many schools are now requiring graduating students to perform some type of community service as a way of expanding a young person's world view and what impact they can have.

- Involving youth in volunteer projects that you may be involved in can bring a new perspective to their lives. Model for them the value of giving!

- Sometimes the simplest thing can make a huge difference in their lives. Asking an older child to show another child how to do something like cook a meal or even help with homework, can strengthen the youth's confidence and sense of him/herself as a young adult.

FOCUS ON THE BIG PICTURE—THE FUTURE

It is never too early to talk with your foster teen about his/her plans for when s/he is no longer in care. It's a subject that some may not want to discuss, for a number of reasons, fear being a big one. You can help youth face their fears and help prepare their path to success. Here are some suggestions:

- Empower the youth to be fully involved in directing his/her own permanency planning and decision making

- Help youth find family/relatives s/he can connect with

- Help youth create a "life-book" filled with their stories about growing up, including photos when possible, and contact information of friends and family members

- Make an effort to become a permanent connection for youth yourself

- Maybe even consider teenage or adult adoption

- Encourage as many positive adult relationships as possible

- Become familiar with programs for Transitional Age youth, such as the Transitional Housing Programs (THPP) and Transitional Housing Programs-Plus (THP Plus) programs, and encourage your teen to participate in them. These programs offer a vital lifeline between foster care and adult independence.

- Encourage participation in the Independent Living Program (ILP) and other foster-youth focused advocacy groups, such as the California Youth Connection (CYC), in order to maximize opportunities for youth to become empowered for success in adult life.

- Know the services and opportunities available to foster youth once they are on their own and make sure your youth knows how to access these services.

- The steps you take to ensure a successful transition for your foster youth will make all the difference!

Chapter 15

Resources

There are many, many resources, especially web-based resources, available to foster youth and foster parents to help make the transition to adulthood much easier. Here are some of the web-based links to become familiar with.

www.tayconnected.com

Lifebook for Transitional Age Youth: www.fcni.org/books

http://familiesnow.org

http://www.johnburtonfoundation.org/

http://www.nrcyd.ou.edu

http://findyouthinfo.gov/

http://www.tipstars.org/

http://www.cacareerzone.com

www.vstreet.com

http://www.newwaystowork.org/documents/ytatdocuments/CareerDevGuidebookJUNE2009%282%29.pdf

http://www.caseylifeskills.org

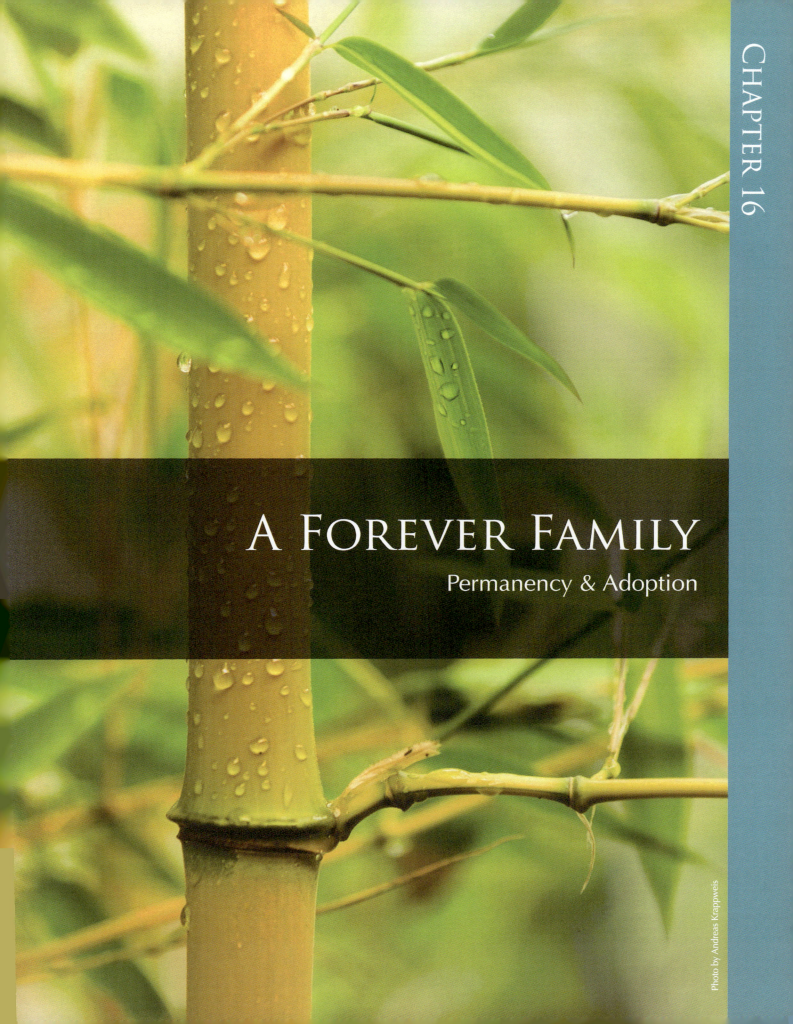

CHAPTER 16

A Forever Family

Permanency & Adoption

Photo by Andreas Krappweis

CHAPTER 16

A FOREVER FAMILY
Permanency & Adoption

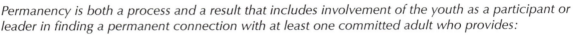

PERMANENCY

The goal of foster care is not to provide a child or youth with a long-term foster home; it is to move a child to "Permanency" as soon as possible. All children need permanent, stable relationships and life circumstances.

So, what do we mean by "Permanency?" The following is a universally accepted definition of permanency as it applies to foster children and youth:

> *Permanency is both a process and a result that includes involvement of the youth as a participant or leader in finding a permanent connection with at least one committed adult who provides:*
> - *A safe, stable and secure parenting or parent-like relationship*
> - *Love*
> - *Unconditional commitment*
> - *Lifelong support in the context of reunification, a legal adoption, or guardianship, where possible, and in which the youth has the opportunity to maintain contacts with important persons including brothers and sisters*
> - *Lifelong Permanent Connection with an adult who consistently states and demonstrates that she or he has entered an unconditional, life-long parent-like relationship with the youth. The youth agrees that the adult will play this role in his or her life*

THE NEED FOR A PERMANENT PLACEMENT

There are 130,000 children in foster care in the United States who cannot return to their birth families and are waiting for a permanent family. These children have needs and backgrounds that require special considerations:

- They tend to be older children with 47% of the waiting children age nine or older;

- They have spent a significant time in foster care; on average, these children have been in the foster care system for 42 months (three and a half years) or longer;

- They are disproportionately children of color, who experience even longer stays in foster care and fewer adoptions than their white peers;

- Nearly 90% of the children adopted from foster care are classified as having "special needs," many with complicated traumatic histories exacerbated by separation from birth family, multiple moves and unresolved grief;

- High needs/issues put children and youth at risk of emotional and mental health challenges that can be barriers to adoption.

While a broad array of individualized permanency options exist, reunification and adoption reamain the preferred choices.

Adoption

The Adopting Foster Parent

As a foster parent, there will inevitably come a time when a child or youth in your care becomes eligible for adoption. It is natural that you might consider becoming the child's adoptive parent and many foster parents do adopt. Here are a few statements from adoptive parents and foster children:

- *"It is a rewarding experience to see the expression on a child's face at the adoption hearing when the Judge says to the child, 'You are now a member of this family!'"*

- *"Personally, the opportunity to adopt has been one of the great privileges of my life. It has not always been an easy journey, but it has been one of the most meaningful and joyful things I have ever undertaken. My daughter could not be more mine if I had given birth to her myself."*

- *"Adopting our foster child was a way to continue the relationship we had developed over the years and to know that this child who we love so much would always be part of our family."*

The law requires Child Welfare Services and the Court to have a concurrent plan in place while a child is in the process of reunification with their family of origin. Concurrent planning is a structured approach to moving children more quickly from the uncertainty of foster care to the stability and security of a permanent family. It emphasizes working toward family reunification, while at the same time establishing an alternative or back-up permanency plan to be implemented if children cannot safely return to their biological parents.

If Family Reunification or Kin-Care are unattainable, three other options may be considered:
- Court guardianship
- Guardianship without court involvement
- Adoption

In many cases, the Juvenile Court will consider adoption as the only option depending on the child's age and adoption suitability.

Even though the need for adoptive families is great, there is no expectation that a foster parent/family must adopt their foster child. In fact, it is very important for foster parents not to be influenced by well-meaning pressure from the child's placement worker or even the child themselves. Most importantly, a decision to adopt must never be made out of a sense of guilt.

Foster-Adoption

Because the first priority for every child in out-of-home placement is reunification with biological family whenever possible, the foster-adoption (fost-adopt) parent must understand that while the process may be emotionally challenging, it is ultimately about the best interest of the child.

Foster-adoption is unpredictable and uncertain. One reason many choose not to opt for this type of placement is that very often the children placed in fost-adopt families are young, including infants, and there is a higher likelihood they will be placed with biological family or next of kin. When these foster children are returned to bio-family, foster parents can be left with a tremendous sense of loss and disappointment.

When hopeful foster/adoptive parents take care to educate themselves about the program, they must ask themselves hard questions, and have realistic expectations of the risks involved. When these parents know about the legal risk in advance, and are willing to assume it in exchange for the possibility that they may ultimately be able to adopt the child, it can be an excellent option. Foster parents may be "Plan B," but that is much better than having no alternative permanency options for a foster child.

Chapter 16

ADOPTION: IT'S A LIFE CHANGING DECISION

Assessing the risks that are present in an adoption is important for potential parents, but this process must be kept in proper perspective or it could be counterproductive. Parents deciding whether or not to fost-adopt should consider the following:

- Over-evaluating or over-emphasizing the risks of an adoption can create unnecessary stress and can put a damper on the happiness and excitement that is part of the journey through the adoption process.

- In evaluating an adoption opportunity, parents must always look closely at medical, financial, legal, and emotional issues; the extensive vetting process, and then determine if the challenges and risks fall within an acceptable range for them. On the other hand, this must be balanced with "what is in the best interest of the foster child/youth!" Does the child/youth's need for permanency outweigh the risk, challenges and inconveniences of adoption?

- Since prospective adoptive parents will usually have very little first-hand experience in understanding all that is involved with the adoption process, seeking the advice of an adoption social worker, counselor, caseworker, adoption attorney or another fost-adopt parent is strongly recommended.

REWARDS AND CHALLENGES OF ADOPTING

When considering whether or not to adopt, it is important to explore the rewards of such an undertaking and the challenges.

Rewards
- Gives the child/youth a permanent "forever-family"
- Assists the child/youth to reach his/her full potential
- Breaks the cycle of abuse and neglect, hopefully providing the child with a healthy future
- Gives you the opportunity to be a significant parent to the child/youth, nurturing and guiding them towards success and happiness
- Adds depth and meaning to your life

Challenges
- Child may struggle with loyalty issues
- The child/youth may have psychological, emotional and/or behavioral issues
- The possibility of attachment or bonding challenges
- The emotional and physical demands
- Redefining success and expectation
- Taking on new legal and financial responsibilities/liabilities
- Rejection by family members and/or peers
- Conflicting cultural and value systems
- Unrealistic expectations of the child/youth of the adoptive family

When considering adoption, you must take the time to do some soul searching and ask yourself:
- What has been your experience with the child/youth you are considering adopting?
- What does your extended family think of the idea?

- What is your motivation?
- Are you being pressured or possibly manipulated to make this decision?
- Can you commit to the possibility of having to manage challenging behaviors long-term?
- Are there other adoptive parents you can talk to?

Once you decide that adoption may be the right choice for you, you will still want to do a lot more investigating in order to make an informed final decision. You should prepare a checklist of questions about the child's biological family history, especially regarding possible genetic/medical issues. You must be very clear about the child's short term and long term needs and if you are ready to unconditionally commit to this child, no matter what happens, as you would for your own biological child. Some other questions to ask yourself include:

- Are you okay with the child's desire to know and interact with their biological parent(s)/family, and allow them to be part of child's life?
- Are you willing to work through a tough transition stage?
- Do you have a solid and persistent support system and network?
- Is the child ready to be adopted? Do they want to be adopted?
- Have you considered the question of "cultural and ethnic" impact, values and conflicts?
- Are you prepared for the potential mental and emotional challenges that may occur during the adoption process?

The Fost-Adopt Process

In most Fost-Adopt programs, the child is usually placed with a pre-identified fost-adopt family before the child's biological parents' parental rights have been permanently terminated. Generally, the fost-adopt parents make a commitment to adopt the child if and when those rights are terminated and the child is legally free to be adopted.

Foster Parents need to be supportive of the biological family at all times. Should the reunification attempt fail, the adoptive foster family will be next in line for the target permanent family. The main reason for concurrent planning and a fost-adopt placement is to prevent multiple moves if family reunification fails. Key features of fost-adopt programs include:

- Placement with a fost-adopt family before the child's biological parents' parental rights have been terminated

- Efforts at family reunification may be ongoing, or biological parents may be appealing a decision to terminate their parental rights

- Generally, children placed in a fost-adopt program are considered less likely than others to return to the biological family

- The foster family agrees to adopt the child if/when the biological parents' parental rights are terminated

- The foster family serves as the primary parent caretaker throughout the concurrent planning process

> It is necessary and vital for the fost-adopt family to support the biological family and to refer to them respectfully since reunification is the first goal of Concurrent Planning. There is a possibility that fost-adopt parents will be working with the biological parents as mentors or to educate them about the specific needs of their child during the early part of the planning process.

A child who is available for adoption through fost-adopt may have some attachment issues and it is good to know that these can be healed, though sometimes not without a lot of patience and persistence. Research does show that dealing with attachment issues while the child is young makes a difference in behavioral problems.

Additionally, once parental rights have been terminated, the child will be less likely to harbor ill will towards the fost-adopt parents if they have shown respect for their parents and support during the reunification process.

It is extremely important that foster families do not state or indicate their willingness or desire to adopt a child before they are absolutely sure they are going to make that commitment. It is very damaging for a child to have families say they will adopt them and then not follow through. The timing of talking with a child about issues of adoption should involve the Child & Family Team.

The Adoption Process

The formal adoption process begins after all efforts toward reunification have been exhausted. Even though you have completed a home study as part of your foster home certification process, another more comprehensive Adoption Home Study must be completed by a licensed Adoption Agency. This could include your Foster Care Provider, an outside Adoptions Agency or a State Adoptions Department.

The Adoption Home Study is a standardized, statewide format which is extremely thorough and comprehensive. It involves a series of mandatory meetings (both individually and as a couple if applicable) with an Adoptions Social Worker. At least one of these meetings will take place in your home. If other people live with you, including any children, they will also be interviewed. You will be asked to provide documents including birth certificates, marriage license, child abuse clearance (the agency will tell you how to do this), health records, criminal background reports and personal references.

You will also be required to provide written information about yourselves, your family and your life experiences. This may include any family history of alcoholism, substance abuse, illegal activity, sexual or child abuse, domestic violence or any criminal record. During this process, you will also talk with the Case Worker about your motivation to adopt and the types of children you feel you can best parent and accept into your family and home.

Once the Home Study is completed and the parents are approved, the adoption can proceed through the Juvenile Court process. There is generally a six-month period where you will have the child/youth with you under the adoption process before it will become finalized.

The last step in the process is the finalization of the adoption through a hearing before the Juvenile Court Judge. Once completed, you will become the legal guardian of your newly adopted child, and legally responsible for him/her as if they were your biological child.

Managing the Adoption Process

The adoption process is not always smooth; in fact, it's inevitable that some bumps will be encountered along the way, including:

- Delays in the court process
- Home study and adoption suitability issues
- Resistance or interference from the child's birth family
- Lack of accurate information or misinformation
- Miscommunications between prospective adopting family, adoptee and the adoption Social Worker
- Decisions made under pressure

One of the most difficult parts of the adoption process for the adoptive parents is managing the anxiety that can occur from court delays, and surprisingly, anxiety may increase as the finalization date gets closer. This anxiety is normal and often what most adoptive parents talk about as being one of the hardest parts of the process. The uncertainty that occurs during the adoption process will naturally cause stress because you have committed yourself and your family to the child for a lifetime with a degree of risk that the adoption might not happen.

It is extremely important that you talk about your anxiety and feelings with your spouse or partner, other adult family members and your Foster Care Provider's Social Worker. It may be helpful to attend adoption support groups or to connect personally with other adoptive parents who are going through the same process or who have completed the adoption process.

The Adoptive Child

Once an adoption is final, the child may react in some ways that you might not expect. Often there is a period of time where everything goes extremely well, often called the "Honeymoon period." The child and adoptive family are euphoric about the adoption, and everyone is on their best behavior. The child and family may have an idea or expectations about what their new life together will be like and when the reality of daily life sets in, these expectations may not be completely met. Many times an adopted child will display challenging behaviors, testing his/her adoptive parents' limits as a way to find out, "do you really love me?"

Many children who have been in foster care and are then adopted, experience "attachment issues" or issues related to the trauma they have experienced which brought them to the attention of the Juvenile Court System. These issues can manifest in difficult behaviors, sometimes extreme or dramatic mood swings, even when things seem to be going smoothly.

Children who have had multiple placements may also manifest challenging behaviors or exaggerated emotions. This is a self-protection tool they have developed with the idea that they will reject their new parents before the parents reject them. They are testing their new adoptive parents to see how unconditional their love is. Parental skills in working with traumatized children/youth can be very effective in stabilizing behaviors and promoting wellness.

On the other hand, the adopted child may not experience any of these struggles mentioned, and instead express deep appreciation for being given a new life. Adoptive parents will begin to immediately see the child's growth and success as a result of having the support and love of their new family.

FAQ: Adoption

How does changing the child's last name affect their identity?

The child may experience mixed emotions. On the one hand, their new name symbolizes their acceptance into their new family and can change the course of the child/youth's history. On the other hand, this change may evoke a sense of loss of identity. It's important to be sensitive to all these possibilities and support the child/youth in dealing with their mixed emotions.

Is there financial support for the adopted child/youth?

Most fost-adopt cases are eligible for financial assistance. These rates are generally lower than what private foster parents receive, but are designed to cover basic care and maintenance. Additionally, there is an Adoptions Assistance Program (AAP) which will cover an array of post-adoption services. Consult your state and/or Foster Care Provider's guidelines for more information.

Does an adopted child/youth have medical insurance provided for them?

An adopted foster child/youth is covered under Medicaid/MediCal up to 21 years of age, including eligibility for mental health services.

Will my adopted child/youth have contact with his/her birth parents/family?

That depends on the conditions of the adoption, and whether it is considered "open" or "closed." The growing trend in this country is toward open adoptions where the adopting family has some contact with the child/youth's biological family. While this may seem a bit daunting to adopting parents, in the long run this contact has been found to be very beneficial for everyone concerned. There are adoption agreements that can be mediated before adoptions that spell out the terms of contact between the adopted child/youth and his/her biological family. These agreements can be can be very helpful in setting up healthy boundaries between the biological family and adopting family.

How should I respond if my child/youth asks questions about their biological family?

Most adopted children/youth will, at some point in their lives, have questions about their family of origin. It is important that adoptive parents not respond with negative emotion to this curiosity as the child/youth's questions have nothing to do with how they feel about you. Telling a child/youth that questions about their biological family bothers you is very inappropriate and can even be damaging for the child/youth. Use your active listening skills and hear what they have to say. Validate their feelings and answer what you can. The adoption may be final, but the adoption process will continue throughout the child's life and yours.

What happens if we experience serious behavioral or emotional problems? Is it possible to send the child/youth back?

No. It is essential to the child/youth's welfare that a sense of unconditional love, support and attachment is established. Therefore, it is important to be proactive and develop a support system for the child/youth and your family so you can handle any behavioral or emotional problems should they arise. For example:

· Involvement and participation in adoption support groups and/or mentoring from an adoptive parent.
· Utilization of the Adoption Assistance Program and contacts in your state.
· Continued collaboration with Social Services and other agency partners involved in the adoption.
· Knowledge of your local mental health system and its resources.
· Most important of all, don't be afraid to ask for help!

Will my adopted child/youth need counseling to help them cope with questions and concerns about their identity?

Many adopted children benefit from counseling at different points in their lives, particularly as they go through periods of developmental change. Be supportive of this and make it a priority. It may also be helpful for your adoptive child/youth to meet and talk with others who have also been adopted as this will help them know that they are not alone.

Will my adopted child/youth still be eligible for any special financial aid for college?

Each scholarship or grant for financial aid has different qualifications, however some are available to any child/youth who was ever in foster care; there are even grants for adopted children.

Tips for Successfully Parenting an Adopted Child/Youth

- Maintain a strong marriage or family support system (i.e., respite, relationship building)

- Maintain a strong, effective community support network (i.e., church, neighbors, extended family, adoptive parent group, etcetera)

- Understand the child/youth's biological and cultural background

- Avoid "put downs" of the child/youth's biological family

- Build a relationship of mutual respect with the child/youth

- Understand your legal responsibilities

- Educate yourself about adoptions, child development, trauma informed interventions, and parent skill building. Become an "expert" on parenting an adopted child.

> The decision to adopt a foster child/youth is a life changing one, certainly for the child/youth, but also for you and your whole family. It is not to be entered into lightly because there are many challenges, however, it is one of the most rewarding, satisfying and loving things you will ever do.

Other Permanency Considerations

Whether you are on a foster-adoption track or not, it is important for foster parents to always attempt to maintain a supportive, nurturing relationship with their former foster children/youth. Always attempt to make your foster parenting experience a "lifelong" relationship. Consider doing the following when your foster child leaves your home:

- Make yourself available for phone calls, email messages, visits and letters.

- Ask your exiting foster youth if you can have his/her contact information after s/he leaves your home.

- Consider being Facebook or twitter friends with your former foster child, or to keep in contact through one of the many other social networking options.

- When appropriate, make yourself available to your foster youth's biological family as a resource and support.

- If your foster youth enters into one of a Transitional Age Youth Programs, allow them to come "home" to visit, for holidays or just for some support and nurturing. Offer to help him/her with lifeskill development activities.

- It may also be appropriate for you to provide a personal reference for a former foster youth.

- Ask your foster children/youth if you can put up pictures of them just like you would one of your own children. Have them send you pictures after they have left your care. Offer to send them pictures as well.

- Attend significant events, (i.e., graduations, weddings, performances, etcetera)

> Remember, it's all about maintaining a permanent, lifelong relationship!

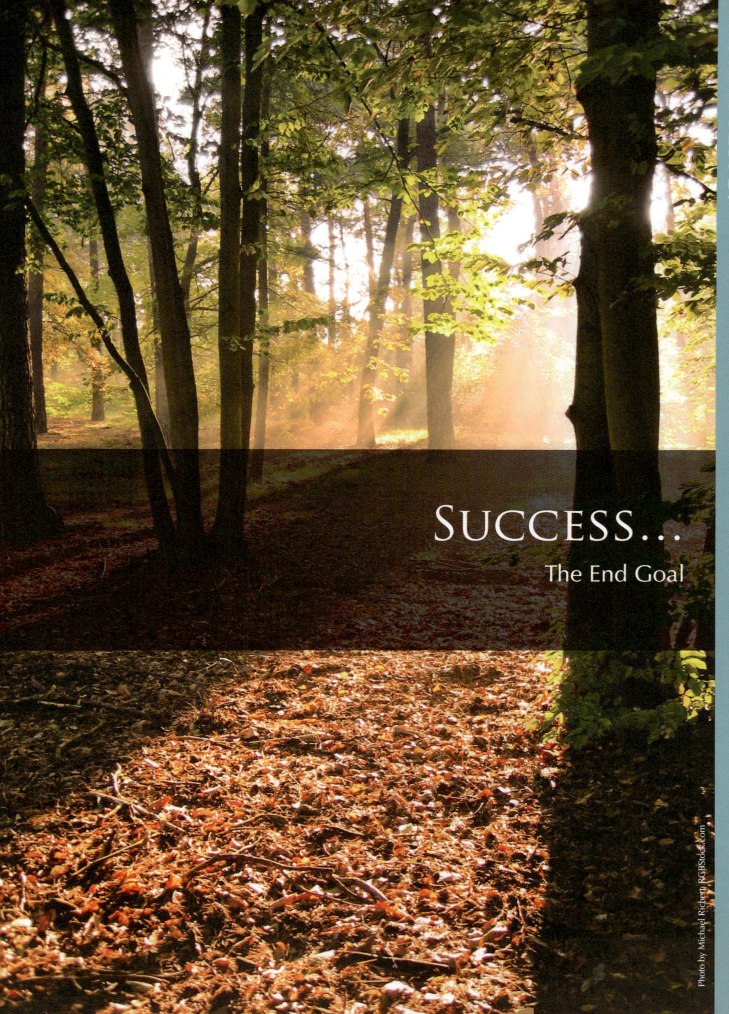

CHAPTER 17

Success...
The End Goal

Chapter 17

Success...
The End Goal

Let's face it, you became a therapeutic foster parent because you care deeply and you want to make a profound difference in the life of a child or youth who has experienced trauma and disappointment. You want to see your efforts make a visible, tangible difference in improving the lives of the children you have cared for—every foster parent wants to be successful! But, what does this mean? That is what we will discuss in this chapter; how "success" is determined in the foster care world.

Important Premises

- ***Safety, Permanency and Wellbeing*** for every foster child and youth is always the goal, the ultimate measure of success.

- ***Foster Care*** is never an end, it is ***only a temporary intervention*** to achieve permanency.

- Your job is to serve as a "***Resource Parent,***" guiding children and youth to permanency and serving as a resource to them after they have left your home.

- As with your biological children, foster children will leave your home. It makes no difference whether they are with you a few months or many years, there is a ***separation and loss*** process which must be anticipated and embraced.

Federal Outcomes For Foster Care

Because the Federal Government is the primary funder of foster care, Congress has set three overarching outcomes for the foster care system, including:
- Safety
- Permanency
- Wellbeing

Foster Parent "success" will be discussed as it relates to Safety, Permanency and Wellbeing.

Safety—The Obvious

Safety underlies the reason all children and youth become engaged with the foster care system. Children who are abused and/or neglected need to be protected from further occurrences of abuse and neglect. Children with mental or emotional problems need to be protected so they can heal and reduce the risk of injury to themselves or others. Youth involved in the juvenile justice system need to receive treatment services to enable them to no longer be a safety risk to the community or to themselves.

Therapeutic Foster Parents successfully provide Safety for foster children and youth by:
- Providing a safe, clean and nurturing home
- Maintaining a comprehensive foster parenting risk-prevention plan
- Fully complying with all health and safety regulations and requirements
- Ensuring that foster youth are never subjected to physical or verbal abuse, threats or humiliation
- Carefully following all "Safety" or risk-prevention plans

- Providing 24/7 Emergency Shelter Care
- Providing effective "care and supervision" to prevent harm or injury; especially with children with a history of self-harm or abuse. This includes knowing who the foster youth is with at all times and preventing risky behaviors
- Protecting your foster child or youth from court disallowed contacts and associations with questionable, unsavory or negative individuals
- Making sure foster children and youth's physical and mental health needs are being met
- Maintaining parental blocks and software to protect foster youth from Internet predators
- Providing healthy, nutritious meals and snacks

Foster parents who are diligent to ensure Safety, are always the most successful!

Permanency—What Is It?

Over the past 10 years, there has been a strong public policy mandate to move foster children and youth to "Permanency," as long term foster care is no longer seen as being in the best interest of the foster child or youth. Fortunately, there is a fairly universal understanding of Permanency.

Permanency is both a process and a result which involves finding a permanent connection with at least one committed adult who provides:
- A safe, stable and secure parenting relationship
- Love
- Unconditional commitment
- Lifelong support in the context of reunification, legal adoption, or guardianship when possible; and in which the foster child/youth have the opportunity to maintain contacts with important persons including brothers, sisters and thier kin

A permanent lifelong connection involves an adult who consistently states and demonstrates that s/he has entered into an unconditional parent-like relationship with a foster youth and the youth agrees to have this lifelong relationship.

Foster Parent Success and Permanency

Therapeutic Foster Parents play a very important, critical part in helping foster children and youth achieve permanence. Please note there are plenty of ways in which you can help your foster child achieve permanency without becoming an adopting or guardian family. Here are some examples of how you can be successful in helping your foster child/youth achieve permanency:

- **Providing Stability:** It cannot be stressed enough the importance of providing a safe and stable home. When a child or youth feels protected and free from abuse, the healing and recovery process will take place much more quickly. You may struggle with your foster child's resistance, rejection and challenging behaviors, but this is an important process in making them ready for permanency! Your family stability will be a life changer. You are successful in providing any length of stability for a foster child/youth.

- **Modeling Proper Parenting:** Most foster children and youth probably do not know what it means to experience a healthy parent-child relationship. A key ingredient to the definition of "Permanency" is to provide a safe, stable and secure parenting relationship. This is your opportunity to model that kind of parenting. Consistency, respect, setting limits, showing compassion, acknowledging successes, praising, guiding, encouraging, showing interest, engaging and having fun are all part of proper parenting. Whether or not you see a positive response, providing model parenting substantially enhances the foster child/youth's success toward permanency.

- **Therapeutic Parenting:** The Therapeutic Foster Parent is undoubtedly one, if not the most significant, role in promoting a successful transition to permanence. All foster children have experienced a degree of trauma from which they need to recover and heal. Therapeutic Foster Care parents guide and help their foster children navigate through the wellness and recovery process, adding so much along the way. It is an absolute success for a TFC parent to see their foster child/youth stabilize in their care and be moved to a permanent or less restrictive situation.

- **Working with the Target Permanent Family:** For years, it was taboo for foster parents to have anything to do with biological parents, kin or adoptive parents. But this is no longer the case. Therapeutic foster parents have an awesome opportunity to transfer skills and knowledge, and serve as a mentor or support to the parents the foster child will be living with long term. This type of "mentoring" relationship only breeds success.

- **Providing Adult Foster Care:** Under the 2008 Federal Fostering Youth Connections Act, states such as California are able to provide continued foster care services until a foster youth turns 21 years old, enabling foster parents to continue providing care for their foster youth who would traditionally be emancipated from "the system" at 18 years of age. This type of foster parenting means providing secure parenting, unconditional commitment and support with lifelong implications—all ingredients of permanency. Continuing to parent your foster youth until they can substantially complete college or become vocationally or financially secure is a huge contribution to said youth's success.

- **Supporting a Foster Youth in Independent Living:** Your former foster youth may choose to participate in a transitional housing or independent living program. Here is yet another opportunity for you to contribute to his or her success. There are countless ways that you can provide your former foster youth your continued support including: make yourself available for them to talk to; invite them to holiday events at your home, so they feel included and connected; remember their birthdays and offer to celebrate with them; and invite them to visit from time to time for a bit of respite and relaxation. Your opportunity to be a supportive parent can go way beyond the period of time that your foster youth actually lives with you.

- **Maintaining a Life-Long Connection:** Fostering a child or youth doesn't need to be a short-term relationship for you or the foster child/youth. Foster parents are always encouraged to make themselves available and accessible to their foster children/youth after they have left the foster home. Maintaining a relationship is especially easier in this era of high-tech communications. Email, text messaging, Facebook and other social networking programs make staying in contact so much easier. Foster parents should be encouraged to make an effort to keep in contact with their foster children/youth if they have a child's/youth's permission to do so. Regular communications and birthday and holiday cards go a long way in sending the message, "I care" and "you are important to me." Ongoing efforts to reach out very often turn into opportunities for you to continue to "parent" through active listening and sharing your counsel and advice.

- **Adoption or Guardianship:** It is no surprise that many short-term foster care placements turn into permanent adoption or guardianship situations. Once positive family relationships are established, it is hard to disrupt them. Security, healing, familiarity, acceptance and concern take hold; plus, change means more trauma for the child or youth to experience. Adopting a foster child or youth is a monumental and life-changing decision, which is made by both the foster family and the foster child/youth. Not every foster family makes the decision to do this, but those who do, provide an invaluable life-long benefit to the child/youth.

Another related permanency action a foster parent can take is to do an "Adult Adoption." Once a foster youth is 18, they can choose to be adopted as an adult. This affords the same rights and privileges of any adopted child, but with a much simpler, less complicated process.

Please refer to the "Forever Family" chapter for more information on adopting.

Wellbeing—The Promotion of Health and Success

There are many ways "Wellbeing" is defined in our culture. There is financial wellbeing, social wellbeing and physical wellbeing. For our purpose, think of the wellbeing of a foster child in terms of a state of being healthy, happy, prosperous and able to succeed in life.

> Every foster child and youth has been subjected to a degree of trauma from which they need to heal. It's great to find a child a permanent family, but if wellbeing is not achieved, they will continue to need help; even many years after the fact. A lack of "wellbeing" could be seriously disruptive to their success for a lifetime!

Seven Components of Wellness

The following seven components of Wellness apply to all of us, but they are especially important conditions for foster children and youth to achieve.

- **Purpose in Life:** Empowered through personal strengths to set and achieve life goals and dreams

- **Achieve Success:** Able to engage in, and experience productive, satisfying education, work and recreation; and enjoy imaginative and creative expression

- **Joyful Relationships:** Able to develop and maintain healthy, supportive and loving long-term relationships

- **Healthy Body:** Practices a healthy lifestyle and diet in order to prevent debilitating illnesses, diseases and injuries; and able to secure appropriate health care when needed

- **Healthy Mind:** Free from, or effectively managing, debilitating, intrusive and troubling feelings and behaviors

- **Stable Living:** Experiencing quality of life through a safe and stable living environment they can call "home," while possessing the lifeskills necessary for self-care and independence

- **Happy & Hopeful:** Experiencing personal satisfaction and joyfulness; able to see the future with positive anticipation and hope

Wellbeing—Mission Accomplished

Foster Parents very often do not realize how valuable and impactful their work is in promoting and achieving foster child/youth wellbeing. Truthfully, it is profound! The following are clear examples of a successful foster parent.

- **Modeling:** Foster Parents are handed the opportunity, seven days a week, to model and demonstrate the seven components of Wellbeing presented above. It makes no difference how long the child or youth is in your care, every minute s/he is observing, absorbing and experiencing your wellbeing. So, "be-well!"

- **Encouragement:** If you are a foster parent who provides hope, ongoing encouragement, strength-based interventions, positive feedback and consultation, coupled with respect and compassion, you are doing much towards enhancing your foster child's wellbeing.

- **Therapeutic Foster Care:** As presented in Chapter 3, TFC is far more than basic foster care seasoned with a little mental health service and behavioral management. It is a medically necessary treatment service where the foster parent plays a very significant role as a professional team member in a highly structured family-based treatment process. When you are a TFC parent, you are completely focused on your foster child/youth's "wellbeing" and making him/her ready for permanence. TFC is so important that it has become the national preferred-placement for traumatized children and youth requiring treatment services. Children and youth receiving TFC are 85% more likely to have a successful transition to permanency.

- **Emergency Shelter Care:** Foster Parents who make their home available 24/7 to receive a traumatized victim of abuse or neglect provide an invaluable service. When a child is removed from his/her living situation for whatever reason, it is essential that they be delivered to a safe, nurturing family environment with parents skilled to meet their needs. Foster parents providing family-based emergency care are basically "first-responders" in the therapeutic wellness-recovery process.

- **Basic Care:** Foster Parents contribute to child and youth wellness continuously by providing every day care. Taking a foster child/youth for physical or dental appointments, serving healthy meals and snacks, helping with homework, signing them up for sports, music or art, or letting them experience a play, concert or cultural event is part of the wellbeing process. Never underestimate the value of your day-in and day-out routines and their positive impact on a foster child/youth's wellbeing.

- **Lifeskills Development:** Teaching a foster child or youth even the basics of successful daily living is contributing towards their wellbeing. Learning good personal hygiene, how to cook a meal and/or how prepare food, having proper social skills and manners, or how to shop for clothing, how to budget and save, and other similar lifeskills are essential for achieving wellbeing.

- **Improvements at Discharge:** Seriously, if a foster child or youth leaves your home having made any improvements in the seven components of wellness listed above, you have been successful! Remember, you never know how much was "caught" and absorbed by a foster child/youth during their time in your care. Seeds are always planted, but some take years to come to fruition!

Never be discouraged as a foster parent. There will always be challenges and sometimes, the feeling of failure. But in the end, it is inevitable that you will positively benefit the child or youth you have served in foster care!

"I love to call you two my mom and dad when I'm talking with my friends or whoever it may be, and I appreciate you guys thinking of me as a son."

–Youth age 15 to Foster Parents

"Aunt Edith"

The following story was written by Jim Roberts, the Founder/CEO of Family Care Network, inc. and is based upon his experience as a Probation Officer. As you will see, this amazing foster family had a profound effect on motivating Jim to start the Family Care Network. It is hoped that this story will be equally inspiring and encouraging to others who have chosen to serve foster children and youth.

I knocked on the door of this unassuming country home, distinguished by its gravel driveway, giant Cottonwood and Locust trees, interesting vines and yard trinkets, beautiful roses, assorted clutter and a massive vegetable garden which boldly consumed about a third of the yard.

The door opened, "Hello, I'm Jim Roberts, the new Deputy Probat—"

"Yes," Edith interrupted, "Maury has told me all about you and I have been looking forward to meeting you. Brother Roberts, please, please come in."

Edith called everyone "brother or sister," I think it had to do with her Pentecostal roots, and everyone, and I mean everyone, even the Judge, called her "Aunt Edith." Edith Dawson was a short, stocky woman in her late 70s, who possessed a beautiful round face adorned with a very engaging smile and bright eyes, crowned with a full head of well-manicured white hair. She wore flowered dresses and walked with a very distinct, almost painful to watch, limp.

As I stepped through her door, Aunt Edith declared, "Let me introduce you to my family." She then began to gesture to a wall of photos, stating, "This is... and these are her children...and her grandchildren... She came to live with us in...And this is..." I stood in amazement, stunned, at the hundreds of pictures which hung on every wall; pictures of children and families, weddings, as well as letters and cards and even children's drawings. These were Edith's and Jimmy's kids, and their kids, and their kids-kids—literally hundreds of them. These were the foster children they had cared for during their over five decades as foster parents—simply amazing!

Edith ushered me into her small living room and parked me on a small, Victorian era sofa. The room was moderately cluttered, but very bright and clean, and there were several vases of freshly cut flowers. It smelled, looked and reminded me of my grandmother's house. "Please, make yourself comfortable," she said as she quickly scooted into an adjacent room. "Do you take cream or sugar in your coffee?" she asked. But before I could even answer her, she appeared in the door carrying a tray with an ornate China coffee/tea pot with two matching China tea cups and a plate of freshly baked chocolate chip cookies. "Now, tell me about yourself," she stated.

Before I knew it, she had me telling her my entire life's story; like a seasoned therapists, she drew out every bit of content from my soul. At some point in our conversation, her husband Jimmy came up the stairs from their large, finished basement. He was a small, frail looking gentleman, with great wit and a wonderful sense of humor. After we were introduced, he made a few witty comments and quickly ventured outside to tend to some chores.

Chapter 17

Now it was Aunt Edith's turn. She described many of her "kids," sharing some very meaningful, heart wrenching stories. She then proceeded to tell me how she and Jimmy had lost their only son in a car accident to a drunk driver. She concluded her comments with a statement that I have never forgotten. "For some reason, God took our son, but then He gave us hundreds of children and blessed us with an unimaginable family." Aunt Edith loved her "kids." She could describe them for you in great detail; what happened to them and where they were right now. And her face radiated joy and pride as she spoke about them all.

I was there to discuss with Edith the possibility of their taking in yet another foster child. The child in question was a pre-adolescent girl who had been severely abused by parents heavily involved in the occult. Edith and Jimmy had taken a break for several years due to poor health, but had recently requested to start fostering again. Given their age and health, there was some hesitation on my department's part to place the child with them, but after speaking with Edith, we acquiesced and made the placement.

The girl would be the Dawson's last foster child. She'd had a rough transition to foster care, but ended up doing very well. She stayed with Edith and Jimmy for several years before being placed with a family member. The timing of her move was good as the Dawsons' health had begun to further deteriorate. Six or seven years after the girl moved on, in 1985, Jimmy passed away. Six months later, Aunt Edith went to join him. Edith's memorial service was a grand celebration. Hundreds upon hundreds attended to give tribute to the remarkable woman, many, if not most of them, were former foster children and their families. Truly, she left a tremendous legacy in the lives of her "kids" with whom she loved no matter how challenging, angry or oppositional they might have been. I think it is fair to say that every child who entered the Dawson family left changed for life!

Aunt Edith is certainly one person I feel remarkably privileged to have known and to have worked with. Her life had a dramatic and profound impact on me, and served as a primary motivator for me to establish the Family Care Network. She demonstrated firsthand, year after year, that foster parents can work with very difficult and challenging children and still make a positive impact on those children's lives. Jimmy and Edith Dawson taught me that children are better served in a foster family than in an institutional setting. For many, many years prior to my joining that probation department, the Dawson home was treated like the local "group home" for difficult kids. Edith once told me, "I don't worry about the behaviors we see when children come into our home, and we have seen it all. What do you expect? They are hurt, scared or angry. Making them feel safe, respected and loved will eventually heal their hearts. It just takes time, and I have lots of it!"

But, here is the rest of the story. You see, the Dawsons were the first foster family I had ever met or worked with. Given that we had very few foster families in the rural community where I worked, they became my standard for foster parenting; they became my benchmark for how foster parents should behave.

The Dawson family is just one example of the thousands of families who have responded to the call to become a resource for foster children and youth. Like the Dawsons, every family possesses unique skills, values and characteristics to positively mold and shape a young life for a better future. Were the Dawsons successful? Absolutely! But their successes were different for each and every child they cared for. You also will be successful through your commitment, patience, flexibility and your willingness to allow an "outsider" in to change your life—just as you will indelibly change your foster child's life.

Terms & Definitions

Terms & Definitions

Adoption Feasibility

Should a child be placed in Permanency Planning Services after reasonable attempts at family reunification have failed or non-reunification has been ordered, the adoption of the child can become the next viable placement option. The Adoptions Unit at the Department of Social Services must evaluate whether adoption is in the best interest of the child. Children 12 years or older will be asked to voice their willingness and desire to be adopted. While the needs of sibling groups are necessarily considered, the needs of each child must be examined separately.

Agency Social Worker

Every Foster Care Provider employs Social Workers as defined by its state regulations. The Social Worker acts as the case manager, coordinating services and providing therapeutic interventions with children and families.

Case Plan

This is the specific plan ordered by the court for each child. It includes the terms, and identifies the type and nature of services to be provided to the child. It can be modified at various stages of the process as family needs change.

Certified Foster Family

A home certified by a private Foster Care Provider for the exclusive use of that agency.

Child And Family Plan

This is a plan developed and periodically revised, by a Foster Care Provider's Social Worker, which serves as a basic framework for activities to be performed on behalf of the child. Specific treatment goals are established along with objectives, or planned activities necessary to meet these goals. An initial treatment plan is developed within the first 30 days of a child's placement and is revised quarterly.

Community Care Licensing (CCL)

In California, CCL is the state agency responsible for licensing and monitoring licensed facilities. In most counties, the responsibility for foster families is contracted to the county Social Services agency. Nonetheless, a county-issued foster home license is a state license.

Concurrent Planning

In all dependency cases, when it appears that family reunification may be questionable, the caseworker is responsible for creating a "Concurrent Plan." The Concurrent Plan addresses alternative permanent placement options, i.e., relative/kin placement, adoption or guardianship.

Court Appointed Special Advocate (CASA)

The Juvenile Court has the option to appoint a CASA to represent the interest of the child. In sum, they may be made a guardian ad litem, and will advocate for the child with the court and other agencies. They usually appear in court and other critical meetings to provide information regarding what is in the best interest of the child. Their primary role is that of a stable adult who remains in contact with the child during the entire process.

COURT REPORTS

Probation Officers and Social Workers communicate with the Juvenile Court through written "court reports." These reports become a part of the court record and are important confidential documents. Copies of court reports are kept at your Foster Care Provider's office, and can be reviewed with your Social Worker.

COURT REVIEW HEARINGS

The Juvenile Court is required to review the case of every child placed out-of-home, a minimum of every six months. Often, these review hearings are set more frequently. The child has the right to be present at all hearings, but often times these hearings are conducted without them as their appearance isn't usually necessary.

CUSTODY/DETENTION HEARING

Whenever a child is removed from home for any reason and CPS or Probation determine not to return the child to his/her home, there must be a hearing within 48 hours (excluding non-judicial days) to determine if the child can be returned home, should be placed in protective custody or in detention.

DEPENDENTS

Nationally, Juvenile Court Law almost universally designates children who are abused and/or neglected as "Dependents" of the Juvenile Court. The care, supervision and treatment of Dependents is the responsibility of state or County Child Welfare Services (CWS). In California, Dependents are referred to as "300s", referring to §300 of the Welfare and Institutions Code.

DISPOSITIONAL HEARING

At this hearing, the court determines what to do with the child and his/her family, and makes specific orders in this regard. This is somewhat equivalent to the "sentencing" phase of adult proceedings.

EMANCIPATION

A court order may be issued after the submittal of a petition to allow a child under the age of 18 years old to live on his/her own and not under the authority of his/her parents, the Child Protective Services Agency, Probation Department or the Juvenile Court. The emancipated person has all of the rights and responsibilities of an adult to enter into contracts. It also releases the parent or guardian from legal responsibility in certain situations. This status can only be granted by a Juvenile Court of Law.

FAMILY REUNIFICATION SERVICES (FR)

Nearly all children categorized as dependents must be provided FR services. A major requirement of the law is to reunify families whenever possible. FR services usually do not go beyond the 18-month hearing.

FOSTER CARE

Foster care refers to the placement of a child in any state or privately licensed facility. This may range from a basic foster family to a highly structured residential treatment facility.

FOSTER FAMILY AGENCY (FFA)

A private, non-profit foster care agency licensed in the state of California to recruit and certify foster families, place children and provide treatment services to children and families. Other states use different terms and there is no national standard definition for private foster care providers. This Handbook refers to FFAs and other private providers as Foster Care Providers.

Terms & Definitions

Fostering Youth Connections
In October 2008, the Federal Fostering Connections to Success and Increasing Adoptions Act (FCA) was passed and signed into law. The FCA provides opportunities for additional federal funding sources while increasing opportunities to better serve Youth in foster care. Under the law, states are eligible to receive federal matching funds for subsidized foster care payments for youth up to age 21. California, along with some other states, has established programs to serve foster youth up to age 21.

Guardian Ad Litem
The person appointed by the Juvenile Court to act as the court's representative to ensure that the best interests of the child will be served. This is usually the placement worker, such as the caseworker or probation officer.

Guardianship
The process whereby an individual or couple is awarded the legal authority to care for a child as their own, but without the permanent status of an adoption. As legal guardians, these parents can administer the affairs of the child without the intervention or fiscal support of the "system." Guardianship can be for a fixed period of time or open ended. Guardianships can be revoked by a court order under certain circumstances.

Home Study
The procedure whereby an individual or a couple is evaluated to determine the suitability of their home for the placement of children. This includes: foster parent applicants, relatives, prospective guardians and adoptive homes. This study usually focuses on two main issues: 1) the psycho-social history and status of the person(s) being considered, and 2) the physical environment of the home.

Independent Living Skills Services (ILS)
Special training provided to foster children 16 years or older, focused on developing skills such as money management, housing, job interviewing, etcetera. These services are available to former foster children until the age of 25 years.

Jurisdiction Hearing
The hearing to determine if a child does come under the court's jurisdiction, if the petition is "true" or not. It is the equivalent to a "trial" in adult proceedings.

Non-Depenedent Minor (NDM)
This is the term for adult foster youth who voluntarily choose to remain in the foster care system until age 21 when these services are authorized by the state.

Non-Secure Detention
Includes custody of children in non-locked facilities such as shelter care homes, group homes and foster homes. Children categorized as 300s, 601s and 602s can be detained in this fashion.

Out-Of-Home Placement
Children removed from the care and custody of their natural parents and placed in shelter homes, juvenile hall, foster homes, residential treatment, hospitals or other situations.

Permanency Planning Hearing

Every Dependent must receive Family Reunification services for at least 12 months. After 15 months of family reunification (or less depending on the age of the child) a Permanency Planning Hearing must be conducted to determine if the foster child can be returned home or ordered into Permanency Placement Services.

Permanency Planning Services (PP)

Once family reunification has failed, the court must order PP services. The nature of these services depends on the needs of the child. Adoption is the preferred service unless there are reasons adoption would not be a good plan for the child. Other options include placement with a relative or guardianship.

Petition/Supplemental Petition

The "paper" filed in court alleging that a child comes under a specific section of the Juvenile Court law and the reason for the petition.

Progress Report

Periodic reports written by responsible parties, (i.e. social workers, probation officers, child care workers, therapists, etc.) which discuss the progress of a case or treatment plan for a specified period of time.

Psychological Evaluation

An evaluation done by a psychologist or psychiatrist which includes an examination of family history, developmental progress, relationships, parenting, psychological development, intellectual functioning, academic functioning and recommendations for treatment services.

Review Hearing

In all out-of-home placements, there must be a review of a child's adjustment and progress at a minimum of every six months.

Secure Detention

Custody of a child in any "locked" facility, (i.e., juvenile hall, probation camp, etcetera). Only wards can be detained this way. Runaway children can no longer be detained in locked facilities, except in certain, special circumstances.

Status Offenders

There are states who serve youth who are non-criminal or "status" offenders. These "offenders" include runaways, incorrigible youth, parent/child conflicts, truants, etcetera (children who come under the court's jurisdiction only due to their status as being minors, under age 18). Once the youth turns 18 years of age, these behaviors are not illegal. In California, these youth are sometimes referred to as "601s."

Termination Of Parental Rights

Before a child can be adopted, the court must first order parental rights terminated. This requires a full court hearing. After failed FR attempts, the presumption is that parents are unable to parent and rights should be terminated if it is in the child's best interest to do so. Such an order frees the child for adoption.

Terms and Conditions of Probation

The court ordered requirements and expectations for each child placed on probation.

Terms & Definitions

Therapeutic Foster Care (TFC)
TFC serves as a family-based treatment program as an alternative to group home or institutional care. It includes highly trained and compensated professional foster parents, intensive one-on-one in-home support services, intensive social worker/case management services and supporting mental health services.

Transition to Independent Living Plan (TILP)
The law requires that a written plan be developed for every foster youth 16 years or older, which sets forth specific goals and tasks the child needs to complete in order to be prepared for independent living. It is the responsibility of government social workers and probation officers to complete TILPs, though the best practice is for it to be done with the youth and Independent Living Program (ILP) worker.

Wards
Youth who have committed criminal acts and are under the jurisdiction of state or County Probation, are referred to as "Wards" of the Juvenile Court. These youth may remain at home under Probation supervision, they may be placed in Juvenile Hall or other institutional, correctional settings, or they may be placed in foster care. In California, Wards are referred to as "602s."

Wraparound Services Program
Wraparound, available in many states, is a family-based alternative to group home or institutional care. It provides a unique placement option, allowing a high-needs foster child/youth to remain in a family setting, typically their own, while they receive very intense services. This strength-based, needs-driven program is an extremely effective intervention, which serves and supports not only the foster child/youth, but the entire family, including siblings. Wraparound is a volunteer program designed to empower families and help them create community connections and supports.

"When we are motivated by goals that have deep meaning, by dreams that need completion, by pure love that needs expressing, then we truly live life."

—Greg Anderson